CIVIL RIGHTS AND PUBLIC ACCOMMODATIONS

CIVIL RIGHTS AND
PUBLIC ACCOMMODATIONS,

The *Heart of Atlanta Motel*
and *McClung* Cases

Richard C. Cortner

UNIVERSITY PRESS OF KANSAS

Published by the University Press of Kansas (Lawrence, Kansas 66049), which was
organized by the Kansas Board of Regents and is operated and funded by Emporia State
University, Fort Hays State University, Kansas State University, Pittsburg State University,
the University of Kansas, and Wichita State University.

Library of Congress Cataloging-in-Publication Data

Cortner, Richard C.
    Civil rights and public accommodations : the Heart of Atlanta Motel and McClung
cases / Richard C. Cortner.
    p. cm.
    Includes index.
    ISBN 0-7006-1077-4 (cloth : alk. paper)
    1. Heart of Atlanta Motel—Trials, litigation, etc. 2. McClung, Ollie—Trials, litigation,
etc. 3. Discrimination in public accommodations—Law and legislation—United
States—Cases. I. Title.

KF228.H43 C67 2001
342.73'085—dc21   00-049956

    British Library Cataloguing in Publication Data is available.

Printed in the United States of America
10 9 8 7 6 5 4 3 2 1

The paper used in this publication meets the minimum requirements of the American
National Standard for Permanence of Paper for Printed Library Materials Z39.48-1984.

For
W. Edward Morgan

CONTENTS

PREFACE

The pervasive system of racial segregation that had been erected in the United States during the years following the end of Reconstruction in the 1870s had slowly but surely begun to be dismantled by the 1960s. Following the U.S. Supreme Court's invalidation of public school segregation in 1954, governmentally supported segregation in other walks of life was increasingly subjected to successful constitutional attack. By 1960, however, there remained extensive racial discrimination in places of public accommodation, such as movie theaters, lunch counters, restaurants, hotels, and motels. Travel by blacks, especially in the South and the border states, was frequently a difficult and harrowing experience because of the scarcity of accommodations available to serve them. As U.S. Senator Hubert Humphrey remarked, blacks were constrained to "draw up travel plans much as a general advancing across hostile territory would establish his logistical support."[1]

Beginning in the early 1960s, protests against discrimination in public accommodations through sit-in demonstrations resulted in massive arrests and prosecutions of the demonstrators by state authorities under criminal trespass laws. In 1963 and 1964, there were over 1,100 demonstrations protesting discrimination in public accommodations, and while the National Association for the Advancement of Colored People (NAACP) defended 13,000 sit-in demonstrators during the early 1960s, there remained 3,000 trespass prosecutions pending in the courts in 1964.[2]

Congress finally responded to the mushrooming crisis in race relations affecting facilities of public accommodation by enacting the Civil Rights Act of 1964, which included public accommodations provisions prohibiting discrimination on the grounds of race, color, national origin, or religion in places of public accommodation. After extensive debate, Congress based the public accommodations provisions of the 1964 act on its power to regulate interstate commerce, derived from the Commerce Clause of the Constitution, on the theory that discrimination in facilities of public accommodation resulted in burdens on interstate commerce, which Congress could remove or prohibit under its commerce power.

As a matter of first impression, it appeared that the public accommodations provisions could have been based more logically on the congressional power to enforce the provisions of the Fourteenth Amendment of the Constitution, especially the Equal Protection Clause of that amendment. The U.S. Supreme Court, however, had ruled in 1883 that the congressional power to enforce the Fourteenth Amendment could not validly be used to prohibit discrimination by private individuals in places of public accommodation.[3] And more recently in cases arising from trespass prosecutions of sit-in demonstrators, the Court had also refused to hold that the Fourteenth Amendment prohibited discrimination in public accommodations or that the trespass prosecution of sit-in demonstrators who were protesting discrimination in public accommodations was barred by the amendment. Rather than base the public accommodations provisions of the 1964 act on the congressional power to enforce the Fourteenth Amendment and invite a revision or reversal of its previous decisions by the Supreme Court, Congress chose what seemed the constitutionally safer course of basing the public accommodations provisions on the Commerce Clause.

The public accommodations provisions of the Civil Rights Act of 1964 were nevertheless subjected to almost immediate challenge on the ground that they were beyond the legitimate scope of congressional power under the Constitution. The constitutional challenge of the public accommodations provisions was launched by the owners of the Heart of Atlanta Motel in Atlanta, Georgia, and Ollie's Barbecue in Birmingham, Alabama. The resulting litigation in *Heart of Atlanta Motel v. United States* and *Katzenbach v. McClung* is the subject of the analysis in the pages that follow.[4] The Supreme Court's decisions on December 14, 1964, unanimously sustaining the constitutionality of the public accommodations provisions of the Civil Rights Act of 1964 produced landmark decisions under the Commerce Clause of the Constitution. And the decisions in the public accommodations cases also resulted in the desegregation of facilities of public accommodation throughout the nation and thus profoundly changed America forever.

During the process of researching and writing this book, I have received assistance from numerous individuals as well as institutions. The staffs of the University of Arizona Library, the Library of Congress, the Tarleton Law Library of the School of Law at the University of Texas–Austin, the Lyndon B. Johnson Library, and the Seeley Mudd Library at Princeton University were uniformly helpful with my research, and I express my gratitude to them.

While my analysis of the litigation in the *Heart of Atlanta Motel* case is based substantially on the file of the Civil Rights Division of the Department of Justice, obtained through a Freedom of Information Act request, the Civil Rights Division file on the *McClung* case has unfortunately been lost. My analysis of the litigation in the *McClung* case was significantly aided by information provided by Robert McDavid Smith, who was the lead attorney for the McClungs. Robert Smith also read the material contained herein regarding the *McClung* case, and I express my deep appreciation to him for his assistance.

I have also benefited greatly from the comments of several individuals who graciously agreed to review all or part of my manuscript. My colleagues in the Department of Political Science at the University of Arizona, Professors Clifford M. Lytle Jr., James Todd, David Wilkens, Laura Langer, and William Mishler, and Professor Lee Epstein of the Department of Political Science at Washington University read all or parts of the manuscript, and I deeply appreciate their helpful suggestions. I have in addition once again had the assistance of my friend Leo Sonderegger, who read the manuscript with the keen eye of a veteran newspaper reporter and editor. Finally, I express my appreciation to Michael Briggs and the highly professional staff of the University Press of Kansas for smoothing the path of publication. As always, of course, I am alone responsible for any errors that may appear in the pages that follow.

This book is dedicated to my old friend Ed Morgan. As a lawyer, Ed was a pioneer in the field of civil rights and civil liberties, and his conduct has always exemplified the highest standards of his profession. The dedication of this book to Ed is in recognition of his contributions to the constitutional right of equality, which was also vindicated by the *Heart of Atlanta Motel* and *McClung* cases.

What follows is an analysis of the litgation of two Supreme Court cases that produced one of the most significant advances in the right of equality during the civil rights era of the 1960s. I hope that the story of *Heart of Atlanta Motel v. United States* and *Katzenbach v. McClung* will illuminate the nature of constitutional litigation and the judicial process as well as the role of the Constitution and law in social change in the United States. And finally, the pages that follow are intended to contribute to a better understanding of an important chapter in constitutional development in America.

INTRODUCTION: PUBLIC ACCOMMODATIONS, THE CONSTITUTION, AND THE SUPREME COURT

During July 1964, Albert Richard Sampson entered the Heart of Atlanta Motel in downtown Atlanta, Georgia, where he had earlier reserved a room for the night, wiring money to the motel to cover the cost of his accommodations. On July 3, a young black man entered Ollie's Barbecue, a restaurant in Birmingham, Alabama, and requested service at the restaurant's counter. Both Albert Sampson and the young man in Birmingham were refused service because they were black. "I can't accommodate any Negroes," Sampson was informed by Moreton Rolleston, the owner of the Heart of Atlanta Motel, who then refunded Sampson's room deposit. Ollie McClung Jr., co-owner of Ollie's Barbecue in Birmingham, explained to the young black man who had requested service that it was the restaurant's policy not to serve blacks on the premises but only on a take-out basis. Denied service at the restaurant, the young man departed.[1]

The refusal of the Heart of Atlanta Motel and Ollie's Barbecue to serve blacks was a violation of the Civil Rights Act of 1964, which included public accommodations provisions prohibiting discrimination by places of public accommodation on the grounds of race, color, religion, or national origin. Whether Congress had the power under the Constitution to prohibit discrimination in public accommodations was hotly debated in 1964, and that issue would be presented to the U.S. Supreme Court in the fall of 1964 in cases involving the Heart of Atlanta Motel and Ollie's Barbecue. The result would be a profoundly important social change, as facilities of public accommodation were desegregated throughout America.[2]

In the cases involving the Heart of Atlanta Motel and Ollie's Barbecue, the Court would be revisiting the issue of the relation of the Constitution to discrimination in facilities of public accommodation, which it first addressed over eighty years previously when it decided the constitutional validity of the Civil Rights Act of 1875. And the issue of discrimination in places of public accommodation and the Constitution would also confront the Court with one of the most vexatious and divisive questions it would be constrained to address in the *Sit-in* cases of the 1960s. The Court's decisions on the validity of the Civil Rights Act of 1875 and in the *Sit-in* cases of the '60s would in turn substantially affect the constitutional power upon which the

Civil Rights Act of 1964 would be based and ultimately the Court's decision regarding the constitutional validity of the 1964 act.

As he lay dying in March 1874, U.S. Senator Charles Sumner, Republican of Massachusetts, reportedly pleaded with Congressman Ebenezer Hoar to continue his support of the bill that would become the Civil Rights Act of 1875. "You must take care of the civil rights bill,—my bill, the civil rights bill,—don't let it fail!" Sumner declared. As the foremost champion of equal rights for blacks during the Civil War and postwar era, Sumner originally proposed in 1870 a civil rights bill that would have prohibited racial discrimination in facilities of public accommodation such as public conveyances, hotels, and restaurants, but also in public schools and churches as well. Although enacted as a memorial to Sumner, the Civil Rights Act of 1875 was considerably less sweeping in its prohibition of racial discrimination than the late senator's original proposal. Dropped from the 1875 act was any prohibition of discrimination in public schools and churches; the act instead declared:

> all persons within the jurisdiction of the United States shall be entitled to the full and equal enjoyment of the accommodations, advantages, facilities, and privileges of inns, public conveyances on land and water, theaters, and other places of public amusement; subject only to the conditions and limitations established by law, and applicable alike to citizens of every race and color, regardless of any previous condition of servitude.[3]

Based on section five of the Fourteenth Amendment, delegating to Congress the power to enforce the provisions of the Fourteenth Amendment through appropriate legislation, the Civil Rights Act of 1875 was nevertheless declared unconstitutional by the Supreme Court in the *Civil Rights Cases* of 1883, over a vigorous dissent by Justice John Marshall Harlan I. To no avail, Harlan charged that "the substance and spirit of the recent Amendments of the Constitution have been sacrificed by a subtle and ingenious verbal criticism," and he vehemently argued that the 1875 Civil Rights Act was constitutionally valid under both the Thirteenth and Fourteenth Amendments.[4]

The majority of the Court nevertheless held that the Civil Rights Act of 1875 exceeded the power of Congress to enforce the provisions of both the Thirteenth and Fourteenth Amendments. "Of course," the Court said, "no one will contend that the power to pass . . . [the Civil Rights Act] was contained in the Constitution before the adoption of the last three Amendments [the Thirteenth, Fourteenth, and Fifteenth Amendments]." The prohibitions contained in the first section of the Fourteenth Amendment, including the Equal Protection Clause's prohibition of the denial to any person the equal protection of the laws by any state, the Court held, were directed at prohibiting state action denying the rights protected by the amendment. "It is state action of a particular character that is prohibited," it pointed out.

> Individual invasion of individual rights is not the subject matter of the Amendment. . . . It does not authorize Congress to create a code of municipal law for the regulation of private rights; but to provide modes of redress against the operation of state laws and the action of state officers executive or judicial, when these are subversive of the fundamental rights specified in the Amendment.[5]

In the Civil Rights Act of 1875, the Court noted on the other hand, Congress had prohibited discrimination by private owners of places of public accommodation, unsupported by any kind of state action. Since the Fourteenth Amendment only prohibited the violation through state action of the rights it protected, the Court held, the Civil Rights Act consequently exceeded the congressional power under section five of the amendment to enforce its provisions through appropriate legislation.

Although the Court had said that the power of Congress to enact the Civil Rights Act of 1875 had not existed prior to the adoption of the Civil War Amendments to the Constitution, it nevertheless pointed out that its discussion of the legitimate scope of congressional power to enforce the provisions of the Fourteenth Amendment was inapplicable to the powers Congress derived from the Commerce Clause and other delegations of power in the Constitution. While the power of Congress derived from section five of the Fourteenth Amendment was limited to enacting corrective legislation prohibiting state action violative of that amendment, the Court noted, "these remarks do not apply to those cases in which Congress is clothed with direct and plenary powers of legislation over the whole subject, accompanied with an express or implied denial of such power to the States, as in the regulation of commerce with foreign States, among the several States, and with the Indian Tribes." "In these cases," the Court continued, "Congress has the power to pass laws for regulating the subjects specified in every detail, and the conduct and transactions of individuals in respect thereof." Whether Congress could prohibit discrimination by private individuals in public accommodations under the Commerce Clause, such as interstate public conveyances, the Court pointed out, was "a question which is not now before us, as the sections [of the Civil Rights Act of 1875] in question are not conceived on any such view."[6]

While conceding that the Thirteenth Amendment, unlike the Fourteenth Amendment, conferred on Congress the power to enforce its prohibition of slavery and involuntary servitude directly against actions of private individuals as well as those of the states, the Court rejected the argument that racial discrimination in facilities of public accommodation was a badge or incident of slavery that Congress could validly prohibit under its power to enforce the Thirteenth Amendment. "It would be running the slavery argument into the ground," the Court said, "to make it apply to every act of discrimination which a person may see fit to make as to the guest he will entertain, or as to the people he will take into his coach or cab or car, or admit to his concert or theater, or deal with in other matters of intercourse or business." The Court continued:

> When a man has emerged from slavery, and by the aid of beneficent legislation has shaken off the inseparable concomitants of that state, there must be some stage in the progress of his elevation when he takes the rank of mere citizen, and ceases to be the special favorite of the laws, and when his rights as a citizen or a man, are to be protected in the ordinary modes by which other men's rights are protected.[7]

While the Supreme Court subsequently repudiated the narrow interpretation of the power of Congress to enforce the Thirteenth Amendment that it adopted in the *Civil Rights Cases*,[8] the state action doctrine as enunciated by the Supreme Court in the *Civil Rights Cases* became an established doctrine in American constitutional law. Under that doctrine, the prohibitions imposed on the states by the Fourteenth Amendment, including the Equal Protection Clause, could be triggered only by some state action violative of the amendment's provisions but not by actions of private individuals unaided or supported by the states. The state action doctrine nonetheless was subjected to considerable strain as the civil rights movement gained momentum in the 1950s and '60s in the wake of the Supreme Court's decision in *Brown v. Board of Education,* declaring public school segregation unconstitutional under the Equal Protection Clause.[9]

As state-supported racial discrimination and segregation were slowly eliminated while the principle of equality embodied in the *Brown* case was expanded, the civil rights movement by the early 1960s came to focus on racial discrimination in facilities of public accommodation such as lunch counters, restaurants, theaters, hotels, and motels. Sit-in demonstrators began to enter places of public accommodation, such as restaurants and lunch counters, and refuse to leave until served. These sit-in demonstrators were then arrested by local police for violating laws prohibiting criminal trespass on another's property.

In the numerous resulting *Sit-in* cases challenging the trespass convictions of the demonstrators, the Supreme Court was urged to construe the state action doctrine enunciated in the *Civil Rights Cases* of 1883 to include the enforcement of state and local trespass laws against those seeking equal access to facilities of public accommodation. The states' enforcement of their trespass laws against sit-in demonstrators, it was argued, was state action violative of the Equal Protection Clause of the Fourteenth Amendment. The Court was therefore urged to hold that discrimination in places of public accommodation supported by such state action violated the Fourteenth Amendment and that all public accommodations could not consequently deny service on the grounds of race or color.[10]

The strongest precedent supportive of such arguments was the Supreme Court's 1948 decision in *Shelley v. Kraemer,* holding that state court enforcement of racially restrictive covenants, which were deed restrictions prohibiting the sale of real estate to blacks and members of other minority groups, was discriminatory state action violative of the Equal Protection Clause. Since racially restrictive covenants were customarily private contractual agreements among owners of homes in residential neighborhoods, if state court enforcement of such covenants was state action violative of the Equal Protection Clause, it was argued in the *Sit-in* cases, state court enforcement of state trespass laws against sit-in demonstrators was similarly state action violative of the Fourteenth Amendment.[11]

The issues presented by the *Sit-in* cases during the early 1960s presented a dilemma to the Department of Justice and especially to U.S. Solicitor General Archibald Cox. Created in 1870, the Office of U.S. Solicitor General is responsible for the legal representation of the federal government before the Supreme Court. The consent of the solicitor general is necessary, with few exceptions, before a case lost by the government in the lower courts may be appealed to the Supreme Court. In addition to writing the briefs and conducting the oral arguments on behalf of the government in the Supreme Court, the solicitor general's office may also intervene as *amicus curiae* in cases in which the government is not a party. And it was in this latter capacity that Solicitor General Archibald Cox participated in the *Sit-in* cases.[12]

Archibald Cox was superbly qualified for the position of solicitor general in the Kennedy administration. Harvard-trained, Cox had served on the *Harvard Law Review* as a law student, had subsequently been a law clerk for U.S. Court of Appeals Judge Learned Hand, and had served as an assistant in the solicitor general's office. At the time of his appointment as solicitor general by President Kennedy, the forty-eight-year-old Cox was the leading expert in labor law on the faculty of the Harvard Law School and had been director of research in the 1960 Kennedy presidential campaign. "My whole life and career," he said, "had trained me to look upon the solicitor's office as second only to God." Cox perceived his role as solicitor general as that of an officer of the Supreme Court with the duty of protecting the Court from adopting constitutional positions that might seem correct in the short term but that might prove harmful in their long-term effects on the development of constitutional law. Consequently, Cox's customary approach to constitutional issues was cautious, self-restrained, and incremental, an approach that frequently appeared to his Justice Department colleagues and to Attorney General Robert Kennedy himself as overly cautious, especially in the field of civil rights.[13]

Yet the attorney general and Cox's Department of Justice colleagues recognized his brilliance and his outstanding conduct of the solicitor general's office. A story Robert Kennedy frequently told on himself had President Kennedy calling Robert Kennedy regarding a legal opinion the White House needed regarding a legal problem it was confronting. "I'll get on it right away," the attorney general assured his brother. "I said I wanted a *legal* opinion," the president responded. "Don't you get on it. Get Archie Cox on it."[14]

Solicitor General Cox's cautious approach to the issues in the *Sit-in* cases as *amicus curiae* nevertheless aroused opposition among those within the Justice Department who were more result-oriented and believed the proper position of the government should be one of total support for the civil rights movement. Cox, on the other hand, resisted taking the position that the Supreme Court should hold that the Fourteenth Amendment compelled desegregation in places of public accommodation and that state enforcement of criminal trespass laws against sit-in demonstrators was state action violative of the Equal Protection Clause. When the Civil Rights Division head, Assistant Attorney General Burke Marshall, and National Association for the Advancement of Colored People (NAACP) general counsel Jack Greenberg attempted to persuade Cox to change his position in the *Sit-in* cases, the solicitor general refused. "If you believe in your position," an irritated Greenberg told Cox, "write it up in the *Harvard Law Review*. But now you're the Solicitor General of the United States, and it is the policy of the Kennedy administration to oppose discrimination wherever it can."[15]

For Cox, however, the issues in the *Sit-in* cases presented more complex considerations than just the proposition that racial discrimination in public accommodations was morally wrong and that the government should support the sit-in demonstrators regardless of the constitutional consequences and the possible effects on the legitimacy of the Supreme Court's authority. A ruling that the Fourteenth Amendment itself required the desegregation of public accommodations, Cox believed, would engender the kind of widespread resistance that the Court's decision in *Brown v. Board of Education,* ordering public school desegregation, had aroused in the South, with the resultant undermining of respect for the Court and its legitimacy as a constitutional tribunal. In addition, Cox believed that there was not a majority on the Supreme Court that would support a holding that the Fourteenth Amendment required the desegregation of public accommodations. "If we went for all or nothing," he felt, "it would have been nothing."[16]

As long as there was a glimmer of hope that Congress might enact legislation requiring desegregation in public accommodations, the solicitor general felt, the best course for the government as *amicus curiae* in the *Sit-in* cases was to pursue a cautious approach that avoided an argument that the Court should decide the core Fourteenth Amendment issue raised in those cases. He instead urged the Court to reverse the trespass convictions in each of the *Sit-in* cases, but not on the ground that the Fourteenth Amendment itself prohibited discrimination in public accommodations when such discrimination was enforced through state trespass laws. Rather, Cox argued, there was sufficient state action supportive of racial discrimination in the particular places of public accommodation involved in each *Sit-in* case, aside from state enforcement of trespass laws, to trigger the Equal Protection Clause and require a reversal of the convictions.[17]

The issues raised by the *Sit-in* cases ultimately proved to be as divisive for the members of the Supreme Court under the leadership of Chief Justice Earl Warren as they were for Solicitor General Cox and his Justice Department colleagues. The justices of the Warren Court represented the forces of continuity and change that are customarily reflected in the membership of the Court, with two members of the Court having been appointed by President Franklin Roosevelt, one by President Truman, four by President Eisenhower, and two by President Kennedy.

The senior associate justice on the Warren Court was Hugo L. Black, who had been appointed by Roosevelt in 1937. The appointment of Black, a two-term U.S. senator from Alabama and a fiery supporter of Roosevelt's New Deal, was initially clouded by the revelation that he had been a member of the Ku Klux Klan. Black's adamant support for civil rights for blacks, including the Court's unanimous decision in *Brown v. Board of Education* in 1954, however, had long since dispelled any fears that he would represent the forces of bigotry on the Court. Instead, Black became one of the most steadfast supporters of civil rights and civil liberties in the history of the Court, and he was best known for his contention that the Fourteenth Amendment was meant to apply all of the provisions of the Bill of Rights as restrictions on the powers of the states as well as his position that the guarantee of freedom of expression in the First Amendment was absolute. By the 1960s, it was widely acknowledged that Justice Black had influenced the course of constitutional development more than any other justice since the 1930s.[18]

Junior only to Justice Black on the Warren Court was Justice William O. Douglas, who had been appointed by Roosevelt in 1939. Born in Minnesota but raised in Washington, Douglas had been a member of the Yale Law School faculty and had served as chairman of the Securities and Exchange Commission, the New Deal's Wall Street watchdog. On the Court, although a loner, Douglas was usually closely allied with Justice Black in supporting civil rights, the application of all of the Bill of Rights as restrictions on the states, and First Amendment freedoms. Only forty years old when he was appointed, Douglas was destined to serve on the Court over thirty-six years, longer than any other justice in the history of the Court.[19]

The sole Truman appointee on the Warren Court was Justice Tom C. Clark of Texas, who had been Truman's attorney general. Unfortunately, President Truman's other appointments to the Court were uniformly mediocre at best, and Tom Clark's appointment to the Court in 1949 was also initially denounced as a mediocre selection or worse. Serving on the Court until 1967, however, Justice Clark compiled a moderate to conservative record that was, while not outstanding, a solidly competent one, and his performance as a justice certainly more than exceeded the expectations of the initial critics of his appointment.[20]

When another of President Truman's appointees to the Court, Chief Justice Fred Vinson, died in September 1953, President Dwight D. Eisenhower had his first opportunity for an appointment to the Court, and he chose Governor Earl Warren of California. Warren had served as district attorney of Alameda County and California attorney general, and had been elected governor of California three times, enjoying broad bipartisan support. Warren had also been the unsuccessful vice-presidential candidate of the Republican Party in 1948. While he possessed a thoroughly engaging personality and had been an eminently successful politician, there was little in Warren's pre-Court record to indicate that he would bring to the Court as chief justice anything more than the philosophical views of a moderate to progressive Republican. Surprisingly, however, and to the apparent consternation of Eisenhower, the Court under Warren's leadership compiled the most liberal record in the protection and extension of civil rights and civil liberties in our history.

The Court's unanimous decision in *Brown v. Board of Education* in 1954, invalidating public school segregation, was largely due to Warren's patient leadership, and after 1954, the Warren Court in case after case systematically dismantled legally imposed segregation in other walks of life. By the late 1950s, Warren, allied with Justice William Brennan, adopted the position that virtually all of the rights in the Bill of Rights should apply to the states via the Fourteenth Amendment (the selective incorporation position), and in the 1960s Warren and Brennan, allied with Justices Black and Douglas, who believed that all of the Bill of Rights applied to the states, led the fight to apply virtually all of the Bill of Rights as restrictions on state power. In 1962, again with Chief Justice Warren in the majority, the Court began what came to be called the "reapportionment revolution" by holding in *Baker v. Carr* that the federal courts could properly hear redistricting and reapportionment suits.[21] After 1962, the result was the reapportionment of state legislatures and the redistricting of congressional districts under the Warren Court's "one person, one vote" standard that resulted in a massive shift of political power to urban and suburban areas of the country, whose inhabitants had previously been denied political representation commensurate with their numbers because of the refusal of rural-dominated state legislatures to reapportion or redistrict.[22] By the time of his retirement from the Court in 1969, Chief Justice Warren thus fully deserved the title Justice Brennan bestowed upon him, that of "Super Chief."[23]

Three additional Eisenhower appointees remained on the Court in the 1960s, Justice John Marshall Harlan II, appointed in 1954, Justice William Brennan, appointed in 1956, and Justice Potter Stewart, appointed in 1958. A lifelong Republican and grandson of Justice John Marshall Harlan I, who had dissented in the *Civil Rights Cases* of 1883, John Marshall Harlan II had long been a member of one of New York's most prestigious law firms and was appointed by Eisenhower to the U.S. Court of Appeals for the Second Circuit in 1954. Upon the death of Justice Robert H. Jackson in the fall of 1954, Harlan received a recess appointment to the Supreme Court from Eisenhower in November but was not finally confirmed by the Senate until March 1955. By the 1960s, Harlan was recognized as the Warren Court's most conservative member while also widely respected for his legal craftsmanship and careful, well-reasoned opinions. Harlan led the rearguard fight against the "incorporation" of the rights in the Bill of Rights into the Fourteenth Amendment as restrictions on the powers of the states. And as a quintessential advocate of judicial self-restraint, he dissented from the Court's decisions extending the jurisdiction of the federal courts over districting and apportionment under the "one person, one vote" standard. "The Constitution," he warned his colleagues in a typical comment, was "not a panacea for every blot upon the public welfare," and the Court was not "a general haven for reform movements." Justice Harlan, like his grandfather, was nevertheless steadfast in his support for the civil rights of blacks and the enforcement of the principles of *Brown v. Board of Education.*[24]

Unlike Justice Harlan, Justice William Brennan was a Democrat who had specialized in labor law in his law practice and was serving as a justice of the New Jersey Supreme Court at the time of his appointment by Eisenhower to the U.S. Supreme Court in 1956. Once on the Court, Brennan soon became a close ally of Chief Justice Warren when each recognized that their liberal views on most issues coming before the Court were frequently the same. Brennan became one of the most adept justices in the Court's recent history in building a consensus of views among his colleagues on the issues confronting the Court, a talent he continued to utilize long after the era of the Warren Court had ended.[25] Justice Brennan's record on the Court was one of unsurpassed support for the rights in the Bill of Rights and the selective incorporation of those rights as restrictions on the states, and for the extension of federal judicial power over political districting and reapportionment. Brennan's legacy on the Court includes his opinion for the Court in *Baker v. Carr* in 1962, establishing federal judicial power over political districting, and his opinion for the Court in *New York Times v. Sullivan* with its vindication of freedom of the press in the field of libel.[26]

Justice Potter Stewart had been the last appointment to the Court by President Eisenhower in 1958. A member of a distinguished Ohio Republican family and educated at Yale and Cambridge Universities and Yale Law School, Potter Stewart developed a moderately conservative record on the Court, allying himself with Justice Harlan at times, but on other occasions pursuing an independent course. Like Harlan, Stewart was steadfast in his support of civil rights for blacks, and he too became known for the lucidity of his opinions—with some of his best opinions being in the field of searches and seizures.[27] Although at times criticized for his lack of a sufficient work ethic on the Court, Stewart nevertheless proved to be an able justice and compiled a solid albeit not spectacular record as a member of the Court.[28]

In 1962, President John F. Kennedy was presented with the opportunity to make two appointments to the Court upon the retirement of Justices Charles Evans Whittaker and Felix Frankfurter. To replace Whittaker, Kennedy selected Byron R. White, whom Kennedy had met while White was a Rhodes scholar in England prior to World War II, and the two had also served on PT boats in the Pacific during the war. Born in Colorado, White had been not only a successful scholar but also an outstanding football player, and had played that sport professionally as "Whizzer White." He was practicing law in Denver when Kennedy launched his bid for the presidency, and White headed the Citizens for Kennedy-Johnson in the 1960 campaign. After Kennedy's election, White was appointed deputy attorney general under Attorney General Robert Kennedy in the Justice Department. While staunch in his support for civil rights on the Court, White generally pursued an independent course and was frequently aligned with the Warren Court's conservative or centrist justices on criminal procedure issues. Justice White, however, supported the selective incorporation of most of the Bill of Rights as restrictions on state power and the extension of federal judicial power over political districting under the one person, one vote standard.[29]

President Kennedy selected his secretary of labor, Arthur J. Goldberg, as the successor on the Court to Justice Felix Frankfurter. Born in Chicago the son of Russian-Jewish immigrant parents, Goldberg worked his way through Northwestern University Law School, graduating at the top of his class. In his law practice, he specialized in labor law and ultimately served as general counsel for the American Federation of Labor–Congress of Industrial Organizations, and his reputation as a labor relations negotiator made Goldberg a natural choice as Kennedy's secretary of labor. On the Court, Justice Goldberg soon established a reputation as a staunch liberal, second perhaps only to Justice Douglas in his support for innovative approaches to constitutional issues, and he lent his support to the selective incorporation of the Bill of Rights as restrictions on state power, the one person, one vote standard in districting cases, and the Warren Court's strengthening of the procedural rights of criminal defendants.[30]

Although in the *Sit-in* cases the Warren Court endorsed Solicitor General Cox's position by refusing to hold that the Fourteenth Amendment standing alone required the desegregation of facilities of public accommodation, the issues raised by those cases ultimately resulted in deep divisions on the Court. These divisions were readily apparent in *Bell v. Maryland*, decided by the Court in June 1964.[31]

Justice Brennan, joined by Justices Clark and Stewart, wrote an opinion in the *Bell* case reversing the trespass convictions of black demonstrators who had sat in at a restaurant in Baltimore; the ground for reversal was that since the convictions had been obtained in the Maryland courts, both the City of Baltimore and the State of Maryland had enacted laws prohibiting discrimination in places of public accommodation. The case should be remanded to the Maryland courts, Brennan held, to allow them to determine whether, under these changed circumstances, the indictments against the demonstrators ought to be dismissed.[32]

In a concurring opinion by Justice Goldberg, joined by Chief Justice Warren and in part by Justice Douglas, the core question of whether the Fourteenth Amendment required the desegregation of public accommodations was reached and decided. The Fourteenth Amendment, Justice Goldberg argued, had been understood by those who framed and ratified it to guarantee blacks access to public accommodations on a nondiscriminatory basis. The citizenship conferred upon blacks by section one of the Fourteenth Amendment, Goldberg maintained, had been intended to confer upon them the right to equal access to public accommodations then required by the common law rule that owners of such accommodations were required to serve all comers on an equal basis. The repeal of this common law rule by the southern and border states, allowing discrimination in places of public accommodation, he argued, violated the Equal Protection Clause of the Fourteenth Amendment. And the enforcement of state trespass laws against blacks asserting their right to equal access to facilities of public accommodation "is as affirmative in effect," Goldberg argued, "as if the State had enacted an unconstitutional law explicitly authorizing racial discrimination in places of public accommodation." Convictions of sit-in demonstrators under state trespass laws therefore violated the Fourteenth Amendment, he concluded, by denying blacks the right to equal access to places of public accommodation in violation of the Equal Protection Clause.[33]

Justice Douglas, joined in part by Justice Goldberg, also concurred in the reversal of the trespass convictions in the *Bell* case, and he too reached the merits of the core constitutional issue involved. The right to equal access to places of public accommodation, Douglas argued, was guaranteed both as a privilege and immunity of national citizenship and by the Equal Protection Clause. The enforcement of trespass laws against sit-in demonstrators by state police, prosecutors, and courts was state action violative of the Fourteenth Amendment, he maintained, just as had been state court enforcement of racially restrictive covenants by the state courts, which the Court had invalidated in *Shelley v. Kraemer* in 1948. "Segregation of Negroes in the restaurants and lunch counters of parts of America is a relic of slavery," Douglas declared.

It is a badge of second-class citizenship. It is a denial of a privilege and immunity of national citizenship and of the equal protection guaranteed by the Fourteenth Amendment against abridgment by the States. When the state police, the state prosecutor, and the state courts unite to convict Negroes for renouncing that relic of slavery, the "State" violates the Fourteenth Amendment.[34]

Justice Black, joined by Justices Harlan and White, on the other hand, dissented from the Court's decision in the *Bell* case reversing the trespass convictions of the demonstrators. The dissenters warned that a ruling by the Court that state enforcement of trespass laws against sit-in demonstrators was state action prohibited by the Fourteenth Amendment would result in resorts to self-help by owners of places of public accommodation, which might lead to a breakdown of law and order in society. State enforcement of trespass laws against sit-in demonstrators, the dissenters maintained, did not constitute state action violative of the Equal Protection Clause of the Fourteenth Amendment. The Fourteenth Amendment, they argued, "does not of itself, standing alone, in the absence of some cooperative state action or compulsion, forbid property holders, including restaurant owners, to ban people from entering their premises, even if the owners act out of racial prejudice."[35]

As the opinions in *Bell v. Maryland* revealed, therefore, Chief Justice Warren and Justices Goldberg and Douglas would have held that the Fourteenth Amendment required the desegregation of public accommodations, while Justices Black, Harlan, and White rejected that proposition. And Justices Brennan, Stewart, and Clark refused to address the question of whether the Fourteenth Amendment prohibited discrimination in facilities of public accommodation, but reversed the convictions in the *Bell* case on other grounds.[36]

While the Court was thus splintered on the issue of discrimination in public accommodations and the Constitution in the spring of 1964, Congress was also engaged in a rancorous debate as it considered the Civil Rights Act of 1964 and whether or not to once again enact a prohibition of discrimination in places of public accommodation as it had in tribute to Charles Sumner in 1875. And the ultimate resolution of that question by Congress would ensure that the issue of the relation of the Constitution to racial discrimination in facilities of public accommodation would soon be confronting the Supreme Court once again.

1

THE IDEA WHOSE TIME HAD COME:
THE CIVIL RIGHTS ACT OF 1964

The legislative proposals that ultimately became the Civil Rights Act of 1964 had originally been introduced by President John F. Kennedy in June 1963. Kennedy's action followed televised coverage of especially brutal police tactics against schoolchildren protesting segregation in Birmingham, Alabama, and the federal intervention to compel the admission of two black students to the University of Alabama despite the defiance of Alabama Governor George C. Wallace. Addressing a national television audience on June 11, President Kennedy announced his intention to seek civil rights legislation from Congress in response to what had become a crisis in race relations in America. "We are confronted primarily with a moral issue," he said. "It is as old as the Scriptures and it is as clear as the Constitution. The heart of the question is whether all Americans are to be afforded equal rights and equal opportunities, whether we are going to treat our fellow Americans as we want to be treated."[1]

Despite the public revulsion regarding the use of fire hoses and cattle prods against black schoolchildren in Birmingham and the assassination of Mississippi National Association for the Advancement of Colored People (NAACP) leader Medgar Evers on the night of the president's civil rights address to the nation, Kennedy's civil rights proposals languished in Congress along with most of the rest of his legislative program. By the fall of 1963 the prospects for meaningful civil rights legislation appeared minimal. The national trauma produced by the assassination of President Kennedy on November 22, however, revived his civil rights proposals in Congress as the most fitting memorial for the slain president. Addressing a joint session of Congress on November 27, President Lyndon B. Johnson thus declared that no "memorial oration or eulogy could more eloquently honor President Kennedy's memory than the earliest possible passage of the civil rights bill for which he fought so long."[2]

There ensued the longest debate regarding a legislative proposal in congressional history. Successful passage of the Civil Rights Act of 1964 required that control of the Rules Committee of the House of Representatives be wrested from its segregationist chairman, Congressman Howard Smith of Virginia, so the bill could be cleared for consideration by the House. In the Senate, a filibuster by southern senators, led by Georgia's Senator Richard B.

Russell, had to be broken to pave the way for a vote on the bill. This could be accomplished, the civil rights forces knew, only if the bill were a bipartisan measure, since Republican support in both the House and Senate was essential to its enactment. Crucial to this bipartisan support for the civil rights bill were the ranking Republican member of the House Judiciary Committee, Representative William McCulloch of Ohio, and the Republican minority leader in the Senate, Senator Everett Dirksen of Illinois.[3]

McCulloch's support for the civil rights bill was obtained in the summer of 1963 through negotiations conducted by Assistant Attorney General Burke Marshall, the head of the Civil Rights Division of the Department of Justice. McCulloch had felt betrayed during the passage of civil rights legislation in 1957 and 1960, when Republican-supported legislation had passed the House only to be watered down in the Senate by Democrats to prevent threatened filibusters by southern senators against the measures. He therefore demanded in the negotiations with Marshall that the Senate would not be allowed to gut any future House-passed civil rights bill and that he be given the sole power to approve any changes in the bill that might be made in the Senate. The Democratic administration must also give equal credit to Republicans for any civil rights bill that was enacted, McCulloch demanded. Marshall and Attorney General Robert Kennedy agreed to these demands, and the bargain for McCulloch's support was sealed.[4]

Senator Everett Dirksen, on the other hand, initially announced his opposition to what most considered the heart of the civil rights bill, Title II's prohibition of discrimination on the grounds of race, color, religion, or national origin in facilities of public accommodation. Dirksen's support for the bill and the Republican votes he could deliver in the Senate to break a southern filibuster were essential to the success of the bill, and he became the object of assiduous courtship by President Johnson, Senator Hubert Humphrey, who as Senate majority whip had charge of the bill, and Attorney General Kennedy and his Department of Justice lieutenants. Dirksen subsequently agreed to support Title II's ban on discrimination in public accommodations in return for relatively minor changes in the bill requiring federal deference to state agencies administering state antidiscrimination statutes. Once the civil rights bill had Dirksen's support, Senator Humphrey reported triumphantly to President Johnson that "we've got a much better bill than anybody even dreamed possible. We haven't weakened this bill *one damned bit*. In fact, in some places we've improved it. And that's no lie! We really have."[5]

Basking in his new role as the champion of the civil rights bill, Senator Dirksen lectured reporters on the moral necessity of enacting the bill. "Today the challenge is here!" he declared. "It is inescapable. It is time to deal with it!" And pointing toward the Senate chamber, he predicted with typical flamboyance, "No one that is on that floor is going to stop this. It is going to happen!" On June 10, when the Senate vote on cloture to end the southern filibuster against the bill occurred, the Democratic leadership permitted Dirksen to make the closing speech in favor of cloture and in support of the bill. Paraphrasing Victor Hugo, as he had earlier to reporters, Senator Dirksen declared: "Stronger than all the armies is an idea whose time has come. The time has come for equality of opportunity in sharing in government, in education, and in employment. It will not be stayed or denied. It is here." To a packed Senate chamber he said, "There is another reason why we dare not temporize with the issue which is before us. It is essentially moral in character. It must be resolved. It will not go away. Its time has come."[6]

The Senate then proceeded to invoke cloture against the southern filibuster by a vote of 71 to 29, ending the longest filibuster in the history of the institution and making the first successful cloture vote on a civil rights measure. Forty-four Democrats voted in favor, while Dirksen delivered 27 Republican votes for cloture. On June 19, the Senate voted to pass the civil rights bill, but, breaking with his Republican colleagues and Senator Dirksen, Senator Barry Goldwater of Arizona, the Republican front-runner for his party's presidential nomination, announced his opposition to the bill.[7]

The prohibitions against discrimination in public accommodations and employment in Titles II and VII of the bill prompted his opposition, Goldwater said.

> I find no constitutional basis for the exercise of Federal regulatory authority in either of these areas, and I believe the attempted usurpation of such power to be a grave threat to the very essence of our basic system of government; namely, that of a constitutional republic in which 50 sovereign States have reserved to themselves and to the people those powers not specifically granted to the Central or Federal Government.

Although he was unalterably opposed to discrimination, Goldwater declared, the bill would lead to the "creation of a police state. And so, because I am unalterably opposed to any threats to our great system of government and the loss of our God-given liberties, I shall vote 'no' on this bill."[8]

Although Goldwater's concerns would be subsequently reflected in the first constitutional challenge to the Civil Rights Act, the House of Representatives agreed to concur in the Senate amendments to the bill on July 2. The vote was an overwhelming 289 to 126. The bipartisan support that had been manifest in the Senate vote was duplicated in the House, with 153 Democrats and 136 Republicans voting in favor of the bill. In approving it, the House had responded to House Judiciary Committee chairman Emanuel Celler's appeal in the concluding speech on behalf of the bill. "I hope that we will have an overwhelming vote for this bill," Celler had said, "so that it can be said the Congress hearkens unto the voice of Leviticus, 'proclaiming liberty throughout the land to all the inhabitants thereof.'" With President Johnson's signature on the bill on the evening of July 2, the Civil Rights Act of 1964 became the law of the land.[9]

In addition to Title II, which prohibited discrimination on the basis of race, color, religion, or national origin in facilities of public accommodation, the most important provisions of the Civil Rights Act of 1964 strengthened federal protection of the right to vote in federal elections (Title I); authorized the Department of Justice to bring suits to desegregate public facilities, such as parks, public schools, and colleges (Titles III and IV); extended the life of the Commission on Civil Rights as a national clearinghouse of civil rights information (Title V); prohibited discrimination in federally assisted programs; created the Equal Employment Opportunity Commission to enforce the prohibition of employment discrimination on the grounds of race, color, religion, sex, and national origin by firms with twenty-five or more employees (Title VII); and created a Community Relations Service to aid states and communities to negotiate the settlement of disputes arising from discrimination (Title X).

The public accommodations provisions of Title II, however, had from the beginning been considered the heart of the Civil Rights Act. Title II was based in part on congressional power to enforce the Fourteenth Amendment's prohibition of the denial of the equal protection of the laws. Discrimination or segregation in places of public accommodation that was supported by state action was prohibited by Title II. And state action was defined as discrimination or segregation supported under color of state law or custom or usage enforced by state officials or required by the action of any state or subdivision of a state.

The public accommodations provisions of Title II were nevertheless primarily based on the power of Congress under the Commerce Clause to regulate interstate and foreign commerce. Facilities of public accommodation were defined by Title II to include any inn, hotel, or motel that provided lodging to transient guests, excepting a building containing five or fewer rooms in which the proprietor resided; restaurants, cafeterias, lunchrooms, lunch counters, soda fountains, or other facilities engaged in selling food for consumption on the premises, including those located in retail establishments or gasoline stations; and motion picture houses, theaters, concert halls, sports arenas, stadiums, and other places of exhibition and entertainment. The operations of inns, hotels, and motels were deemed by Title II to affect interstate commerce if they served or offered to serve interstate travelers. Restaurants and other eating establishments were deemed to affect commerce if they served or offered to serve interstate travelers or if a substantial portion of the food they served, or gasoline or other products they sold, had moved in interstate commerce. Motion picture houses, theaters, concert halls, sports arenas, and the like affected commerce, Title II provided, if they customarily presented films, performances, athletic teams, exhibitions, and other sources of entertainment that moved in interstate commerce. Discrimination on the basis of race, color, religion, or national origin was prohibited in all of these facilities of public accommodations.

The initial decision of the Kennedy administration, and the subsequent decision by Congress, to base Title II's public accommodations provisions primarily on the Commerce Clause, rather than on the congressional power under section five of the Fourteenth Amendment to enforce the provisions of that amendment, was the subject of sometimes heated debate during congressional consideration of the Civil Rights Act of 1964. The primary reason for basing the public accommodations provisions on the Commerce Clause rather than the Fourteenth Amendment, however, was supplied by the Supreme Court's decision in the *Civil Rights Cases* of 1883 and the Court's ruling in those cases that racial discrimination by private owners of places of public accommodation was beyond the legitimate reach of congressional power under section five of the Fourteenth Amendment.[10] Rather than pursuing the risky course of basing the 1964 act on section five of the Fourteenth Amendment and hoping the Court would reverse its decision in the *Civil Rights Cases,* both the administration and ultimately Congress made the safer choice to base the public accommodations provisions on the Commerce Clause—a choice undoubtedly reinforced by the splintering of the Court in the *Sit-in* cases on the issue of whether the Fourteenth Amendment prohibited racial discrimination in facilities of public accommodation.[11]

Unlike congressional power under section five of the Fourteenth Amendment, the power of Congress under the Commerce Clause can be exercised to regulate or prohibit actions of private individuals that obstruct or impose burdens on interstate commerce. And congressional power under the Commerce Clause had been broadly construed by the Supreme Court, beginning with opinions by Chief Justice John Marshall and then in subsequent decisions of the Court, especially since the 1930s.

In his classic exposition of the meaning of the Commerce Clause in *Gibbons v. Ogden* in 1824, Chief Justice John Marshall had interpreted the power of Congress over interstate commerce expansively to include "every species of commercial intercourse" and declared that no "sort of trade can be carried on . . . to which this power does not extend." Interstate commerce, he said, was "that commerce which concerns more States than one" or which affected other states. The power of Congress to regulate interstate commerce, Marshall continued, was the power "to prescribe the rule by which commerce is to be governed. This power, like all others vested in Congress, is complete in itself, may be exercised to its utmost extent, and acknowledges no limitations, other than are prescribed in the constitution." The power over commerce, he said, "is vested in Congress as absolutely as it would be in a single government, having in its constitution the same restrictions on the exercise of the power as are found in the constitution of the United States." And, Marshall indicated, the people must rely primarily on the political process to prevent abuses by Congress in its exercise of its commerce power.

> The wisdom and discretion of Congress, their identity with the people, and the influence which their constituents possess at elections, are, in this, as in many other instances, as that, for example, of declaring war, the sole restraints on which they have relied, to secure them from abuse. They are the restraints on which the people must often rely solely, in all representative governments.[12]

In *McCulloch v. Maryland,* decided in 1819, Chief Justice Marshall similarly interpreted the Necessary and Proper Clause expansively to give to Congress a broad and flexible choice of the means through which it implemented its other delegated powers, including its power under the Commerce Clause. "We admit, as all must admit, that the powers of the government are limited, and that its limits are not to be transcended," Marshall conceded.

> But we think the sound construction of the constitution must allow to the national legislature that discretion, with respect to the means by which the powers it confers are to be carried into execution, which will enable that body to perform the high duties assigned to it, in the manner most beneficial to the people. Let the end be legitimate, let it be within the scope of the constitution, and all means which are appropriate, which are plainly adapted to that end, which are not prohibited, but consist with the letter and spirit of the constitution, are constitutional.[13]

Although Chief Justice Marshall thus very broadly construed the power of Congress under the Commerce Clause as supplemented by the Necessary and Proper Clause, this arsenal of national power was not exercised by Congress during much of the nation's history. Indeed, the scope of congressional power over commerce was not the focus of constitutional litigation in the

Supreme Court regarding the Commerce Clause until the latter part of the nineteenth century. Until that time, the primary focus of decisions by the Supreme Court was the extent to which the Commerce Clause imposed limitations on the powers of the states. It was only when Congress began to rely on the Commerce Clause as a source of power upon which to base modern national regulatory legislation—such as the Interstate Commerce Act of 1887 and the Sherman Anti-Trust Act of 1890—that the Commerce Clause as a source of national power became a major focus of Supreme Court decisions, and Marshall's expansive interpretation of the commerce power became more relevant to constitutional issues confronting the Court.

In deciding the validity of modern regulatory measures enacted by Congress under the Commerce Clause, the Supreme Court in many cases construed the commerce power in the spirit of Marshall's opinion in *Gibbons v. Ogden*. In such cases, the Court held that the congressional power under the Commerce Clause extended not only to the regulation of interstate commerce itself but also to the regulation of local or intrastate activities if their regulation was necessary to the effective regulation of interstate commerce or the protection of commerce from burdens and obstructions. In *Southern Railway Co. v. United States* in 1911, for example, a unanimous Court sustained the validity under the Commerce Clause of the Safety Appliance Act of 1893.[14] The act required the railroads to install safety appliances on all their cars and locomotives. Rejecting an argument that the act was invalid because it regulated safety appliances on cars and locomotives used in intrastate commerce as well as those used in interstate commerce, the Court held that since railroad cars and locomotives engaged in intrastate commerce used the same tracks as interstate trains, Congress under the Commerce Clause could validly regulate the subject of safety appliances on intrastate trains in order to ensure the safety of trains engaged in interstate commerce.

Similarly, in the famous *Shreveport Case* of 1914,[15] the Court construed the commerce power to include the regulation of intrastate railroad rates if such regulation was necessary to protect interstate commerce from discrimination resulting from the intrastate rates. The railroads operating between Houston and Dallas, Texas, and Shreveport, Louisiana, were found to be charging substantially lower freight rates between Dallas and Houston and points in east Texas than they charged for freight shipped from Shreveport to Dallas or Houston and intermediate points in Texas. The Interstate Commerce Commission (ICC) ordered the railroads to equalize the rates in order to remove the resulting discrimination against interstate commerce from Shreveport into Texas, but the roads objected on the ground that the ICC's order was constitutionally invalid under the Commerce Clause, since it involved federal regulation of purely intrastate rail rates.

n violation of the Tenth Amendment. Similarly, while the Court con-
that Congress could validly regulate local activities that directly af-
or burdened interstate commerce, local activities that affected
rce only indirectly could not be validly regulated under the Com-
Clause. And, the Court again held, manufacturing and production ac-
and enterprises generally had only indirect effects on interstate
rce and were consequently beyond the legitimate reach of congres-
power under the Commerce Clause.

en Congress exercised its power under the Commerce Clause by en-
the Child Labor Act of 1916, barring the interstate shipment of prod-
oduced by child labor, for example, the Supreme Court invalidated
. In *Hammer v. Dagenhart,* decided in 1918, the Court ruled that the
gulation of the use of child labor in production or manufacturing en-
es violated the Tenth Amendment, which reserved the power to regu-
ch enterprises to the state and local governments.[20]

ing the 1930s, when Congress regulated coal production and the labor
ns and standards associated with coal mining, the Court again invali-
the congressional legislation. In *Carter v. Carter Coal Co.* in 1936, the
ruled that manufacturing and production activities, including coal
g, and the labor relations and conditions associated with them, were lo-
ivities that had only indirect effects on interstate commerce and were
eyond the scope of congressional power under the Commerce Clause.[21]
hough the Supreme Court initially resisted the unprecedented exercise
ional power by President Franklin Roosevelt and the New Deal Con-
n response to the Depression of the 1930s, by the spring of 1937 the
began to retreat from the dual federalism and direct-indirect effects
nes that it had previously used to curtail the commerce power. In the
hrough case of *National Labor Relations Board v. Jones and Laughlin*
Corp.,* decided in April 1937, the Court upheld the constitutionality of
ational Labor Relations Act of 1935 under the Commerce Clause.[22] In
nes and Laughlin* case, the Court sustained under the Commerce
e congressional protection of the right of workers to organize unions
bargain collectively in a steel manufacturing plant, despite the Court's
r rulings that manufacturing and production activities affected com-
only indirectly and were consequently beyond the reach of Congress
the Commerce Clause.

subsequent decisions, the Court made explicit what had been implicit
Jones and Laughlin case—that the doctrines that had previously lim-
he reach of the commerce power were repudiated and that the Court
eturning to the conception of the commerce power enunciated by
Justice John Marshall in *Gibbons v. Ogden.* In *United States v. Darby,*

In the opinion of the Court, Justice Charles Evans
become chief justice in 1930) rejected the arguments o
the validity of the ICC order. Under the Commerce
Congress,

> in the exercise of its paramount power, may preven
> strumentalities of interstate and intrastate commerci
> being used in their intrastate operations to the injury
> merce. This is not to say that Congress possesses the
> late the internal commerce of a state, as such, but
> power to foster and protect interstate commerce, an
> ures necessary or appropriate to that end, although
> tions of interstate carriers may thereby be controlled

The principle that the power of Congress under th
could validly be exercised to regulate local or intrastate
ulation was necessary to effectively regulate interstate c
tect commerce from burdens and obstructions was
Supreme Court to local activities substantially related t
currents or streams of interstate commerce. This curre
merce doctrine was endorsed by the Court in *Swift an*
in 1905 regarding the scope of the Sherman Anti-Trus
sequently reaffirmed by the Court in *Stafford v. Walla*
the Packers and Stockyards Act,[18] and in *Chicago Boa*
1923, sustaining the Grain Futures Act.[19] In each of t
sustained congressional regulation under the Comm
were concededly local activities, when viewed in isolati
substantially or intimately related to recurring curren
Congress had deemed it necessary to regulate in orde
rents of commerce from burdens or obstructions.

Despite the Supreme Court's broad reading of the s
power in such cases as the *Shreveport Case* and the curr
merce cases, prior to the 1930s it also limited the reach o
of Congress through the doctrine of dual federalism and
fects doctrine. Under the dual federalism doctrine, the
provisions, reserving to the states and the people all pow
national government, were considered to limit the sco
gated to Congress. Manufacturing and production ente
activities were reserved to the states for regulation unc
ment, the Court held, and attempts by Congress to re
subjects under the Commerce Clause were unconstituti

decided in 1941, the Court sustained the validity of the Fair Labor Standards Act (FLSA) of 1938 under the Commerce Clause.[23] The FLSA prohibited the shipment in interstate commerce of goods produced in violation of the minimum wage, maximum hour, and child labor regulations embodied in the act. Rejecting an argument that the FLSA regulated labor standards in manufacturing and production enterprises in violation of the Tenth Amendment, the Court reversed *Hammer v. Dagenhart* and repudiated the doctrine of dual federalism upon which that decision had rested. The power of Congress under the Commerce Clause, the Court held, was supplemented by the power conferred on it under the Necessary and Proper Clause. "The power of Congress over interstate commerce is not confined to the regulation of commerce among the states," the Court said. "It extends to those activities intrastate which so affect interstate commerce or the exercise of the power of Congress over it as to make regulation of them appropriate means to the attainment of a legitimate end, the exercise of the granted power of Congress to regulate interstate commerce."[24]

Following the repudiation of the doctrine of dual federalism in the *Darby* case, the Court in 1942 also scuttled the direct-indirect effects doctrine in *Wickard v. Filburn* and upheld the Agricultural Adjustment Act of 1938 under the Commerce Clause.[25] Roscoe Filburn, the operator of a small farm in Ohio, was allocated 11.1 acres on which to grow wheat under the commodity production control provisions of the Agricultural Adjustment Act. Filburn, however, planted 23 acres of wheat and produced 239 bushels in excess of his quota under the act, and he was ordered to pay a penalty or store his excess wheat to keep it off the market. Although Filburn had intended to consume on his own farm the wheat he grew, using it as food, seed, and feed for his livestock, the Court held that his wheat production could be validly reached and regulated under the Commerce Clause. While Filburn's overproduction of wheat might be local in nature, the Court said, "and though it may not be regarded as commerce, it may still, whatever its nature, be reached by Congress if it exerts a substantial economic effect on interstate commerce, and this irrespective of whether such effect is what might at some earlier time have been defined as 'direct' or 'indirect.'"[26]

A local activity's effect on interstate commerce was also not to be gauged by viewing that activity in isolation from all similar activities nationwide, the Court held. While Filburn's minimal overproduction of wheat would have only a slight effect on commerce, if all similarly situated farmers across the country were to overproduce wheat in like amounts, the Court noted, the effect on commerce would be substantial because the total volume of excess wheat would lower the price for which wheat sold in interstate commerce. Also, if Filburn and all similarly situated farmers grew like amounts of wheat for home consumption, the effect on commerce would again be substantial, the Court said, since the amount of wheat that would otherwise have been purchased in interstate commerce would be substantially reduced, producing an adverse effect on the interstate price of wheat. There was consequently no doubt, the Court concluded, "that Congress may properly have considered that wheat consumed on the farm where grown if wholly outside the scheme of regulation would have a substantial effect in defeating and obstructing its purpose to stimulate trade therein at increased prices."[27]

In numerous decisions in the decades following the *Jones and Laughlin, Darby,* and *Wickard v. Filburn* cases, the Supreme Court repeatedly affirmed that the modern scope of congressional power under the Commerce and Necessary and Proper Clauses included the power to regulate not only interstate commerce itself but also local activities that substantially affected, burdened, or obstructed interstate commerce. Under these decisions, discrimination in facilities of public accommodation, such as hotels, motels, and restaurants, while concededly local occurrences, could nonetheless affect interstate commerce by discouraging interstate travel by blacks or by reducing the market for products in interstate commerce. This well-established breadth of congressional power under the Commerce Clause was consequently a major factor contributing to the decision of the Kennedy administration, and subsequently Congress, to base the public accommodations provisions of Title II of the Civil Rights Act of 1964 on the Commerce Clause rather than on the more doubtful source of constitutional power under the Fourteenth Amendment.

The Kennedy administration's choice of the Commerce Clause rather than the Fourteenth Amendment as the constitutional basis of the public accommodations provisions, however, initially drew strong objections from many congressional Republicans whose support for the civil rights bill was essential to its passage. The Republicans regarded the Fourteenth Amendment as one of the great Republican achievements of the Civil War and Reconstruction era and its addition to the Constitution in 1868 as the high-water mark of Republican efforts to protect civil rights and to guarantee racial equality. Consequently, there was essentially a visceral affinity on the part of congressional Republicans for "their" Fourteenth Amendment as the proper constitutional basis upon which to enact the public accommodations provisions of the civil rights bill. The purpose of the public accommodations provisions was after all equality of access to places of public accommodation, they argued, and it was the Equal Protection Clause of the Fourteenth Amendment, rather than the Commerce Clause, that addressed the issue of equality in civil rights most directly in the Constitution, and accordingly the Fourteenth Amendment was the most appropriate constitutional provision upon which to base the public accommodations provisions.[28]

Republican opposition to the Commerce Clause as the basis of the public accommodations provisions was also based on the fact that it had been the Commerce Clause upon which Congress had relied in enacting many legislative programs to which the Republicans had been opposed, such as the National Labor Relations Act of 1935 and the Fair Labor Standards Act of 1938. Indeed, it had been congressional power under the Commerce Clause that had been the constitutional underpinning of much of the New Deal–era legislation that had greatly expanded, over Republican opposition, the power of the national government to regulate economic affairs. Congressional Republicans thus identified the Commerce Clause with an overintrusive federal government that the Democrats had created, and any further extension of the reach of the commerce power through the civil rights bill drew almost instinctive Republican resistance.[29]

To support their opposition to the Commerce Clause as the basis of the public accommodations provisions, Republicans had to meet the argument that a reliance on the Fourteenth Amendment as the constitutional basis of those provisions would make them vulnerable to constitutional attack under the Supreme Court's decision in the *Civil Rights Cases* of 1883. In response, however, Republicans contended that facilities of public accommodation were licensed by the states throughout the nation and that the licensing of places of accommodation by the states was state action, which made discrimination in those facilities violative of the Fourteenth Amendment. Congress, they argued, could therefore validly enact corrective legislation against such state action under section five of the Fourteenth Amendment. At the same time, however, Republicans supported a civil rights bill that would be limited in scope and would not impose unduly intrusive federal restrictions on free enterprise.[30]

The tide turned against reliance on the Fourteenth Amendment and in favor of the Commerce Clause as the basis of the public accommodations provisions during hearings on Title II of the civil rights bill before the Senate Commerce Committee in 1963. Especially effective in convincing Republicans to accept the Commerce Clause as the basis of Title II was a brief submitted to the committee by Professor Paul A. Freund of the Harvard Law School, analyzing the constitutional and policy implications of reliance on either the Fourteenth Amendment or the Commerce Clause as the constitutional basis of Title II. Freund convincingly demonstrated that public accommodations provisions based on the Commerce Clause were almost certain to be sustained by the Supreme Court, given the broad interpretation of the congressional commerce power since the 1930s. On the other hand, he argued that relying on the Fourteenth Amendment as the basis for Title II of the civil rights bill would raise problems under the Court's decision in the *Civil Rights Cases* of 1883.[31]

More importantly, however, Freund contended that basing the public accommodations provisions on the Fourteenth Amendment on the theory that state licensing of places of public accommodation was state action, thus making discrimination in such places violative of the Fourteenth Amendment, would have far-reaching and unintended consequences if the theory was accepted by the courts. If such a theory was sustained by the Supreme Court, he pointed out, the result would be that discrimination in any business, profession, or occupation licensed by a state would automatically violate the Fourteenth Amendment. And the impact on the free enterprise system would be broader and more intrusive than would be acceptable to congressional Republicans. In addition, Freund noted, licensing practices varied considerably from state to state, with the result that there would be no uniformity in the application of public accommodations regulations if they were based on the Fourteenth Amendment under the licensing theory. Finally, he argued, the states could completely escape a public accommodations measure predicated on state licensing by repealing licensing requirements altogether.[32]

All of these problems, Freund maintained, could be obviated by basing the public accommodations provisions on the Commerce Clause rather than the Fourteenth Amendment. Unlike the far-reaching and intrusive impact on the free enterprise system that would result from a reliance on the Fourteenth Amendment, he argued, if the public accommodations provisions were based on the Commerce Clause, Congress could carefully calibrate the reach of federal regulation and limit its scope. Reliance on the Commerce Clause as the basis of Title II, Freund concluded, would consequently be the best method to implement the policy preferences of the Republicans in limiting the degree of federal regulatory intrusion upon the business and commercial community.[33]

Armed with the arguments of Professor Freund and other constitutional experts, Attorney General Robert Kennedy was able to make a persuasive case for the administration's choice of the Commerce Clause as the basis of the public accommodations provisions during his testimony before the Senate Commerce and Judiciary Committees during the summer and fall of 1963. The initial Republican aversion to basing Title II on the Commerce Clause was thus successfully overcome.[34]

While the public accommodations provisions of the Civil Rights Act of 1964 were based partially on the Fourteenth Amendment (in prohibiting racial discrimination in public accommodations supported by state action), the primary basis of Title II rested on the Commerce Clause and the theory that discrimination in places of public accommodation adversely affected or burdened interstate commerce. The battleground on which the constitutionality of the public accommodations provisions of the Civil Rights Act would be fought would consequently be the Commerce Clause and not the Fourteenth Amendment.

As the Civil Rights Act approached final passage in Congress, President Johnson was concerned that the government's enforcement of the act would meet massive resistance in the South. On June 19, when the act passed the Senate, Johnson remarked to NAACP head Roy Wilkins, "Our troubles are just beginning. I guess you know that." He was considering sending spokesmen to communicate to the southern governors that "we've got to have observance instead of enforcement," Johnson told Wilkins. "If they'll observe the law, then we won't have to take pistols and enforce it."[35]

Three young civil rights workers, Michael Schwerner, Andrew Goodman, and James Chaney, had been murdered in Mississippi in June, and the president was especially concerned that violent resistance to the Civil Rights Act might occur in that state. Before signing the act later in the evening of July 2, Johnson urged Federal Bureau of Investigation director J. Edgar Hoover to beef up the FBI presence in Mississippi to monitor the Ku Klux Klan. "You ought to have the best intelligence system—better than you've got on the Communists," the President said, and continued,

> We ought to have intelligence on that state because that's gonna be the most dangerous thing we have this year. If I have to send in troops, or somebody gets rash and we have to go like what we did in Little Rock [when federal troops were required to desegregate the public schools in 1957], it'd be awfully dangerous.[36]

If the enforcement of the Civil Rights Act was to occur in the courts, rather than in the streets as President Johnson feared, the primary burden would fall on the Civil Rights Division of the Department of Justice, headed by Assistant Attorney General Burke Marshall. Trained at Yale Law School, Burke Marshall had been a successful partner in the Washington, D.C., law firm of Covington and Burling, specializing in antitrust law. Deputy Attorney General Byron White recommended Marshall to Attorney General Robert Kennedy to be head of the Civil Rights Division. Marshall's interview for the job with Kennedy was, however, a disaster. With neither man possessing a gift for small talk, Kennedy and Marshall sat through the first ten minutes of the interview in silence. "I blew it," Marshall later confessed to his wife, while Kennedy subsequently complained, "I have nothing in common with that man."[37]

When Marshall was nonetheless appointed head of the Civil Rights Division, civil rights leaders expressed dismay over the appointment of a man they perceived to be a corporate lawyer with no record of support for civil rights or identification with the civil rights movement. Attorney General Kennedy and Deputy Attorney General White, however, had deliberately decided to select an outstanding lawyer without any ideological ties to the civil rights movement to be the head of the Civil Rights Division. "We thought it would be more interesting," White said later, "to get a first-class lawyer who would do the job in a technically proficient way that would be defensible in court—that Southerners would not think of as a vendetta, but an even-handed application of the law."[38]

Burke Marshall had been attracted to government service by President Kennedy's call for citizen service to the country and, as Marshall said later, "the subject matter of civil rights and the bringing to bear the processes of the law on that, you know, is a matter of great interest—at least, it seemed to me to be obvious at the time—1961, that that was going to be the most interesting lawyers' work going on in the country." Marshall continued,

> As I say, I did anticipate that [civil rights] was going to be the most in-teresting and demanding lawyers' work going on in the country, and so I think I anticipated that all right; but to say that I anticipated the real historical upheaval that was going to take place in the next five years, I didn't anticipate that.[39]

If massive resistance to the Civil Rights Act materialized, Burke Marshall and the Civil Rights Division would be stretched perilously thin in the enforcement of the act. The Civil Rights Division consisted in 1964 of only fifty-five attorneys, with the responsibility of enforcing not only the Civil Rights Act of 1964 but all other federal civil rights statutes as well.[40] The Civil Rights Division could of course call upon local U.S. attorney's offices for assistance, as well as the investigative assistance of the FBI, but nevertheless the manpower available to meet any massive resistance to the Civil Rights Act was limited at best. Before the act became law, Burke Marshall ordered the deployment of Civil Rights Division attorneys to various anticipated trouble spots in the South to gather information that could be used if resistance to the act was widespread or if violence broke out. When the Civil Rights Act became law on July 2, therefore, Burke Marshall and the Civil Rights Division, along with the president, the attorney general, and the country at large, waited with anticipation to see how reaction to the act would unfold.[41]

2

THE GENESIS OF THE
HEART OF ATLANTA MOTEL CASE

When the passage of the Civil Rights Act of 1964 became inevitable with the U.S. Senate's approval of the act on June 19, the reactions throughout the South were largely predictable. "This is a sad day for individual freedom and liberty," Alabama Governor George C. Wallace declared. "It is ironical that this event occurs as we approach the celebration of Independence Day. On that day we won our freedom. On this day we have largely lost it." He predicted that the "American people will rise up in indignation when they realize the awful consequences of this legislation." Florida Governor Farris Bryant denounced the Senate for inflicting a "great injury to national unity by passing a bill which strikes first and hardest at the South and which probably will not strike at all at most of the states from which the proponents come," while Louisiana Governor John A. McKeithen lamented what he said was "a bad day for Louisiana and all other southern states." And Mississippi Governor Paul B. Johnson predicted that the Civil Rights Act would "divide the people" and result in "civil strife and chaotic conditions."[1]

President Johnson's signing of the Civil Rights Act on July 2 occurred in the presence of Attorney General Robert Kennedy, Martin Luther King Jr., Senators Hubert Humphrey and Everett Dirksen, and a bipartisan group of over a hundred other members of Congress who had supported the act. "My fellow citizens," the president said, "we come now to a time of testing. We must not fail. Let us close the springs of racial poison. Let us pray for wise and understanding hearts." Earlier in the day, Johnson had remarked in a telephone conversation with NAACP executive secretary Roy Wilkins regarding the Civil Rights Act that "[w]e've got a long, hard fight ahead, but if we work together, we'll find the answers. 'Cause we're right. We're right."[2]

The very real fear in the Johnson administration that the Civil Rights Act might meet with massive and perhaps violent resistance in the South was manifested by an off-the-record meeting held in the Cabinet Room of the White House immediately following the signing of the act by President Johnson. In attendance, among others, were the president, Attorney General Kennedy, Deputy Attorney General Nicholas Katzenbach, Burke Marshall, Secretary of Commerce Luther Hodges, and former Florida governor Leroy Collins, head of the Community Relations Service, as well as the leadership of virtually all civil rights groups, including A. Phillip Randolph, James

Foreman, Martin Luther King Jr., Whitney Young, Roy Wilkins, and Clarence Mitchell. President Johnson pointed out in his remarks to the group that now that the Civil Rights Act was the law of the land, the rights of blacks were legally enforceable in the courts, thus making desegregation demonstrations unnecessary and possibly self-defeating. And Johnson emphasized that it was critical that the Department of Justice be allowed to carefully select the cases that would test the validity of the Civil Rights Act in order to avoid decisions in the lower federal courts ruling the act unconstitutional and thus encouraging resistance to the act's enforcement, even though the Supreme Court might ultimately overrule the lower courts and uphold the validity of the act. In response, the black leaders in attendance pledged their full cooperation with the Justice Department in testing the validity of the Civil Rights Act.[3]

It was evident from this White House meeting that the strategy of the Justice Department was to carefully seek to control the selection of the cases that would test the validity of the public accommodations provisions and to avoid if possible the filing of unsuitable cases as the result of pressure from demonstrations by blacks against segregated facilities, cases that might well be lost in the lower federal courts. This strategy was nevertheless in the end unsuccessful, since both of the cases that ultimately tested the validity of the public accommodations provisions in the Supreme Court were not initiated by the Justice Department but rather by owners of facilities of public accommodation. And while the case that tested the applicability of the Civil Rights Act to motels and hotels was eminently suitable from the government's standpoint, the case that tested the act's applicability to restaurants clearly was not, and indeed resulted in a decision in the lower federal court invalidating the public accommodations provisions as applied to restaurants, an event the government had sought to avoid.

The various civil rights organizations, including the Student Non-Violent Coordinating Committee (SNCC), the Congress of Racial Equality (CORE), the Martin Luther King–led Southern Christian Leadership Conference (SCLC), and the National Association for the Advancement of Colored People (NAACP), were reported in the press as prepared to test compliance with the public accommodations provisions of the Civil Rights Act. The targets of the civil rights groups, it was reported, would be those facilities of public accommodation that had proven most obdurate in their resistance to desegregation in the past. These included, the *Wall Street Journal* reported, such establishments as the Woolworth lunch counter in Jackson, Mississippi, the Leb's and Pickrick restaurants in Atlanta, Georgia, and some other southern outlets of cafeteria, hotel, and motel chains. Civil rights forces in Birmingham, Alabama, faced an especially daunting task in testing compliance with the Civil Rights Act, the *Wall Street Journal* noted, since they would be confronted with "tackling hundreds of segregated facilities."[4]

There were scattered vows of defiance regarding the Civil Rights Act, although they were unexpectedly few in number. Louis W. Hollis, a Jackson, Mississippi, official of the segregationist Citizens' Councils of America, predicted that compliance with the public accommodations provisions would be no more effective than Prohibition had been. "Most businessmen feel the law will be declared unconstitutional and are going to treat it like they did the Supreme Court decision of May 17, 1954 [holding public school segregation unconstitutional]," Hollis said. "It will be like the speakeasies of Prohibition when people went on drinking as though there was no Prohibition."[5]

As one of the most rapidly growing urban centers in the South, Atlanta, Georgia, was the focus of much attention regarding how the Civil Rights Act would be received. Although Atlanta cultivated a national image of good race relations as the "city too busy to hate," the reality of race relations in the city prior to the Civil Rights Act belied its national image. Upon assuming the office of mayor of Atlanta in 1962, the progressive Ivan Allen found that while the city buses, golf courses, and, to an extent, parks had been desegregated, Atlanta's hotels, restaurants, and department stores remained largely segregated, as were city hall employees, and black Atlanta police officers lacked the power to arrest whites. Mayor Allen attempted to negotiate desegregation agreements between the owners of the city's facilities of public accommodation and its increasingly militant civil rights groups, but by 1963, he admitted that only limited progress toward desegregation had been achieved.[6]

Allen said later,

Atlanta *had* made strides during the first three years of the sixties, but the battle lines had been drawn quite clearly at the restaurants and the hotels. Everything I had tried in those areas had failed. There had been endless meetings with the hotel and restaurant people over the past three or four years, and no matter what agreement was reached everyone involved would be split in every direction.

The hotel and restaurant associations would not even respond to the pragmatic argument that unless they opened their doors to everyone, Atlanta's convention and tourist business—not to mention its favorable national image—would plummet.[7]

When Mayor Allen received a request from President Kennedy through an intermediary to testify before Congress in favor of the then pending civil rights bill, Allen's initial response was that it would be political "suicide" for him to do so, since compliance with the president's request would almost certainly result in his defeat for reelection as mayor in 1965. After personal persuasion by President Kennedy, however, Allen reluctantly agreed to testify, becoming the first public official from the deep South to do so.[8]

Meanwhile, demonstrations and sit-ins by civil rights groups escalated in Atlanta, coordinated by the Summit Leadership Conference, a coalition of the older, traditional civil rights groups such as the NAACP and the newer, increasingly militant groups, such as SNCC. In May 1963, the Atlanta Chamber of Commerce unanimously adopted a resolution urging the city's businesses to desegregate in order to "maintain the city's healthy climate." In response, eighteen leading hotels and motels and thirty restaurants agreed to desegregate, although the hotels and motels agreed to desegregate for conventions only. In a subsequent survey, however, the Atlanta Council on Human Relations found that most of the hotels, motels, and restaurants that had agreed to desegregate in the spring of 1963 had in fact resegregated.[9]

Demonstrations protesting the continued segregation of most of the city's facilities of public accommodation, especially restaurants, increased during December 1963 and January 1964. The demonstrators targeted the Toddle House restaurants as well as Lester Maddox's Pickrick restaurant, Leb's, and the restaurant at the Heart of Atlanta Motel, where three hundred demonstrators were arrested.[10] While the Toddle House management subsequently agreed to desegregate its nationwide chain of 222 restaurants, Lester G. Maddox, the forty-nine-year-old owner of the downtown Atlanta Pickrick restaurant, and Charles Leb, owner of Leb's, adamantly refused to desegregate their operations.[11]

At a civil rights rally sponsored by the Summit Leadership Conference in mid-December, Martin Luther King Jr. declared that while Atlanta billed itself as "the city too busy to hate, something strange and sad has happened to Atlanta. While boasting of its progress and virtue, Atlanta has allowed itself to fall behind about every major Southern city in progress toward desegregation."[12]

In early December, the Atlanta Board of Aldermen adopted a resolution urging the voluntary desegregation of the city's public accommodations, and in January, Mayor Allen announced that he would seek the passage of a city public accommodations ordinance. On January 10, Allen met with thirty-five hotel and motel owners as well as the owners of one hundred of the city's restaurants. Following the meeting, fourteen major hotels and motels announced that they would desegregate, and these were subsequently joined by Atlanta's Holiday Inns, bringing the total to sixteen. And on January 21, the *Atlanta Constitution* reversed its earlier editorial opposition to the civil rights bill. While criticizing the demonstrations occurring in the city, the *Constitution* acknowledged that the voluntary desegregation of Atlanta's public accommodations had failed.[13]

Following the January 10 meeting with Mayor Allen, no action was taken by the Atlanta Restaurant Association, in contrast to the desegregation pledged by the motels and hotels. The Restaurant Association instead called upon its members to "search their hearts, minds, and consciences and make their own decision as to what their future course of action will be." As demonstrations targeting segregation in the city's restaurants continued to escalate, however, the position of the Restaurant Association appeared to harden. In a full-page ad published in the *Atlanta Constitution* in late January, the association defended

> the basic right of an individual, any individual of whatever race, creed or color, to engage in business, to purvey any commodity or service which is lawful, to cater to a clientele of his own choosing and, once selected, to honor his obligation to continue to provide the goods and/or services which first prompted the customers' allegiance to the establishment.

And in an obvious reference to the civil rights bill pending before Congress, the association warned that the "ever-increasing trend toward centralized control and regulation must stop before socialism is an accomplished fact." The ad closed with a denunciation of the civil rights demonstrations, which were "calculated to upset the tranquility of our city," and the "coercive pressures exerted by the city administration and certain civic leaders against the restaurant owners of Atlanta." When President Johnson signed the Civil Rights Act in July, the Atlanta Council on Human Relations found that only twenty desegregated eating facilities existed in the city.[14]

When the Civil Rights Act became law, Lester Maddox pledged that his Pickrick restaurant, which specialized in serving fried chicken, would never desegregate, and he vowed to defy the law. "I'll do just as I have in the past—throw the Negroes out—even if it falls my due to go to jail," Maddox announced. Leb's restaurant, another frequent target of civil rights demonstrators, on the other hand, desegregated in response to the act. Charles Leb, the owner of the restaurant, posted a sign protesting that the Civil Rights Act "forces me to serve Communist-led hoodlums," but he nevertheless posted another sign announcing, "I am now integrated."[15]

The reaction to the Civil Rights Act in Atlanta was nevertheless on the whole quite receptive, despite the avowed intransigence of Lester Maddox. As the measure had moved toward passage by Congress, the *Atlanta Constitution* had denied that the act was a punitive measure directed at the South. "It is a bill with which we can live and we must prepare ourselves to do just that," the *Constitution* said editorially. "The alternative is chaos. Orderly accommodation to the law of the land is the only way. It is also our greatest opportunity." And Atlanta Mayor Ivan Allen, who had testified in favor of the act before Congress, predicted that the city would "cooperate and will respect the law."[16]

On the day President Johnson signed the act, the Atlanta Chamber of Commerce's executive committee urged Atlanta businesses to "adjust promptly and peacefully" to the act. "For the past several years the Atlanta Chamber of Commerce has urged its members and all Atlanta businessmen to adopt voluntarily the concept of doing business without regard to race, color, or creed," the committee pointed out. Atlanta businesses and individuals should "exercise good judgment as well as patience during this transition period so that peace and good order will prevail," it said, and predicted that Atlanta business "will adjust promptly and peacefully in the interest of a continuance of law and order in Atlanta." The Chamber of Commerce's action drew editorial praise from the *Atlanta Constitution*, which observed that the Chamber had "maintained its record of wise and forthright leadership." The "business and economic leadership of Atlanta has again taken a quiet and reasoned lead in pointing to the wise way," it added, "and setting an example that will be a help to all individual businesses and citizens of the city."[17]

The Atlanta Chamber of Commerce was subsequently joined by many other civic and business organizations in the city in urging peaceful compliance with the Civil Rights Act. Included among these organizations were the Atlanta Restaurant Association, which reversed its earlier opposition to desegregation, the Atlanta Hotel and Motel Association, the Atlanta Convention Bureau, and the Greater Atlanta Council of Churches. The Atlanta Hotel and Motel Association announced that its members "unanimously resolve to continue its tradition of law observance by full compliance with the civil rights act." Atlanta's black leadership also joined these organizations in urging the preservation of peace and good order in the city as the 1964 act was implemented. The Atlanta Negro Summit Leadership Conference thus called upon the black community to act with "dignity and responsibility" in exercising its "newly acquired freedom and equality." The Leadership Conference predicted that "massive testing [of compliance with the act] will be unnecessary." "We feel that the provisions of the public accommodations section will be accepted by such large numbers of establishments that massive testing will be unnecessary," the conference said. "With white obedience to the law, and Negro respect for law and order," the *Atlanta Constitution* said, "let the changes come the best way—without defiance or rancor—and we will find, as the South has found at each step forward in this field, that the change is far less difficult than we have feared."[18]

Despite the solidarity of the leadership of Atlanta in support of peaceful compliance with the Civil Rights Act, Lester Maddox continued to vociferously vow that he would never comply with the act and desegregate his downtown Pickrick restaurant. And another source of resistance to the public accommodations provisions was the Heart of Atlanta Motel.

The motel had been built in 1956 by Allen Glover Webb, Moreton Rolleston Jr., and other investors. Webb engaged in extensive business travel and found he preferred motels to hotels. He therefore concluded that other travelers would welcome motel accommodations in downtown Atlanta. The target of earlier civil rights demonstrations, the Heart of Atlanta Motel's restaurant, leased to a separate company, had desegregated by the time the Civil Rights Act became law, but the motel itself maintained a policy of segregation. It had been the target of picketing in 1962 by delegates to the NAACP's national convention in Atlanta when the motel, along with most of the downtown hotels, refused to accommodate blacks. When fourteen of the leading Atlanta hotels agreed in 1963 to accommodate conventions that included blacks, the Heart of Atlanta Motel declined to join the agreement. The motel thus continued to be a target of protests against its policy of segregation, and Moreton Rolleston, who also served as the motel's attorney, had sworn out warrants and had demonstrators prosecuted for trespass in the Fulton County Superior Court.[19]

Forty-six years old in 1964, Moreton Rolleston Jr. was born in 1917 in Athens, Georgia. He received his undergraduate college education at Emory University in Atlanta, graduating in 1939. Rolleston then entered the Emory University law school and received his law degree, and was admitted to the Georgia bar in 1941. During World War II, he served in the U.S. Navy and attained the rank of lieutenant commander.[20]

As the inevitability of congressional passage of the Civil Rights Act became apparent in the spring and early summer, Moreton Rolleston had begun preparing a constitutional challenge of the act as soon as it became law. About two hours after President Johnson signed the act on July 2, Rolleston rushed to the federal courthouse in Atlanta, where the United States District Court for the Northern District of Georgia, Atlanta Division, was headquartered. Since the president did not sign the act until approximately 6:45 P.M., however, the courthouse had already closed for the day and was not scheduled to reopen until Monday, July 6, following the Fourth of July holiday. Not to be deterred, Rolleston proceeded to the home of the chief clerk of the U.S. district court and, at 8:55 P.M., filed with the clerk a complaint challenging the constitutionality of the 1964 act. Rolleston's suit thus became the first constitutional challenge to the Civil Rights Act filed anywhere in the country, and apparently this had been the motive for his alacrity.[21]

In his complaint in the federal district court on behalf of the Heart of Atlanta Motel Corporation, Rolleston described the 216-room motel's location in the city block bounded by Courtland Street, Harris Street, Piedmont Avenue, and Baker Street in downtown Atlanta. The business of the Heart of Atlanta Motel, he contended in the complaint, "is so intermingled with wholly local business and so essentially local in character as to be outside the stream of interstate commerce," adding:

> When Heart of Atlanta rents sleeping accommodations to a guest who has come from another state, that guest has literally "come to rest;" his interstate movement is completed by the time he reaches the premises of the motel; and he has ceased to be in the stream of interstate commerce when he comes to threshold of [the] Heart of Atlanta Motel.

Since the motel's operations were therefore not a part of interstate commerce, Rolleston asserted, the public accommodations provisions of the Civil Rights Act were unconstitutional as applied to the motel.[22]

The public accommodations provisions were also unconstitutional as applied to the Heart of Atlanta Motel, Rolleston alleged, because they would deprive the motel of its property without due process of law and take its property without just compensation, in violation of the Fifth Amendment of the Constitution. Because the motel would be deprived of its property right to operate as it saw fit, according to Rolleston, and because 95 percent of its white customers would not patronize the motel if it served blacks, he alleged damages in the amount of $11 million in addition to seeking injunctive relief barring the application of the Civil Rights Act to the motel. In an amended complaint filed on July 15, he also argued that the 1964 act violated the Thirteenth Amendment of the Constitution by imposing involuntary servitude on the owners of the Heart of Atlanta Motel.[23]

"Heart of Atlanta Motel has never rented sleeping accommodations to members of the Negro race, is not now renting sleeping accommodations to members of the Negro race and does not intend to do so unless ordered by this court to comply with the provisions of the Civil Rights Act of 1964," Rolleston's complaint continued. And since the act authorized the U.S. attorney general to obtain injunctions against places of public accommodation that discriminated on the basis of race, the complaint alleged, the Heart of Atlanta Motel would suffer irreparable injury unless the district court held the public accommodations provisions of the 1964 act unconstitutional and issued an injunction prohibiting the enforcement of the act against the motel.[24]

Interviewed by the FBI on July 11, an informant reported that Moreton Rolleston was "very opinionated but is very fair and forthright," as well as being "a hard driver" and extremely "ambitious." Rolleston, the informant continued, was "a strict segregationist but is fair about this matter," and he was "very adamant and positive about never accepting Negroes as guests at the Heart of Atlanta Motel." He would "go to any extreme through legal means to avoid desegregation," the informant predicted, but he would not "defy a court injunction in this connection and after all legal efforts have failed, he will desegregate the Heart of Atlanta Motel." Rolleston, the informant added, had resigned from the Atlanta Hotel Association when it initiated desegregation negotiations with blacks because he felt the association was attempting to dictate policy to its members.[25]

In contrast to Moreton Rolleston's lawful and peaceful challenge to the Civil Rights Act, Lester Maddox as the owner of the Pickrick restaurant adopted defiant, headline-grabbing, and at times unlawful tactics in resisting the act. On July 3, three black theology students at the Interdenominational Theological Center at Atlanta University, George F. Willis Jr., Woodrow T. Lewis, and Albert L. Dunn, attempted to enter Maddox's restaurant, but they were confronted by Maddox, who pointed a revolver at them and shouted, "Get out of here and don't ever come back." At the same time, a crowd of white customers, armed with pick handles, menaced the three young men. Included in the crowd was a small boy, dragging a pick handle and shouting, "I'm gonna kill me a nigger." Two additional blacks were turned away from the Pickrick by Maddox on July 6. "Stop right where you are," he shouted. "You're not going to eat in my place tonight, tomorrow night, or any other time."[26]

On July 8, Assistant Attorney General Burke Marshall in a letter to FBI director J. Edgar Hoover requested an investigation of Lester Maddox and the Pickrick restaurant:

Your Bureau has previously advised this [Civil Rights] Division that three Negroes were forcibly ejected from the premises of the Pickrick Restaurant in Atlanta, Georgia, by Lester Maddox, the proprietor, on July 2 [actually July 3], 1964. At our request you have heretofore interviewed the three Negroes involved and are interviewing a representative number of newspapermen who witnessed the incident. You are also obtaining copies of press photographs at our request. Your Bureau has further advised this Division that Mr. Maddox on July 6, 1964, again refused to admit Negroes to the Pickrick Restaurant. On this as well as the prior occasion Mr. Maddox was armed with a pistol and pickaxe handles were made available on the premises of the restaurant for white persons to use in intimidating Negroes.[27]

"A full investigation is desired to determine whether Lester Maddox and others have engaged and are engaging in a pattern or practice of resistance to the provisions of Title II of the Civil Rights Act of 1964," Marshall said. The FBI investigation should include a determination of the ownership and management of the Pickrick restaurant and the production of a sketch and acquisition of photographs of the restaurant, showing street locations, entrances and exits, parking lots, and layouts of the rooms in the building, Marshall indicated. The restaurant employees should be interviewed, he added, to determine what instructions they had received concerning service to blacks, any efforts of blacks to obtain service at the restaurant, when the pick handles were first displayed, where they came from, and what they were used for, and whether Maddox belonged to any segregationist organizations and whether segregationist activities, meetings, or literature had been held or were available at the restaurant. The Bureau should also determine, Marshall requested, whether Maddox had a permit to carry a gun and when it was issued. Also all available witnesses to the ejection of blacks from the restaurant should be interviewed and any film of such incidents should be obtained. Finally, he concluded, the Bureau should determine "the sources which supply the food prepared by the Pickrick Restaurant. Determine the approximate amount of each category of food procured each month and what part of it comes from sources outside the State of Georgia."[28]

Although their tactics of resisting the Civil Rights Act differed, Lester Maddox and Moreton Rolleston both claimed that their resistance to the act was essential to the preservation of traditional American liberties against the onslaught of the federal government. Maddox would thus subsequently deny that his actions were motivated by racial hatred or bias:

> The photographs of Lester Maddox and his son, armed with pistol and pick handle in defense of what was theirs, were widely circulated, and everywhere the liberal press made me out a racist and bigot and rabble-rouser. I knew then, just as I know now, that I was trying to protect not only the rights of Lester Maddox, but of every citizen, including the three men I chased off my property, for if they could violate my right of private property, then there would be nothing to prevent me from violating theirs.

Maddox had previously been an unsuccessful candidate for mayor of Atlanta and lieutenant governor of Georgia, but he would now exploit his image as the symbol of resistance to desegregation to become the next governor of Georgia.[29]

Maddox's claim that his resistance to the Civil Rights Act was a principled one without motivation by racial bigotry was belied by his sponsorship on July 4 of a "Patriot's Day Rally against Tyranny." The rally was held in the

Lakewood Park section of Atlanta, the city's largest white working-class neighborhood, and was attended by Alabama Governor George Wallace, former Mississippi governor Ross Barnett, and, at Maddox's invitation, Ku Klux Klan Grand Dragon Calvin Craig. In an address written by a Klan member, George C. Wallace denounced the Civil Rights Act as "the most monstrous piece of legislation ever enacted." The act was "a fraud, a sham and a hoax," he declared, which would "live in infamy." The act, Wallace asserted, was derived from the *Communist Manifesto,* a fact that the left-wing media was suppressing. The "liberal left-wingers" had passed the act, he said, so "let them employ some 'pinknik' social engineers in Washington to figure out what to do with it. We must destroy the power to dictate, to forbid, to require, to demand. . . . We must revitalize a government founded in this nation on faith in God!"[30]

Lester Maddox opened his remarks to the rally by saying simply, "Never, never, never," and receiving a rousing ovation. "America will triumph," he declared. "Freedom will prevail. This will be a day you will never forget. Let's be flag-wavers for freedom. We are on our way back to constitutional government, and there's no stopping. We won't be satisfied until victory is won." The rally turned ugly, however, when three black men were found in attendance and were severely beaten with metal chairs, with several in the crowd shouting, "Kill them," before the blacks were rescued by the police.[31]

On the advice of the Atlanta chapter of the NAACP, George F. Willis Jr., one of the three blacks who had been threatened by Maddox at gunpoint on July 3, filed charges against Maddox in the Fulton County Criminal Court. At a preliminary hearing on the charge conducted by Judge Osgood Williams on July 7, Maddox was bound over for trial on the charge and released on a one-thousand-dollar bond. George Willis testified at the hearing that when he attempted to exit his automobile at the Pickrick, Maddox pointed a revolver in his face and said, "Get the hell out of here or I'll kill you." Maddox nevertheless claimed in the hearing that he drew his revolver to "protect my life, liberty, and property." The Civil Rights Act, he asserted, would turn the country into a "police state. I have no intention of following through on that bill." An all-white jury would subsequently acquit Maddox on the weapons charge in April 1965.[32]

Acting on behalf of the three theological students, the NAACP filed suit under the Civil Rights Act against Maddox on July 9. NAACP attorney Constance Baker Motley, who represented the students, noted that the suit seeking an injunction under the Civil Rights Act to require the desegregation of the Pickrick restaurant was the first such suit filed in the nation. United States District Court Judge Frank A. Hooper, in response to the suit, ordered Maddox to show cause why an injunction should not be issued at a hearing on July 17, the same day on which arguments were scheduled in the *Heart of Atlanta Motel* case that had been initiated by Moreton Rolleston.[33]

In response to Rolleston's suit, on July 10 the Civil Rights Division of the Department of Justice filed a counterclaim in the district court for an injunction enforcing the Civil Rights Act against the Heart of Atlanta Motel and a motion to dismiss Rolleston's complaint. On the same day, the Civil Rights Division intervened in the NAACP's suit against Lester Maddox and the Pickrick restaurant and also sought an injunction under the Civil Rights Act compelling Maddox to cease discriminating on the basis of race at the Pickrick. Judge Frank Hooper certified that both cases would be heard by a three-judge district court in accordance with the provisions of the Civil Rights Act.* Chief Judge Elbert P. Tuttle of the U.S. Court of Appeals for the Fifth Circuit appointed himself, Judge Hooper, and Judge Lewis R. Morgan of the U.S. District Court for the Northern District of Georgia as the three-judge panel to hear the *Heart of Atlanta Motel* and *Pickrick* cases on July 17. All of the judges hearing the cases would thus be from Georgia.[34]

Judge Tuttle was born in Pasadena, California, in 1897 and received both his undergraduate and law school education at Cornell University. He was admitted to the Georgia bar in Atlanta in 1923 and soon became active in Republican party political circles. In the 1952 Republican national convention, Tuttle was one of the leaders of the pro-Eisenhower forces, and he was rewarded with an appointment as general counsel of the Treasury Department after Dwight D. Eisenhower's election to the presidency. In September of 1954, Tuttle was appointed by Eisenhower as a judge on the U.S. Court of Appeals for the Fifth Circuit, and he became chief judge of the circuit in 1960.[†] While on the court of appeals, Tuttle was recognized as a leader in the field of

---

*A three-judge U.S. district court was required in the *Heart of Atlanta Motel* and *Pickrick* cases by a congressional statute requiring that such a court be convened to hear a suit attacking the validity of a federal statute and seeking an injunction against its enforcement and by the provisions of the Civil Rights Act of 1964 requiring a three-judge court to hear suits seeking the enforcement of the public accommodations provisions of the act. Such courts are appointed by the chief judges of the circuits in which suits requiring them are filed. Appeals from the decisions of three-judge courts proceed directly to the U.S. Supreme Court, bypassing the U.S. courts of appeals, which normally hear appeals from decisions of U.S. district courts. In 1976, Congress repealed the requirement of three-judge courts in cases involving attacks on the validity of federal statutes and seeking injunctions against their enforcement.

†During Tuttle's service on the Court of Appeals for the Fifth Circuit, the fifth circuit embraced the states of Alabama, Florida, Georgia, Louisiana, Mississippi, and Texas, and was thus involved in most of the important civil rights cases of the era. In 1981, the fifth circuit was divided and a new eleventh circuit headquartered in Atlanta was created, embracing the states of Alabama, Florida, and Georgia. The current fifth circuit includes the states of Louisiana, Mississippi, and Texas.

civil rights as the Court of Appeals for the Fifth Circuit became the focus of litigation directed at dismantling racial segregation in the South following the Supreme Court's decision in *Brown v. Board of Education* in 1954.[35]

Joining Chief Judge Tuttle on the three-judge court that would hear the *Heart of Atlanta Motel* and *Pickrick* cases was U.S. District Judge Frank A. Hooper. Hooper was born in Americus, Georgia, in 1895, and he received his undergraduate college education at Georgia Tech University. Hooper earned his bachelor's, master's, and doctor's degrees in law from Atlanta Law School and was admitted to the Georgia bar in 1916. A Democrat, he served in the Georgia House of Representatives in the 1920s, and was a judge on the Georgia Court of Appeals and the Superior Court for the Atlanta Circuit before he was appointed to the U.S. District Court for the Northern District of Georgia by President Truman in 1949. Although he was a supporter of segregationist U.S. Senator Richard Russell, who had sponsored his appointment to the district bench, Judge Hooper had been firm in his enforcement of the Supreme Court's mandate in *Brown v. Board of Education* and had presided over the desegregation of Atlanta's public school system.[36]

The final member of the three-judge court was U.S. District Judge Lewis R. Morgan. Born in LaGrange, Georgia, in 1913, Morgan received his undergraduate college education at the University of Michigan and his law degree from the University of Georgia. Admitted to the Georgia bar in 1935, he served as an executive assistant to a Georgia congressman, as city attorney of LaGrange, and as county attorney of Troup County from 1957 to 1961, at which time he was appointed to the district bench by President Kennedy in August 1961. Because of his relatively brief tenure as a U.S. district judge prior to the *Heart of Atlanta Motel* and *Pickrick* cases, Morgan's position on civil rights was largely unknown in 1964, but with Judges Tuttle and Hooper on the three-judge court with Judge Morgan, it could be predicted that the Civil Rights Act was likely to receive a favorable reception from the court.[37]

On July 10, Assistant U.S. Attorney General Burke Marshall wrote FBI director J. Edgar Hoover, pointing out that the Heart of Atlanta Motel had filed a suit challenging the Civil Rights Act and that the Civil Rights Division had counterclaimed, seeking "an injunction requiring the plaintiff to comply with the terms of the Act and to cease refusing accommodations and service to Negroes." He continued, "A hearing on the Government's Motion for a Preliminary Injunction has been noticed for 10:00 A.M. on July 17, 1964, in Atlanta. It will be necessary for the Department to present evidence at this hearing in support of the motion." Marshall therefore requested that the FBI conduct an investigation to secure photographs of the Heart of Atlanta Motel and its facilities, a sketch of the motel and its grounds, the incorporation papers of the motel as well as the names of its officers and directors, copies of any leases of facilities in the motel to other persons, and the names and addresses of the lessees. He also requested that the Bureau photograph all billboards advertising the motel and report on which highways they were displayed and obtain other evidence of the motel's advertising, on radio or television and in newspapers, magazines, and other sources, that was designed to attract interstate travelers. In addition, the Bureau was requested to determine if the motel's reservation system involved interstate communications and what arrangements existed for regular airport limousine service to and from the motel. Marshall also indicated that the Civil Rights Division possessed information that there were a restaurant, a cocktail lounge, a gift shop, and a Gulf gasoline station on the Heart of Atlanta Motel's premises. He therefore asked that the FBI determine the sources of the gifts sold in the gift shop, the food and liquor served in the restaurant and cocktail lounge, and the gasoline sold at the gas station, and the cash value derived from the sale of these products and goods that were received from interstate commerce.[38]

Olin C. Cooper, minister of the Methodist church in Norman Park, Georgia, wrote Attorney General Robert Kennedy on July 17, facetiously congratulating the Justice Department on its intervention in the *Pickrick* and *Heart of Atlanta* cases:

> We are so glad that you are intervening in the Maddox case in Atlanta. Thanks for doing so. We are very anxious to carry the state overwhelmingly for Goldwater and we know of nothing that will help us more than you and Martin Luther King to be teamed together at this time on a case as unconstitutional as the Maddox case and that of the Heart of Atlanta Motel. Good luck.[39]

As the first cases to test the validity of the Civil Rights Act, the *Heart of Atlanta Motel* and *Pickrick* cases received national publicity, and a large crowd appeared at the Atlanta federal courthouse on the day scheduled for hearing the cases, July 17. U.S. marshals had to turn away many people, since the courtroom was rapidly filled to capacity. At the hearing in the *Heart of Atlanta Motel* case, the United States was represented by Assistant U.S. Attorney General Burke Marshall, who was assisted by Civil Rights Division attorneys St. John Barrett and Harold Green and U.S. Attorney Charles L. Goodson. The Heart of Atlanta Motel continued to be represented by Moreton Rolleston.

The government called as a witness Albert Richard Sampson, a black Atlanta resident who was the executive director of the Atlanta branch of the NAACP and the associate editor of the *Atlanta Enquirer*. Sampson testified that on July 7 he telephoned the Heart of Atlanta Motel to reserve a room, then drove to South Carolina and from Charleston wired money to the motel to cover the cost of a room. He then flew back to Atlanta and took a shuttle bus from the airport to the Heart of Atlanta Motel. There were two clerks at the motel desk, Sampson said, and one of them informed him that the motel had a federal lawsuit against the Civil Rights Act pending and that consequently the motel would not be able to accommodate him. "I'm very sorry," the clerk said. "We can't accommodate you." Sampson then demanded his money back, but the clerk refused, and Sampson threatened to call the police.[40]

At that point Moreton Rolleston appeared, Sampson testified:

He came in and he pointed out to me—he checked both the guest list, my telegram receipt, and he took me over to the side and he pointed out to me that they had, that he had a suit against the federal government on this same basic situation and he said that if the courts decide for me to open up, I'll open up; but until then, I can't accommodate any Negroes. And at that time, he gave me my money back and I left the hotel.

The government also called Charles Edward Wells, a black minister from Macon, Georgia, who testified that he had gone to the Heart of Atlanta Motel on July 11, accompanied by another minister, John H. Gillison. Wells said that, like Sampson, he had been told that a federal lawsuit was pending and until it was settled the motel would not serve blacks.[41]

Moreton Rolleston briefly cross-examined both Sampson and Wells, and then began his argument before the three-judge court. It was his position, he told the court

and I'd like to state it very clearly, number one, whatever the order of this court or any other court is, federal, state, or any other court, this plaintiff corporation will obey. Number two our policy had been to exclude Negroes on the basis of race from this motel before the passage and before the act became law. Our policy since that time, we have announced that we would not take [black] guests, because we filed a suit within two hours after the law was signed into law, and on the theory that even though we recognize that any law is valid and, until declared to the contrary, once the matter is in the breast of the court, it was our interpretation we could stand on whatever the court decided, and there was an early hearing set, and that was what we were standing on.[42]

Rolleston then addressed the basis upon which he challenged the constitutionality of the public accommodations provisions of the Civil Rights Act.

Really, there's only one issue that I'm—would rely on today, although I would like to discuss it briefly—discuss briefly all of the issues, and that is that where a United States Supreme Court decision on a subject has been handed down and still valid and unreversed, no court, state, local, or any other, has the right under our Anglo-Saxon jurisprudence and judicial proceedings to reverse that other decision of the United States Supreme Court except the United States Supreme Court itself.

"There's an old principle that we lawyers hear about, or adage anyway," Rolleston continued. "'Beware of a man that comes into court with one case.' I'm really here with one case."

"What you call a 'white horse' case," Judge Elbert Tuttle interjected.

"A 'white horse' case," Rolleston said. "Whatever you want to call it. But I'm riding this 'white horse,' and that's the . . . [*Civil Rights Cases*][43] decided . . . in 1883 involving the Civil Rights Act of 1875. I submit that this court, regardless of how it will decide the constitutionality of the present law, is bound by that case." The three-judge court, he argued, "can't presume either, I submit, that the United States Supreme Court will reverse itself. That's up to them, whatever they want to do about it."[44]

The Civil Rights Act of 1875, which the Supreme Court invalidated in the *Civil Rights Cases,* Rolleston argued, was virtually identical to the public accommodations provisions of the Civil Rights Act of 1964. Consequently, that was why he had "my one 'white horse' case, because they decided the same issue exactly which is presented by the Civil Rights Act of 1964."

Judge Tuttle interrupted to point out that the Court had said in the *Civil Rights Cases* that the act of 1875 was based on the congressional power to enforce the Fourteenth Amendment, with the result that the Court did not consider the Commerce Clause as the basis of the 1875 act at all. The public accommodations provisions of the Civil Rights Act of 1964, on the other hand, were based on the Commerce Clause, he noted. "Now what has the Supreme Court of the United States done with the Commerce Clause since that time?" Tuttle asked.

"They have distorted it, may it please the court," Rolleston replied.

"So that without doing violence to that decision [in the *Civil Rights Cases*]," Tuttle persisted, "the Court has now made it really inapplicable for anyone to argue that this [1964] act, which is ostensibly placed, based on the Commerce Clause, cannot be supported by the Commerce Clause other than the Fourteenth Amendment."[45]

Rolleston replied that in the *Civil Rights Cases* the Supreme Court had explicitly said that no one would contend that the act of 1875 could have been enacted by Congress prior to the ratification of the Civil War Amendments to the Constitution, and this meant that the 1875 act could not have been validly based on the Commerce Clause, since the Commerce Clause was a part of the Constitution prior to the ratification of the Civil War Amendments. But Judge Tuttle responded that the Court's language in the *Civil Rights Cases* simply meant that the Court "did not pass on whether . . . [the 1875 act] could be sustained under the Commerce Clause. It said no one has contended it was supported under the Commerce Clause." Rolleston, however, pointed out that the Supreme Court had also said in the *Civil Rights Cases* that Congress lacked the constitutional power to enact a code of law regulating all private rights between man and man in society because that would mean that Congress had superseded the legislatures of the states. "And we say that this is really the basis of this, of this [1964] act."[46]

Rolleston was then asked from the bench whether or not his motel was a part of interstate commerce or whether its operations affected commerce, and in response he denounced the modern decisions of the Supreme Court broadly interpreting the power of Congress under the Commerce Clause. Such decisions, he declared, had the effect of gradually wiping out the powers of the state and local governments. And at that point he made it plain that his challenge to the Civil Rights Act was essentially an ideological protest against the expansion of the power of the federal government. "This is really the gravamen of the case. This is the guts of it," he said. "We could get along with Negro guests. They would hurt our business as we've alleged, and it's true. We could get along with them." "But the next step after this act," he asserted,

there may just be one more step, that's taking over all legislation by Congress, so setting up the stage for a dictatorship in this country. I'm telling you, this extension of the Commerce . . . [Clause] to every man, woman, and child in this room and in the United States, business and personal affairs, is not authorized by the Constitution.[47]

Rolleston also argued that the Civil Rights Act deprived the Heart of Atlanta Motel of its liberty without due process of law and its property without just compensation, in violation of the Fifth Amendment. "We used to could say who could come there and who could not come there and we would turn them away for whatever reason we wanted," he said. "We don't have that liberty under the prohibitions of this act if the act is good. We say that the taking of our liberty has been done by an act of Congress." The act also imposed involuntary servitude on the motel in violation of the Thirteenth Amendment, Rolleston insisted. "We say that we had the right to run the motel like we wanted to before the act was passed. We now have the right to run the motel like the government says. Sure, we have the alternative of quitting and giving up a four million dollar business; but can that be required of a business by law?"[48]

Rolleston continued:

> May it please the court, our legal position is that there has been a case decided which is controlling on facts that are in this case and on a law which is almost exactly the same, and that the court is bound in following our legal procedures to follow it and throw this case to the United States Supreme Court to do what they may. But at this stage of the game, it ought to go up there.

Rolleston added, "I would like to say one other thing, may it please the court. The name of Kennedy will be, go down in history of all times regarding civil rights."

"Mr. Rolleston—" Judge Tuttle interrupted.

"John F. Kennedy," Rolleston continued.

"—is that proper argument?" Tuttle asked.

"Yes, sir, I think so," Rolleston replied.

"Just—"

"We are not disposed to cut you off, but actually, what—what's proper about it?" Tuttle inquired.

"Well, sometimes in the affairs of men it takes more than the individual to express a thing, and I want to quote a man," Rolleston said.

> Mr. Robert Kennedy, the defendant in this case, wrote in the prefaced word to the memorial edition of the *Profiles in Courage,* that one thing that President Kennedy admired was courage. It took courage to pass this law. It took a little courage maybe to file a suit against the federal government. And I know this court will follow the motto over the Supreme Court of Georgia's bench which says in Latin, when translated, "Let justice be done though the heavens may fall."

In conclusion Rolleston then said, "And I know this court, if it agrees with our legal interpretation will do that in spite of the consequences which could arise out of such a decision. And I thank you."[49]

Assistant Attorney General Burke Marshall then opened the argument on behalf of the United States. "The first point made by Mr. Rolleston turns on the *Civil Rights Cases* which involve the constitutionality of a bill passed in 1875," he said. "As you mentioned, Judge Tuttle, it shows on the face of those cases that they were not deciding any question about the power of Congress to pass a law under the Commerce Clause." Marshall cited the

Supreme Court's 1937 decision in *NLRB v. Jones and Laughlin Steel Corp.*,[50] sustaining the constitutionality of the National Labor Relations Act (NLRA) as a leading precedent supporting the constitutional validity of the Civil Rights Act of 1964 under the Commerce Clause. The NLRA, Marshall argued, was similar to the Civil Rights Act

> in the sense that it was intended to deal with a national problem that had been marked by a good deal of emotion and controversy and even violence in the streets. The Court said in . . . [the *Jones and Laughlin*] case that . . . in the course of regulation of commerce the Congress was not limited just to the regulation of institutions which are in the stream of commerce, or which themselves move in commerce, like railroads and buses and that kind of thing, but that it can regulate and pass legislation to eliminate burdens and obstructions due to injurious actions springing from other sources.[51]

"The *Jones and Laughlin* case was the first decision by the Supreme Court," Judge Tuttle interjected, "that went so far as to hold that what had theretofore been considered purely local, like manufacturing, mining, and farming and the like, might still be under congressional regulation."

"Well, Judge Tuttle," Marshall said,

> you say the first case. I think that the history of the Commerce Clause goes back to *Gibbons* versus *Ogden*.[52] I think that the decision in *Jones and Laughlin* and the following ones after that were in the keeping of the spirit and the view of congressional power which goes back to John Marshall's opinion in *Gibbons* against *Ogden*.

Marshall also cited *United States v. Darby*,[53] in which the Supreme Court upheld the Fair Labor Standards Act of 1938 under the Commerce Clause, and *Wickard v. Filburn*,[54] in which the validity of the Agricultural Adjustment Act's regulation of wheat production by a farmer primarily for home consumption was also sustained by the Court. "These cases," he said, "hold that Congress has the power to regulate commerce not only in the sense that they can regulate things that move in interstate commerce generally, but that they can pass legislation that deals with problems that affect interstate commerce."[55]

"Mr. Marshall," Judge Frank Hooper asked,

> to what extent do the courts have the right to say when Congress has said a certain act does affect commerce, what right do the courts have, or do not have, to say whether that factual assumption is correct? Now

in the *Jones and Laughlin* case, the Court said this, among other things: "Undoubtedly the scope of this [commerce] power must be considered in the light of our dual system of government and may not be extended so as to embrace effects upon interstate commerce so indirect and remote that to embrace them in view of our complex society would effectively obliterate the distinction between what is national and what is local and create a centralized government." Now what I'm interested in is whether under the Civil Rights Act Congress says that a certain thing does affect commerce, is that conclusive on the court, or is it . . . not?[56]

Marshall replied that while Congress could not foreclose a constitutional question from being considered by the courts, the determinations of Congress regarding what local activities affected interstate commerce should be given great weight by the courts. The Civil Rights Act of 1964 "was under consideration by Congress for over a year," he pointed out.

It was debated at great length. It is an issue and a problem that involves great emotions. There are great political problems with it. And all of that went into the determination by the Congress to deal with it, Judge Hooper. The decision of Congress on that was made by men that included very conservative men as well as very liberal men. And I think that that kind of a decision is entitled to great weight and has been given great weight by the Supreme Court.[57]

Judge Hooper responded by pointing out that in the *Heart of Atlanta Motel* case the government and Moreton Rolleston had stipulated the facts in the case, a stipulation that included the fact that 75 percent of the guests of the Heart of Atlanta Motel were interstate travelers. "But suppose you later have a case where it's almost negligible," Hooper said. "In that type of case— I was just thinking about the precedent of this case—in that kind of case, where would the courts draw a line between what is substantial and what is not substantial?"[58]

Marshall replied that under the 1964 act's provisions relating to hotels and motels, making that kind of a distinction was not required of the courts because the act applied to all hotels, motels, and inns that served transient guests, regardless of how many of the guests were traveling in interstate commerce. "Now the question is, can Congress do that?" he said. "Can Congress make the factual determination that in order to deal with the problem they have to regulate all hotels—"

"Sir, do not all hotels furnish lodgings to transient guests?" Judge Hooper asked.

"I would think so, Judge Hooper, or virtually all of them," Marshall replied.

"Do you have ready reference to any Supreme Court case that I think states this proposition," Judge Tuttle intervened, "something along these lines, that when a determination is made by Congress on—of this nature, the courts are required to support it if there's any reasonable relation of the determination by Congress to the problem it seeks to legislate on?"

"I think that's right, Judge Tuttle," Marshall responded. "I think that—"

"I think that's the principle," Judge Tuttle added; "I don't have the case."

"I think the principle goes back to *Gibbons* against *Ogden*," Marshall said. "I think that language can be found in *Gibbons* against *Ogden*."

"So that what we are required to do," Tuttle continued, "is to determine whether there was any reasonable basis for Congress to ascertain that the hotel industry reasonably affects interstate commerce."

"Yes," Marshall answered. "And this problem I think, Judge Tuttle, not only the hotel industry, but this problem within the hotel industry of racial discrimination . . . , could Congress reasonably have made that determination. I think that's the question."

"That this would . . . have an adverse effect on interstate commerce," Tuttle said.

"That's right," Marshall agreed.[59]

Marshall continued,

In the *Darby* case, Judge Hooper—no, I'm sorry. It's *Wickard* against *Filburn,* where there is no question but that the activities of the farmer who was regulated, that particular farmer, were intrastate. He grew wheat on his own farm for consumption on his own farm. He grew more wheat than the quota that was allowed him under the Agricultural Adjustment Act. The question was whether Congress had the power to regulate that farmer, that particular farmer, and the Court held unanimously that . . . Congress did. And among other things, it said, the Court pointed out, citing *Gibbons* against *Ogden,* that effective restraints on the exercise of this [commerce] power must proceed from political rather than from [the] judicial process.

Marshall further argued:

I think our system works that way. If Congress is arbitrary and unreasonable and the court can make that determination that there is an arbitrary or unreasonable relationship between what Congress was trying to do and some, some commercial problem affecting commerce, then I think it would be the court's duty to strike down the act. But unless it can make that determination, I think it's up to Congress—[60]

"You are saying," Judge Hooper interjected, "that it is not necessary under this statute as to hotels to show that they take any transients moving in commerce, in interstate commerce?"

"It has to be shown they take transients, Judge Hooper," Marshall replied.

"Transients, that means people who are moving in interstate commerce," Hooper persisted.

"No, Judge Hooper," Marshall responded. "It means people that are moving, it means that the hotel . . . caters to transients. It takes in people that usually come from some other place, but the some other place does not under the act, Judge Hooper, have to be shown to have been another state."[61]

"Now as I said," Marshall continued,

these cases [such as *United States v. Darby* and *Wickard v. Filburn*] expressly held that Congress has the power to reach some activities that are completely intrastate if they have to do that in order to control a problem, deal with a problem that they properly can deal with under the Commerce Clause. And those holdings of those cases in turn go back to the *Shreveport Rate Cases*[62] in 1914 where the question of the validity of an order of the Interstate Commerce Commission over purely intrastate rates in Texas was involved. And that was upheld by the Supreme Court in the . . . [*Shreveport Case*] in 1914. And these cases carry that on, Judge Hooper.[63]

There were four ways that Congress could have reasonably determined that racial discrimination in hotels and motels affected interstate commerce and could therefore be validly regulated under the Commerce Clause, Marshall then argued. First was the negative impact of racial discrimination in hotels and motels on interstate travel by blacks, he said. The scarcity of accommodations for blacks traveling in interstate commerce reduced their interstate travel, thus adversely affecting interstate commerce and justifying congressional regulation to remove that burden on commerce. The existence of racial discrimination in hotels and motels as well as other places of public accommodation also adversely affected interstate commerce, he argued, by imposing artificial restrictions on the market for interstate products, a market that would substantially expand if the racial discrimination restricting that market were removed. Racial discrimination in hotels and motels and other places of public accommodation also produced protests, demonstrations, and disputes against the practice, and these disputes adversely affected the business of the targets of the disputes as well as that of business establishments generally in the areas in which they occurred, he argued. And the reduction of business activity produced by racial disputes reduced the demand for goods and products from interstate commerce and thus adversely affected that commerce. Finally, Marshall said, the pervasiveness of racial discrimination in the South had retarded that region's economic growth to the detriment of the national economy as a whole and of interstate commerce. Businesses that might have relocated in the South, or have built plants or other businesses there absent racial discrimination, he said, had declined to do so, with resulting adverse effects on interstate commerce that Congress also had the legitimate power to remove under the Commerce Clause.[64]

The Supreme Court had held, Marshall continued,

> that Congress may exercise the commerce power to prevent injuries to the public health, morals, or welfare. That the fact that they are doing something else, that they are advancing the cause of justice or meeting a problem of health, morality, or the public welfare by regulating commerce doesn't make the regulation invalid.

"Well," Judge Hooper interrupted, "has the Supreme Court said on several occasions that the general welfare clause is a matter of state law and not the federal law, that the welfare clause was to be construed in the light of specific powers which are given to Congress?"

"Well, Judge Hooper," Marshall replied,

> I did not intend to put any emphasis on the separate power of Congress under the general welfare clause. I said that in regulating commerce, in regulating commerce and in the exercise of that power, the purpose— this is what they said in the *Darby* case—could include such purposes as to promote public health, . . . public morals, or promote public welfare.

"Oh, surely . . . Right," Hooper agreed.[65]

The fact is, Marshall continued,

> that a great deal of legislation passed under the Commerce Clause does that. The Food and Drug Act, that's mainly a health measure. I mean it's done by regulation of commerce, but it is dealing with the problem of health. The Meat Inspection Act, the Packers and Stockyards Act . . . was upheld in 1922, Fair Labor Standards Act, the whole [National Labor Relations Act], and of course the Mann Act and other things.

In closing, Marshall also denied that the Civil Rights Act deprived those subject to its provisions of liberty or property without due process of law or took their property without just compensation. And he also denied that the act imposed involuntary servitude within the meaning of the Thirteenth Amendment.[66]

In a brief rebuttal, Moreton Rolleston argued that under the provisions of the Civil Rights Act the operations of every motel and hotel in the country were being regulated. "And I'm, I'll state to the court, . . . I'm sure the court will almost take judicial notice, there isn't a motel or hotel in the United States that doesn't take transient guests, so they are all covered by the act. What it amounts to." The Commerce Clause had been made a part of the Constitution to solve the problem of a stagnant commerce that had resulted during the Articles of Confederation, he argued, and it was intended to give Congress the power to regulate trade among the states. "Now we have seen the Commerce Clause by all the cases I have cited and other counsel here have cited for the government in the various ways they have nibbled and nibbled and nibbled until they have the whole piece of cheese," Rolleston asserted. "And this is the last step. There isn't anything left of . . . intrastate commerce if this act can be valid and enforced to the full extent, and it will be liberally followed." In conclusion, Rolleston therefore again urged the court to hold the Civil Rights Act unconstitutional as beyond the legitimate power of Congress under the Commerce Clause.[67]

"Anything further on either side?" Judge Tuttle asked.

Well, for once counsel were not overly optimistic. We have a little time to spare. The court will take this case under advisement and announce the decision as promptly as possible. I'll ask this question, although this is a motion I guess for a preliminary injunction, is there anything further to be proved or further argument to be made? Could this not be considered a final motion and trial on the permanent injunction? What do counsel have to say about that?

"As far as the plaintiff is concerned, there's nothing else, your honor," Moreton Rolleston said.

"We are in agreement on that, Judge Tuttle," Burke Marshall said. "I think the whole case is before the court now."

"The court will stand in recess until 1:30," Judge Tuttle then announced, and the hearing before the three-judge district court in the *Heart of Atlanta Motel* case was at an end.[68]

When the three-judge court reconvened on the afternoon of July 17, it proceeded to hear the *Pickrick* case involving Lester Maddox's refusal to comply with the Civil Rights Act. The government was represented by the same attorneys who had participated in the *Heart of Atlanta Motel* case, while the NAACP was represented by its chief counsel Jack Greenberg, associate counsel Constance Baker Motley, and Michael Meltsner, who were joined by local black attorney William Alexander. Lester Maddox and the Pickrick restaurant were represented by Sidney T. Schell and William G. McRae. In contrast to the *Heart of Atlanta Motel* case, in which only two witnesses were called by the government, twenty-seven witnesses were presented in the *Pickrick* case to testify regarding the events at the Pickrick restaurant and its refusal to comply with the Civil Rights Act. The government demonstrated that the Pickrick during 1963 had purchased more than $250,000 worth of food and that 50 to 75 percent of that food had moved in interstate commerce. Evidence presented at the hearing also indicated that the Pickrick offered to serve interstate travelers, although it actually served relatively few of them. The restaurant was thus clearly covered by the Civil Rights Act, the government argued, and was operating in violation of the provisions prohibiting racial discrimination in restaurants serving food a substantial portion of which had moved in interstate commerce or offering to serve interstate travelers.[69]

Lester Maddox's attorneys argued, on the other hand, that "the plaintiffs have no right to complain against these defendants' conduct in choosing to select for themselves the type of customers to which they will sell goods and render services at said restaurant." Congress, they insisted, could not validly coerce one person to sell private property to another against his will without imposing involuntary servitude in violation of the Thirteenth Amendment. "The Constitution was designed to preserve the freedom of a man to discriminate," William McRae argued, citing the First Amendment's guarantee of freedom of association. "What greater freedom is there than to select your own associates, to serve whom you want to serve?" And in a rather bizarre argument, McRae also denied that the Pickrick's operations affected interstate commerce. "A fellow eats some food at the Pickrick and then evacuates it, and it'll go into the Chattahoochee River as waste," he said, "and there's no more commerce in that than there is in food coming to the Pickrick in the first place." The hearing in the *Pickrick* case stretched into Monday, July 20, when the three-judge court took the case under advisement as it had the *Heart of Atlanta Motel* case.[70]

The three-judge federal court did not prolong the suspense regarding its decisions in the *Heart of Atlanta Motel* and *Pickrick* cases; its decisions were announced on July 22. A front-page banner headline in the *Atlanta Constitution* announced the results: "Federal Court Orders Maddox and Motel to Serve Negroes."[71] In the *Heart of Atlanta Motel* case, the court dismissed Moreton Rolleston's claim for $11 million in damages against the government, ruling that even if the claim were valid, which was doubtful, it could be pursued only in the U.S. Court of Claims. With regard to the Commerce Clause as the constitutional basis of the Civil Rights Act, the court's decision was a full vindication of the arguments of Assistant Attorney General Burke Marshall. Citing *McCulloch v. Maryland*[72] and quoting from *United States v. Darby*, the court pointed out that the

> power of Congress over interstate commerce is not confined to the regulation of commerce among the states. It extends to those activities intrastate which so affect interstate commerce or the exercise of the power of Congress over it as to make regulation of them appropriate means to the attainment of the legitimate end, the exercise of the grant of power of Congress to regulate interstate commerce.

It was therefore unnecessary to hold that racial discrimination by hotels and motels was itself interstate commerce, the court said, but rather it was sufficient to find that such discrimination was a local activity that adversely affected or burdened interstate commerce and that the prohibition of the discrimination was an appropriate means by which Congress could implement its power to regulate and protect commerce.[73]

The initial determination of whether a particular regulation was the appropriate means to attain a legitimate end, the court added, was one for Congress to make. "Courts may not overturn such determinations," it said, "unless they conclude that under no reasonable theory could Congress find them 'appropriate to the attainment' of its power to regulate commerce." The operations of the Heart of Atlanta Motel, the court noted, had only recently been found to affect interstate commerce, by the U.S. district court in Atlanta in a case based on the Sherman Anti-Trust Act.[74] And since it was "undisputed that in the adoption of the Civil Rights Act of 1964, Congress has seen fit to exercise its full power as granted it under the Constitution, the scope of its operation in this field must, therefore, be taken to be at least as broad as that which it exercised in the adoption of the Sherman Act." The U.S. Supreme Court had also held in *Hotel Employees v. Leedom*[75] that the National Labor Relations Board could not exclude hotel and motel employees from its jurisdiction under the National Labor Relations Act, the court added, because labor disputes in hotels and motels could adversely affect interstate commerce.[76]

Since the operations of motels and hotels such as the Heart of Atlanta Motel had been clearly held to affect interstate commerce under the Sherman Act and the National Labor Relations Act, the court ruled, racial discrimination in hotels and motels could validly be prohibited by Congress under the Commerce Clause in order to remove the adverse effects and burdens such discrimination imposed on commerce. "It is clear that the attack by the complainant on the constitutionality of [the public accommodations provisions] of the Civil Rights Act must fail," the court concluded. "It is equally clear that the United States is entitled to the injunction prayed for in its counterclaim." The court then issued a permanent injunction barring the Heart of Atlanta Motel from refusing service to its guests on the grounds of race or color. "So that the plaintiff may have an opportunity to prepare its record for appeal and, if so advised, seek a stay of this order," the court said, "it is ordered that the foregoing injunction shall become effective twenty (20) days from the day hereof, on, to-wit, the 11th day of August, 1964."[77]

Although the decision of the three-judge court was unanimous in the *Heart of Atlanta Motel* case, Judge Frank Hooper only concurred in the decision of the *Pickrick* case upholding the application of the Civil Rights Act to Lester Maddox's restaurant on the basis that the restaurant offered to serve interstate travelers. Judges Tuttle and Morgan in the opinion for the court pointed out that the *Pickrick* case raised constitutional issues similar to those presented in the *Heart of Atlanta Motel* case. They noted, however, that unlike in the motel case, the validity of the Civil Rights Act's application to the Pickrick depended upon a factual determination that either the restaurant served or offered to serve interstate travelers or served food or other items a substantial portion of which had moved in interstate commerce. The evidence indicating that the restaurant served many interstate travelers, the court acknowledged, "was slight." There had been testimony that from 2 to 3 percent of the automobiles parked in the Pickrick's parking lot were from out of state, and individuals requesting service in the restaurant were not queried regarding their origins. On the other hand, the court found that "there was no doubt" that the Pickrick offered to serve interstate travelers, since it was located on the main business route of Interstate 41 and it also had several large advertising signs on two business route portions of federal highways.[78]

In contrast to the rather thin evidence that the Pickrick actually served many interstate travelers, the court found that it was "clear beyond question" that a substantial portion of the food the restaurant served had moved in interstate commerce. The restaurant had had $500,000 in gross sales during the previous year, the court pointed out, and its food purchases had exceeded $250,000. Relying on decisions sustaining the application of the National Labor Relations Act to local businesses in which labor disputes would diminish the purchases of interstate products by those businesses, the court also sustained the application of the Civil Rights Act to the Pickrick. "There remains," the court said,

only the question whether, if Congress now has, as we recognize it has, the power to extend regulatory control over labor policies of otherwise local businesses because, in their operations, they either utilize or buy and sell substantial quantities of products that have been in interstate commerce, we can say that it is irrational for Congress to conclude, as it has done in adopting this law, that the prevention of racial discrimination in such otherwise local businesses, is also within its regulatory power because of the effect of such practices on interstate commerce.[79]

Finding that such a conclusion by Congress was not irrational, the court held that the Civil Rights Act's application to the Pickrick was a valid exercise of the commerce power and that, regarding the act's definition of restaurants covered by its public accommodations provisions, it was "clear that this definition includes the Pickrick Restaurant." The court also summarily rejected the contentions of counsel for Lester Maddox that the act violated the First Amendment's guarantee of freedom of association and that the act imposed involuntary servitude in violation of the Thirteenth Amendment. "No question of freedom of association under the First Amendment or involuntary servitude under the Thirteenth Amendment is involved," the court ruled. "It follows, therefore, that defendants' attack on the constitutionality of the act as applied to their operation must fail," the court concluded, adding that an injunction would issue prohibiting the Pickrick from refusing service on the grounds of race or color effective August 11.[80]

Both Moreton Rolleston and Lester Maddox had thus lost their challenges to the Civil Rights Act. Rolleston, as he had promised during his argument before the three-judge court, promptly announced that the Heart of Atlanta Motel would comply with the court's injunction requiring the motel to serve blacks. "We'll obey the court order," he informed the press. Maddox, on the other hand, was defiant. "I'm not going to integrate," he declared. "I've made a pledge. They won't ever get any of that chicken." He complained that the government was "hiring white, black, and half-breed lawyers to fight against me" while paying for them with his tax money. "If I lose everything, I'm not worried," he added. "Lyndon Johnson said he was going to eradicate poverty, didn't he?"[81]

In a letter to J. Edgar Hoover on July 29, Burke Marshall praised the work of the FBI in gathering evidence in the *Heart of Atlanta Motel* and *Pickrick* cases. "I wish to commend the Atlanta Field Office of the Federal Bureau of Investigation for the excellent work it did in investigating violations of the Civil Rights Act of 1964 by the Heart of Atlanta Motel and the Pickrick Restaurant in Atlanta, Georgia," Marshall wrote. "The evidence obtained by the Bureau in these cases furnished the basis for the judgment of a three-judge district court sustaining the constitutionality of Title II of the Civil Rights Act on July 23rd [actually July 22]."[82]

He continued,

> I was particularly impressed by the work of the Atlanta Special Agents in obtaining and systematizing the evidence necessary to establish that the food served at the Pickrick Restaurant had moved in interstate commerce. As a result of this work the Government was able to offer into evidence a schedule prepared by one of your agents definitely establishing that over 57 per cent of the supplies purchased by the restaurant in June 1964 originated from outside the State of Georgia.

"The importance of the Government's victory in these cases cannot be overemphasized," he concluded. "The role played by the Bureau in making this victory possible is deeply appreciated."[83]

Both Moreton Rolleston and Lester Maddox's attorneys applied to Justice Hugo Black, in his capacity as the circuit justice superintending the Fifth Federal Judicial Circuit, to issue stays of the injunctions that the three-judge court had issued against the Heart of Atlanta Motel and the Pickrick restaurant, pending appeals of the decisions of the lower court to the Supreme Court. On August 10, however, Justice Black denied both applications for stays of the lower court's injunctions. The Supreme Court, Black acknowledged, had the power to declare the public accommodations provisions of the Civil Rights Act unconstitutional if they exceeded the power of Congress under the Constitution, and he also conceded that the courts could enjoin an act of Congress pending final determination of its constitutionality if necessary to prevent irreparable injury.[84]

"But such a temporary injunction against enforcement is in reality a suspension of the act, delaying the date selected by Congress to put its policies into effect," Black said.

> Thus judicial power to stay an act of Congress, like judicial power to hold that act unconstitutional, is an awesome responsibility calling for the utmost circumspection in its exercise. This factor is all the more important where, as here, a single member of the Court is asked to delay the will of Congress to put its policies into effect at the time it desires.

The policies he was being requested to suspend were also not the result of "sudden, impulsive legislative action," he noted, "but represent the culmination of one of the most thorough debates in the history of Congress."[85]

Without addressing the validity of the public accommodations provisions of the Civil Rights Act under the Commerce Clause and the Fourteenth Amendment, Justice Black said,

I believe that the broad grants of power to Congress in the Commerce Clause and the Fourteenth Amendment are enough to show that Congress does have at least general constitutional authority to control commerce among the states and to enforce the Fourteenth Amendment's policy against racial discrimination. Under these circumstances, a judicial restraint of the enforcement of one of the most important sections of the Civil Rights Act would, in my judgment, be unjustifiable.

Black said he agreed, however, with the contentions of the appellants and the U.S. solicitor general that the constitutional issues raised in the *Heart of Atlanta Motel* and *Pickrick* cases should be promptly determined by the Supreme Court. "For that reason I would welcome motions to the Court to expedite both cases," he concluded, "in the hope that they would be made ready for argument the first week we meet in October. The applications for stays are denied."[86]

As a native of Alabama, Justice Black was the frequent recipient of at times scurrilous letters and postcards from southerners denouncing both him and the Supreme Court. When the Civil Rights Act became law in July, for example, Black received a letter from a Mississippian denouncing the "monstrous civil rights law," and saying that it was

probably too much to hope that the Supreme Court in view of its past ideological decisions, the protection of communists and criminals, the outlawing of God in our institutions and other crazy decisions, will declare this vicious law unconstitutional. But we hope that the Court will at last realize its legal function and strike down the terrible and unamerican provisions of this iniquitous measure.

After Black refused the applications for stays in the *Heart of Atlanta Motel* and *Pickrick* cases, a fellow Alabamian wrote to him that perhaps "you judges are the most hated persons of all times. Although popularity is not what you seek, I'm sure you wish to be remembered as judges and not being labeled social reconstructionists. Surely no less than eternal damnation awaits those who betray that which they have been entrusted." And a Louisianian asked, "You mean a dirty stincken lazy nigger who has never done anything in his life can tell a hardworking and successful businessman that he must share his property? No, it will never be done." Another fellow Alabamian accused Black of doing "the bidding of the masters of the USSR," warning him, "You are out of harmony with God, but in harmony with end-time events, Satan himself being the Master Mind." Another correspondent forwarded to the justice a newspaper clipping reporting his decision to refuse the stays, with "Stooge" and "Does What Bobby [Kennedy] Says" penciled in.[87]

When Justice Black's decision denying the applications for stays in the *Heart of Atlanta Motel* and *Pickrick* cases was announced, Moreton Rolleston adhered to the position that he had taken throughout the litigation and pledged obedience to the three-judge court's injunction that went into effect on August 11. "We have the same plan we always had," he said. "We're going to obey the court like any other law-abiding citizen whether we like it or not. We'll obey this order the same as any court order." Lester Maddox, on the other hand, appeared initially uncertain over what course to pursue.[88]

Maddox informed the press that he did not know "what we will do tomorrow," the first day the injunction against the Pickrick would be in effect. "We had planned to open tomorrow as usual as of five minutes ago. Now I don't know what I'll do. I kept thinking the Constitution would be upheld and private property preserved," he added. "We have a police state as of this hour and President Johnson is responsible for having brought it about." He claimed to be "shocked to hear others extending the opinion that I must as an American forego my rights under the Constitution and become subservient to those who demand that I must surrender my rights as an American and my property. We will never integrate. Pickrick will never integrate." When asked by reporters if he would close his restaurant, Maddox said that the "federal government will close my establishment. We are just really hurt that our government will tell us that we no longer can select our customers. It's involuntary servitude; it's slavery of the first order, it shows complete, utter disregard for the United States Constitution." He blamed his problems on "the Communists" and added that he believed that "ultimately the public accommodations title of the Civil Rights Act will be declared unconstitutional."[89]

William Alexander, one of the black attorneys for the black plaintiffs on whose behalf the NAACP had sued Maddox under the Civil Rights Act, said that he was "very happy" regarding Justice Black's refusal to stay the injunction against the Pickrick. "We expected it," he said. His clients "had made no plans yet" about attempting to eat at the Pickrick, Alexander said, but "if they decide to go down there for some of that chicken, they will go. I doubt it will be tomorrow." On August 11, with the injunction against the Pickrick in effect, however, three blacks—Albert Sampson, Charles Wells, and Albert Dunn—were denied service by Maddox at the restaurant. Sampson and Wells had testified in the three-judge court hearing against the Heart of Atlanta Motel. Maddox intercepted the three men at the door of the Pickrick, shouting, "You're not here to eat. You're here to run us out of business."

"The government has told you to integrate," Sampson replied. "We would like to enter."

"You're not about to enter," Maddox shouted. "If you live a hundred years you'll never get a piece of fried chicken here," he said, and accused the three men of being "Communists."[90]

On August 12, at the request of Attorney General Robert Kennedy, Judge Frank Hooper ordered Maddox to show cause why he should not be held in contempt of court for refusing to obey the injunction of the three-judge court. Maddox denied that he was in contempt and denounced the order to show cause as having been prompted by "several agitators and the attorney general . . . and inspired by Communists." He would continue to operate his restaurant "unless some of these paid agitators . . . close my business." If additional blacks demanded service at the Pickrick, he announced, he would close the restaurant and "I will not reopen" until the Supreme Court rendered its decision on the validity of the public accommodations provisions. "If they say I have to integrate," he declared, "then my business is gone."[91]

On Thursday, August 13, Maddox posted a sign in the window of the Pickrick announcing that the "first Communist-inspired racial agitators to enter this restaurant and demand service will put us out of business." At 1:40 in the afternoon, Calvin Jones and Gary Robinson, two young black men wearing suits and ties, sought service at the restaurant. Maddox met them at the door, and with his face red with anger, shouted, "You sorry, no good devil, you just put 66 people out of work. You are a Communist. You've stolen my job. You've stolen my business. Now get out of my door." He burst into tears and announced to a crowd of whites who had congregated at the Pickrick that "my president, my Congress, and the Communists have closed my business down." His sobbing wife threw her arms around Maddox and shouted, "They've ruined everything we've worked for all of our lives." Forty-four of the sixty-six employees at the Pickrick were black.[92]

In what appeared to be a preplanned stunt, Maddox then set up a lectern in front of his restaurant and, using the establishment's public address system, spoke to the crowd of whites gathered in front of the Pickrick. He blamed the president, the government, and "renegade white people in public office and weak, cowardly businessmen" for forcing the closure of his business. Forcing him out of business violated "all of the Ten Commandments," he declared. But "the righteous cry out and the Lord heareth. That's why I'm not afraid today." He praised his employees and promised to care for them, and called upon "good Americans everywhere" to contribute to his efforts to provide for his employees and pay his legal fees in his fight against the Civil Rights Act. As for himself, he added, because of the contempt of court charges against him, he might "get a rest out there in the penitentiary."[93]

Supporters of Maddox complained bitterly to the Department of Justice regarding the proceedings again him and the Pickrick restaurant. In a telegram to "millionaire Robert Kennedy," one Atlantan said that

> a pleasant, hard-working, little man, his wife, and 70 employees are without jobs tonight. Lester Maddox today permanently closed the Pickrick restaurant having been denied his constitutional rights. May you always be on the "inside" politically so this will not happen to your business interests. Congratulations and pleasant dreams.

Another Atlantan said in a telegram to the attorney general, "You have broken Maddox. Now get off his back. Many quite law-abiding citizens are truly concerned about private property rights." And a Chamblee, Georgia, resident declared in a telegram to Kennedy, "I hope and pray you and Johnson will never have another moment of happiness. For betraying your own race and horrible treatment of Lester Maddox for a few votes."[94]

On August 14, Maddox moved a flower-covered casket in front of the Pickrick and began to sell red autographed pick handles as "Pickrick drumsticks," to be purchased for use as "souvenirs or otherwise." He announced the money he raised from the sales would be used for "fighting back the attack of my government and the Communists." When a three-judge court heard arguments on August 20 from Maddox's attorneys regarding whether he should be held in contempt of court for violating the federal injunction ordering him to desegregate, however, his attorneys encountered a hostile reception from the court. "We are not going to permit the enforcement of what we conceive to be an unconstitutional statute passed under a power of Congress that it did not have, [to be] enforced against the business people of the South if we can prevent it," William McRae declared to the court. "We are not going to let this be rammed down the throat of the southern people without a test of it."

"You'd better cool down a bit, here," U.S. Court of Appeals Judge Griffin Bell admonished McRae.

> You're not speaking for the southern people, you're here to represent your client. We won't have any political speeches here in court this morning. You can go out somewhere on the sidewalk and get a box or a platform and make as many speeches as you want to but don't make any political speeches in this courtroom.[95]

McRae then offered to call Lester Maddox to testify that he was losing two hundred dollars a day because he had been forced to close his restaurant, but Judge Bell again challenged him. "He didn't have to close," Bell said.

"He closed because of the coercive court order," McRae insisted.

"No, sir," Bell responded, "this court ordered him to obey the law and serve on a nondiscriminatory basis. He closed of his own free will. He could have served on a nondiscriminatory basis." He warned McRae, "Don't say he was forced to close down again."

"He could either close, serve Negroes, or go to jail," McRae retorted. Judge Bell then demanded to know what irreparable damage Maddox and his business would have suffered if he had obeyed the Civil Rights Act and the injunction. "We are not going to integrate to find out," McRae truculently replied. "We're not going to integrate until the Supreme Court says we must." Later, however, McRae asked reporters not to quote his last remark. "We'll never integrate," he said. "We'll think of something else." On August 25, the three-judge court decided that the contempt proceedings against Maddox should properly be heard by a single district judge. U.S. District Judge Frank Hooper then postponed the contempt proceedings pending the decisions of the Supreme Court regarding the validity of the Civil Rights Act.[96]

Maddox had vowed to fight the suit against the Pickrick "all the way to the U.S. Supreme Court to see if Lester Maddox is right or the Constitution is dead." While the publicity he had received as a result of his resistance to the Civil Rights Act had successfully launched him on the path to the governor's office in Georgia, he had nevertheless in fact abandoned his constitutional challenge of the act after Justice Black had refused the application for a stay of the injunction requiring him to cease discrimination in his operation of the Pickrick restaurant. The constitutional test of the public accommodations provisions of the Civil Rights Act as they applied to restaurants serving interstate food would therefore not come from Lester Maddox and the Pickrick restaurant in Atlanta but from a hitherto unheard of restaurant serving barbecue in Birmingham, Alabama.[97]

3

PUBLIC ACCOMMODATIONS AND
OLLIE'S BARBECUE IN BIRMINGHAM

It was perhaps appropriate that the second challenge to the constitutionality of the public accommodations provisions of the Civil Rights Act of 1964 to reach the Supreme Court would originate in Birmingham, Alabama. The city had long possessed a reputation as one of the most rigidly segregated cities in the South, and the obdurate resistance and violence that Birmingham's whites directed at any manifestation of black demands for equality had led some to label the city as "Bombingham." Birmingham police commissioner Eugene T. "Bull" Connor's vow to "keep the niggers in their place," and his nationally televised implementation of that vow by the use of police dogs, fire hoses, and cattle prods against the Martin Luther King Jr.–led demonstrations against segregation in the city, had been a major factor in prompting President Kennedy to propose in 1963 the legislation that would become the Civil Rights Act of 1964. Indeed, in a meeting with civil rights leaders following his proposal of civil rights legislation, Kennedy had joked, "I don't think you should all be totally harsh on Bull Connor. After all he has done more for civil rights than almost anybody else." Another civil rights leader reported the president as saying, "But for Birmingham, we would not be here today."[1]

When the Civil Rights Act became law on July 2, Birmingham Mayor Albert Boutwell reacted somewhat mildly. "However distasteful the Act is to many who are affected by it, and who regard it as unjust and unconstitutional," he said, "nonetheless the testing of its provisions, without significant disorder so far, demonstrates clearly the common sense and dedication to law and order of our citizens, white and Negro." And two days later, rather unexpectedly, most of Birmingham's restaurants peacefully and quietly desegregated in compliance with the act.[2]

In a joint statement, the Birmingham Hotel Association and Motel Association also pledged to comply with the Civil Rights Act, as most public accommodations in the city followed the lead of the restaurants and desegregated. The Reverend Fred L. Suttlesworth, who had been a leader in the demonstrations protesting segregation in Birmingham, declared that the desegregation of most of the public accommodations in the city indicated the "end of [Alabama Governor George] Wallace's pledge of 'segregation today, segregation tomorrow, segregation forever.'"[3]

Time magazine reported that throughout the South, "from Charleston to Dallas, from Memphis to Tallahassee, segregation walls that had stood for several generations began to tumble in the first week under the new civil rights law." J. L. Meadows, a seventy-year-old black chauffeur, walked into the Dinkler-Tutwiler Hotel's Town and Country Restaurant in Birmingham, ordered a meal, and was served without incident, while white diners stared at him agog. "I've been driving white folks down here for 21 years," Meadows said, "and now I'm going to eat where I've been taking these white folks."[4]

In Jackson, Mississippi, two leading hotels and a motel desegregated in compliance with the Civil Rights Act, but the proprietor of the Robert E. Lee Hotel was defiant. He ordered the Confederate flag hauled down from the hotel and posted a sign reading, "Closed in Despair. Civil Rights Bill Unconstitutional." In Tuscaloosa, Alabama, movie actor Jack Palance made an appearance and signed autographs for both black and white fans. He and his wife then attended a movie at the desegregated Druid theater, but a rumor soon spread that a black woman had accompanied the couple. A mob of almost one thousand whites soon gathered outside the theater and hurled rocks at the theater cashier's booth and marquee. The windows of Palance's rented automobile were smashed and its tires slashed, and the Palances were escorted to the police station by Tuscaloosa police to protect their safety.[5]

Despite such pockets of resistance to the Civil Rights Act, the NAACP's Constance Baker Motley reported that voluntary compliance with the act had been "unexpectedly good. I would have lost every penny I've got if I had made a bet." The response to the Civil Rights Act, the *Christian Science Monitor* confirmed, had "exceeded the most optimistic hopes of backers" of the act. "The prospect for voluntary compliance," it said, "has taken a sharp turn for the better. Americans who glumly foresaw collisions on all sides and massive resistance to the new law are rubbing their eyes." And NAACP official Sara Luper declared that this "is the first time the 4th of July has really meant anything to the Negro."[6]

Moreton Rolleston in Atlanta, however, was not alone in planning a constitutional attack on the public accommodations provisions of the Civil Rights Act as it was pending enactment. While the act was still being debated in Congress, the Birmingham Restaurant Association retained the Birmingham law firm of Lange, Simpson, Robinson and Somerville to explore the question of whether the public accommodations provisions applicable to restaurants could be successfully attacked on constitutional grounds if the act became law. A member of the firm, Robert McDavid Smith, researched the issue and reported to the Restaurant Association his conclusion that an attack on the provisions applying to restaurants serving or offering to serve interstate travelers would be futile, since the power of Congress to regulate such restaurants under the Commerce Clause was well established. The only provision of the act applicable to restaurants that might possibly be vulnerable to a constitutional challenge, Smith said, was the provision making the act applicable to restaurants serving food a substantial portion of which had moved in interstate commerce. It might be possible to convince the courts, Smith felt, that a restaurant's serving of food that had moved in interstate commerce constituted such a remote and insubstantial link to or effect on interstate commerce as to be beyond the valid scope of congressional power under the Commerce Clause.[7]

Robert Smith's conclusions were of little comfort to the Restaurant Association, since virtually all of the association's member restaurants served or offered to serve interstate travelers and consequently, under Smith's analysis, were in no position to launch a successful challenge of the public accommodations provisions. The association nevertheless ultimately suggested to Smith that Ollie's Barbecue in Birmingham met his criteria for a restaurant that might succeed in a constitutional challenge of the act because of the nature of the restaurant's operations. Ollie's Barbecue was located in the predominantly black south side of Birmingham and was remote from any state or interstate highways, railway or bus stations, or airports and was therefore likely to have virtually no interstate customers. In addition, Ollie's engaged in no advertising and could thus not be said to be offering to serve interstate travelers. The Restaurant Association consequently suggested to Robert Smith that the owners of Ollie's Barbecue, who were not members of the association, be contacted to determine their willingness to be plaintiffs in a suit challenging the restaurant provisions of the Civil Rights Act.[8]

The owners of Ollie's Barbecue were forty-eight-year-old Ollie McClung Sr. and his son, twenty-four-year-old Ollie McClung Jr. At his wife's request, Ollie McClung Sr. had taken their children to Sunday school in December of 1946, and he himself remained for the church services. As a result, McClung underwent a profound religious conversion. "I had my spiritual experience," he said later, and his whole life changed. Prior to 1946, Ollie's Barbecue had served beer, but on New Year's Day 1947, McClung loaded a truck with all of the beer the restaurant had on hand and hauled it to the city garbage dump. The restaurant not only stopped serving alcoholic beverages of any kind but it also ceased its previous practice of opening on Sunday. "I now felt I was in partnership with the Lord," McClung said, "and if the Lord felt He could do better in six days than in seven, we would do the same thing." McClung became a lay minister of the Cumberland Presbyterian Church, and in 1961–62, he traveled across the country preaching his fundamentalist beliefs to congregations as varied as Chinese-Americans in San Francisco and Native Americans in Oklahoma, as well as many black congregations. "Some of the hardest preaching I have ever done," he said, "has been in colored churches."[9]

Ollie McClung Sr. was deeply concerned when congressional passage of the Civil Rights Act of 1964 seemed assured. He believed strongly that all laws must be obeyed, yet he felt that his business would be destroyed if he complied with the act. Ollie's Barbecue had never served blacks on the premises even though it was located in a predominantly black section of Birmingham. If he desegregated, McClung believed, his restaurant would be flooded with black customers, especially teenagers, and his white customers would cease their patronage as a result. After much conscience-searching and prayer, McClung called his twenty-six black and ten white employees to a meeting and explained his position regarding the Civil Rights Act. "I told them," he said later, "that I felt the Lord had blessed our business over the years and that He had blessed each one of us greatly. I told them that I didn't feel the Lord felt we should change our method of doing business." McClung's employees were not paid wages but rather each shared in a percentage of the restaurant's profits. None of the employees voiced any objection to continuing to operate Ollie's Barbecue on a segregated basis, and the practice therefore continued.[10]

On July 3, the day after the Civil Rights Act became law, several blacks requested service at Ollie's Barbecue, but Ollie McClung Jr. informed them that blacks were not served on the premises, and they ultimately left. When informed of the incident, Ollie McClung Sr. became concerned that the policy of segregation at the restaurant would be publicly perceived as a blatant flouting of the law. "I felt we were doing right," he said, "but I didn't want anybody thinking that I was violating the law. I wanted to erase any such thinking." As a result, when he was contacted regarding his willingness to become a plaintiff in a lawsuit attacking the Civil Rights Act, Ollie McClung readily agreed, but only after another meeting of his employees and their indication of overwhelming support for such a suit.[11]

Since Robert McDavid Smith had already been retained by the Restaurant Association, the McClungs also retained him to represent them in the planned lawsuit. Associated with Smith as counsel in the suit was fellow Lange, Simpson, Robinson and Somerville attorney William G. Somerville Jr. Joining Smith and Somerville as counsel for the McClungs was James H. Faulkner of the Birmingham law firm of Bowers, Dixon, Dunn and McDowell. Faulkner was not retained by the McClungs themselves, but rather was retained by Alabama Governor George Wallace as a means of indicating the segregationist governor's support for the challenge of the Civil Rights Act.[12]

During the litigation in the *McClung* case, the lead attorney for the McClungs would be forty-three-year-old Robert McDavid Smith. Smith was a native of Birmingham, where he was born in 1920. He earned his bachelor's degree at the University of North Carolina in 1942. Smith received his law degree from the University of Alabama Law School in 1948, subsequently earned a master of law degree from Harvard Law School, and was admitted to the Alabama bar in 1949.[13]

Under Title II of the Civil Rights Act, the United States attorney general was authorized to initiate judicial proceedings to enforce the public accommodations provisions of the act when he had "reasonable cause to believe that any person or group of persons is engaged in a pattern or practice of resistance to the full enjoyment of any of the rights secured by this title, and that the pattern or practice is of such a nature and is intended to deny the full exercise of the rights herein described." It was the exercise of this power by Attorney General Robert Kennedy and the Department of Justice that inadvertently triggered the litigation in the case that would be styled *Katzenbach v. McClung* in the Supreme Court of the United States.[14]

On July 16, the *Birmingham News* reported that there had been to date no test cases filed under the Civil Rights Act in Alabama, and that indications were that the Department of Justice would refer any cases that might arise to the Community Relations Service, created by the 1964 act to mediate racial disputes, for negotiated settlements until the Supreme Court passed upon the constitutionality of the act. This prediction was proved erroneous, however, when on July 29 the Department of Justice filed suit under the Civil Rights Act in the U.S. District Court for the Northern District of Alabama in Birmingham. The government's suit sought an injunction ordering the cessation of racial discrimination in virtually every restaurant and eating establishment in Tuscaloosa.

This was the first exercise by the Justice Department in Alabama of its power to initiate proceedings against "a pattern or practice" of violating the public accommodations provisions of the Civil Rights Act, and the suit included twenty-one individual defendants and five corporate defendants. The defendants ranged from the Admiral Benbow Inn and the Holiday Inn Hotel Restaurant to four drug stores that operated lunch counters. Only two of the principal eating establishments in Tuscaloosa were not included in the Justice Department's suit because they had voluntarily desegregated. Ten of the defendants in the suit said that they had voluntarily desegregated as well but had been forced to resegregate after receiving threats from "irritated whites."[15]

The initiation of the Justice Department's suit against the Tuscaloosa eating establishments raised with the McClungs and their attorneys the concern that a similar suit might be initiated by the Justice Department in Birmingham against those restaurants that had not voluntarily desegregated, and if that occurred, it would be difficult or impossible for the McClungs and their counsel to demonstrate the uniquely local nature of their business, which it was felt differentiated it from the much larger restaurants associated with hotels and motels operated by national chains and catering to interstate travelers. The decision was therefore made to avoid these circumstances by filing a suit on behalf of the McClungs, challenging the Civil Rights Act, before the Justice Department took action under the act against the remaining segregated Birmingham restaurants.[16]

Counsel for the McClungs filed a suit in the U.S. District Court for the Northern District of Alabama on July 31, seeking an injunction prohibiting Attorney General Kennedy and the Department of Justice from enforcing the Civil Rights Act against Ollie's Barbecue.[17] In the complaint seeking an injunction in *McClung v. Kennedy,* counsel for the McClungs described the physical location of Ollie's Barbecue in Birmingham and the nature of its operations. The restaurant had been established by J. O. McClung, the father of Ollie McClung Sr., in 1926 at another location, but the restaurant had moved to 902 Seventh Avenue South in 1927. The restaurant itself was described in the complaint as a one-story building located on a tract of land running 200 feet on Seventh Avenue South and 190 feet along Ninth Street, and the restaurant and the land on which it was located represented an investment of $200,000. Ollie's Barbecue, the complaint continued, specialized in the sale of barbecued meat and homemade pies, along with nonalcoholic beverages, and it served approximately 500,000 meals per year and grossed $350,000 annually. The parking lot of the restaurant could accommodate 190 vehicles, while the establishment could seat approximately 200 persons at tables, booths, and counter seats. Thirty-six employees worked at Ollie's Barbecue, twenty-six of whom were black.[18]

In their complaint, counsel for the McClungs next denied that the operations of Ollie's Barbecue were a part of interstate commerce or that they affected interstate commerce. "Plaintiffs' business is essentially local in character," counsel for the McClungs argued.

> It is located some eleven blocks from the nearest federal or interstate highway, except for a truck route one block away from which it derives no trade. It is approximately 17 blocks from the nearest bus station and more than five miles from the nearest airport. Plaintiffs do no advertising and make no effort to attract transient customers.

The McClungs' restaurant, their counsel also pointed out, had attracted large numbers of local customers "by virtue of the excellent quality of the food" it served, the excellence of the service it offered, and "the wholesomeness of the surroundings." Ollie's Barbecue, as far as the McClungs were aware, did not serve interstate travelers within the meaning of the Civil Rights Act, counsel noted, and the McClungs purchased "all of the food served in their restaurant locally, and all such food is delivered to them locally."[19]

Despite this assertion, the attorneys of the McClungs conceded that

> while all of . . . [the restaurant's] purchases of food are made locally, i.e., within the State of Alabama, and the operation of the restaurant in no way affects interstate commerce in the sense required for any such regulation thereof to constitute a lawful exercise of the power of Congress to regulate commerce . . . , some of the food served by plaintiffs probably originates in some form outside the State of Alabama.

The McClungs' counsel thus also conceded that Ollie's Barbecue was covered by the provisions of the Civil Rights Act prohibiting racial discrimination in restaurants serving food a substantial portion of which had moved in interstate commerce, "and as a result the plaintiffs would suffer serious and irreparable injury." Indeed, in an affidavit subsequently submitted to the court in support of the complaint in the *McClung* case, Weaver Saterbak, the office manager of the Birmingham branch of George A. Hormel and Company, certified that during the twelve-month period of July 1, 1963, to July 1, 1964, Ollie's Barbecue had purchased $69,683 worth of pork and beef from the Hormel Company, and that all "the meat sold to Ollie's was received by Hormel at its Birmingham branch from other facilities of Hormel located outside the State of Alabama."[20]

The McClungs had "maintained the policy of reserving, and on occasion exercising, the right to refuse service to any person not acceptable to . . . [them] and whose presence on . . . [their] premises would, in . . . [their] opinion be either detrimental to their business or contrary to the desires and preferences of its customers," counsel pointed out in the complaint. The McClungs, it was admitted, "have never served Negroes any food or beverages for consumption" in the restaurant, "and have elected not to do so voluntarily in the lawful and legitimate exercise of their right to operate their business and to use their property" as they saw fit. Since the enactment of the Civil Rights Act, the complaint said, several blacks had requested service at the McClungs' restaurant but had been denied service. Neither the McClungs nor certain of their employees, it was asserted, "are willing to serve members of the Negro race."[21]

Ollie's Barbecue, the complaint continued, was located in a black residential area of Birmingham, which also had several industrial concerns employing large numbers of black workers. The restaurant was also three blocks from a black high school enrolling between 1,200 and 1,300 students, and the restaurant was within five blocks of two black grammar schools, one public and one Catholic. The McClungs had served black customers on a "take-out" basis so that the food sold to blacks had to be eaten off the premises of the restaurant, the complaint said, and in light of the large amount of food sold in this manner to black customers, it was evident that the food was enjoyed by them. If the McClungs were required to serve blacks on the premises of the restaurant, it was argued, "such persons would occupy plaintiffs' restaurant in large numbers, contrary to the desires of the plaintiffs, their employees, and their regular customers and to the exclusion of plaintiffs' present customers. Plaintiffs' business and property would thereby suffer great injury."[22]

Title II of the Civil Rights Act as applied to Ollie's Barbecue, the complaint asserted, was an unconstitutional exercise of the power of Congress under the Commerce Clause, since it regulated local activities that were reserved to the states for regulation, in violation of the Tenth Amendment of the Constitution. And since no law of Alabama or any local ordinance required the segregation of the McClungs' restaurant, their policy of refusing to serve blacks on the premises of their establishment was an exercise of their property rights under the Fifth Amendment, which would be violated if the Civil Rights Act required them to serve blacks. Any such service to blacks would additionally be against the will of the McClungs and their employees, the complaint maintained, and thus would impose involuntary servitude in violation of the Thirteenth Amendment.

The complaint on behalf of the McClungs concluded:

Plaintiffs further aver that the property rights upon which they rely are ancient and fundamental, won in a progression of blood struggles against tyranny in various forms, and that, there being no legitimate powers given to Congress by the Constitution to interfere with plaintiffs' said rights in the manner attempted in said act, any effort to enforce said act against these plaintiffs would be invalid, in contravention of natural law and in violation of the Tenth Amendment of said Constitution. Plaintiffs aver, therefore, that the so-called Civil Rights Act of 1964 as applied to them, their property, and their business, is illegal, invalid, and violative of their rights under the Fifth, Tenth, and Thirteenth Amendments to the Constitution of the United States as well as other provisions thereof, and should be so held by the court.[23]

Robert McDavid Smith and his fellow cocounsel representing the McClungs had to face the threshold problem of whether their suit for an injunction against the Civil Rights Act could properly be entertained by the

U.S. district court in Birmingham under its equitable jurisdiction. The Department of Justice had not investigated the operations of the McClungs' restaurant, nor had there been any threat of any enforcement action against the McClungs by the department under the Civil Rights Act. Indeed, as government lawyers would subsequently point out, the Department of Justice had never heard of Ollie's Barbecue prior to the filing of the suit on behalf of the McClungs on July 31. Since there had been no threat to enforce the Civil Rights Act against Ollie's Barbecue, it was therefore doubtful that counsel for the McClungs could successfully argue that the McClungs faced the irreparable injury to their legal interests that was normally required before injunctive relief could be obtained in a federal court.

It was in light of these circumstances that the government's response to the McClungs' suit was to file a motion to dismiss the suit on the ground the complaint failed to state a claim upon which relief could be granted, rather than to file a counterclaim for an injunction as it had in the *Heart of Atlanta Motel* case. Clearly, the Department of Justice preferred to defend the validity of the Civil Rights Act in cases of its own choosing, and *McClung v. Kennedy* was not such a case.[24]

Indeed, at the time the *McClung* case was filed in Birmingham, it appeared that the Department of Justice had a much stronger case involving the application of the Civil Rights Act to a restaurant in the *Pickrick* case in Atlanta. Lester Maddox's Pickrick restaurant not only served a larger volume of food that had moved in interstate commerce, but its location on the business route of an interstate highway and its advertising along highways also indicated that it at least offered to serve interstate travelers. Lester Maddox's attorneys had filed a notice of appeal in the *Pickrick* case at the end of July, and the Department of Justice undoubtedly preferred to defend the application of the Civil Rights Act to a restaurant in the Supreme Court in the *Pickrick* case rather than the factually weaker *McClung* case, although this was of course precluded when Lester Maddox and his attorneys failed to pursue the appeal to the Supreme Court.[25]

Since the *McClung* case was an attack on the constitutional validity of a federal statute in which an injunction was sought against the statute's enforcement, a three-judge federal district court was required to hear the case. Normally, the panel of three judges to hear the *McClung* case would have been selected by Fifth Circuit Court of Appeals Chief Judge Elbert Tuttle, but Tuttle was absent from the circuit when the case was filed. In his absence, Acting Fifth Circuit Chief Judge Richard T. Rives appointed the panel, and he selected Fifth Circuit Court of Appeals Judge Walter P. Gewin and U.S. District Judges Seybourn H. Lynne and H. Hobart Grooms, both of the U.S. District Court for the Northern District of Alabama. Judges Lynne and

Grooms were both from Birmingham, while Judge Gewin was from Tuscaloosa, with the result that the three-judge district court in the *McClung* case
was entirely composed of judges from Alabama. The *McClung* case was
scheduled for a hearing on September 1.[26]

Senior among the three judges who would hear the *McClung* case was
U.S. District Judge Seymour H. Lynne. Born in 1907, Lynne practiced law
from 1930 to 1934 in Decatur, Alabama, and then served as a judge on the
Morgan County Court from 1934 to 1940, when he became a member of
the Eighth Circuit Court of Alabama. After service as a lieutenant colonel in
the Army during World War II, Lynne was appointed to the U.S. District
Court for the Northern District of Alabama by President Truman in 1946.
As a U.S. district judge, Seybourn Lynne had proven to be consistent "in
finding no merit in Negroes' civil rights complaints." He had, for example,
dismissed a suit challenging segregated waiting rooms in railway stations as
unlawful. "This is but another in the growing list of cases," Judge Lynne had
said, "wherein both the tutored and untutored apparently entertain the mis-
taken notion that the proper function of the federal courts is propaganda
rather than judicature." And Lynne had also dissented from the federal court
decision ordering the desegregation of Montgomery's public bus system.[27]

Joining Judge Lynne on the three-judge court in the *McClung* case was
Judge H. Hobart Grooms. Born in Kentucky in 1900, Grooms received his
law degree from the University of Kentucky and was admitted to the Alabama bar in 1926, practicing law in Birmingham. A Republican, Grooms
was active in the Republican party in Alabama and was appointed to the U.S.
District Court for the Northern District of Alabama by President Eisenhower
in August 1953. Like his Democratic colleague, Seybourn Lynne, Grooms
had compiled a record of hostility to civil rights claims during his tenure on
the district bench.[28]

The final member of the *McClung* court was U.S. Court of Appeals Judge
Walter Gewin. Born in Nanafalia, Alabama, in 1908, Gewin received his college education at Birmingham-Southern College and Emory University and
earned his law degree from the University of Alabama in 1935. He was a
member of the Alabama legislature from 1939 to 1943 and was the deputy solicitor of Hale County from 1941 to 1951. In 1958, Gewin was elected president of the Alabama Bar Association, and he was appointed to the U.S. Court
of Appeals for the Fifth Circuit by President Kennedy in 1961. Because of his
relatively brief tenure as a federal judge, Gewin's civil rights record was un-
formed in 1964, but given the prevailing racial attitudes in Alabama, he could
be expected to be comfortable with the civil rights views of his colleagues,
Judges Lynne and Grooms. The composition of the three-judge court in the
McClung case consequently did not augur well for the Civil Rights Act.[29]

At the hearing on September 1, the McClungs continued to be represented by Robert McDavid Smith, William Somerville, and James Faulkner, while the government was represented by Civil Rights Division attorneys St. John Barrett and K. William O'Connor, and U.S. Attorney Macon L. Weaver. In preparation for the hearing before the three-judge court, counsel for the McClungs had attempted to demonstrate that the McClungs were in fact facing irreparable injury justifying injunctive relief by serving on counsel for the government numerous requests for admissions. The requests for admissions sought the concession by government counsel that the Civil Rights Act applied to restaurants like that of the McClungs, that the attorney general and the Department of Justice were committed to the enforcement of the act against such restaurants, that the district court had jurisdiction to adjudicate the McClungs' complaint, that they had no adequate remedy at law, and so on. Through the requests for admissions counsel for the McClungs thus sought to establish that injunctive relief would be proper and that a real case or controversy in fact existed for the three-judge court to adjudicate.[30]

Counsel for the government, on the other hand, refused to comply with most of the requests for admissions. Counsel for the McClungs, they argued, were attempting through requests for admissions to create what otherwise did not exist in the *McClung* suit; that is, a real case or controversy in which the McClungs were threatened with irreparable injury to their legal interests by the enforcement of the Civil Rights Act against them. The government's motion to dismiss the *McClung* suit was of course predicated on the contention that there was in fact no imminent threat of the enforcement of the act against the McClungs, and that consequently they faced no immediate threat of irreparable injury justifying the granting of injunctive relief by the federal court. In defense of the legal premises underlying their motion to dismiss the *McClung* suit, counsel for the government thus vigorously resisted most of the requests for admissions that they perceived to undermine those premises.[31]

The first part of the hearing before the three-judge court on September 1 consequently involved arguments on both sides regarding whether the government properly refused to respond to most of the requests for admissions. One of the requests for admissions, for example, had asked if it was the position of Attorney General Kennedy that the Civil Rights Act applied to racial discrimination in restaurants serving food that had moved in interstate commerce, and if so, what percentage of the food served by a restaurant would have to have moved in commerce to trigger the provisions of the act. Counsel for the government had refused this request for admission, and the issue was contested during the hearing. "Now, at some point we have to know his [the attorney general's] contention in this regard," Robert Mc-David Smith argued.

It isn't hypothetical because we have already presented to your honor an affidavit which shows that a portion of the meat served by this plaintiff here did cross state lines. Now it is incumbent upon us to show there is a case or controversy on the point they raise. Now, the case or controversy in this instance happens to arise out of the official position of the defendant Kennedy. I can't think of anything more relevant than what he contends or what his judgment is as to the application of the act.[32]

"Let me ask you this, Bobby," Judge Seybourn Lynne inquired. "You think it is the function of requests for admissions to request that an adversary state his legal positions?"

"No, sir, I think you have to consider this in the context of the other requests made," Smith replied.

We think that the legislative history [of the Civil Rights Act] abundantly shows that he [the attorney general] does contend that a restaurant that serves food, twenty percent of which has crossed state lines, is covered and we expect the legislative history to show that he intended all restaurants to be covered. So, for that reason we thought this was an appropriate request. This comes down to the question in the case or controversy. The controversy here is does this act mean to cover every restaurant in the United States if any food, no matter where it came from, has crossed state lines—

"Then your position is you are not seeking a legal opinion but you are seeking to determine what he contends the law is?" Judge Walter Gewin asked.

"That is correct," Smith responded.[33]

"If your honor please," St. John Barrett replied on behalf of the government,

had counsel asked by interrogatory or request for admissions whether or not the attorney general was preparing, had prepared or contemplated bringing an action with respect to this restaurant, I would concede—I won't concede that would be a proper request, but it would be a request for a fact which is the state of mind, I suppose, of the attorney general with respect to this particular client. But when he says that a case or controversy is whether or not the act extends to all restaurants, he is stating an abstract legal proposition and the fact he is trying with these discovery devices to somehow jell this abstract legal question into the context of something resembling a lawsuit, merely illustrates the essence of what he is doing.[34]

Barrett continued:

Now it is true that an affidavit has been filed today saying that some of his [McClung's] meat comes from outside the State of Alabama. But we don't know where the rest of his produce comes from. Whatever the percentage this is to the total, we don't know what the true facts are. And the attorney general has made no effort in connection with the enforcement of this act to ascertain the true facts or to determine whether or not he should or should not bring a lawsuit [against the McClungs].[35]

"These plaintiffs," Barrett told the court,

are merely seeking to—by asking this court to assume injunctive equitable jurisdiction, is seeking to commit this court to rule on the validity [of the Civil Rights Act] in anticipation of a defense that the restaurant might raise in the future if hereafter the attorney general should determine to file a lawsuit with respect to this restaurant. File such a suit that would have to be in this very court and he asks that the court now on purely hypothetical facts pre-commit itself as to what it would do if such a lawsuit was filed. . . . They are coming in and seeking to create a lawsuit as it were.

"I am with you on your objection," Judge Lynne said. "But I think that they are requesting you to admit a legal contention and I think that is the function of a request for admissions."

"In essence they are trying to make us sue them," Barrett insisted, "either sue them or commit ourselves to say that they are not suable. That is exactly what it seems to me it boils down to. You just don't frame a case or controversy by making that sort of demand on a court."[36]

St. John Barrett was successful in persuading the three-judge court to sustain the government's objections to most of the plaintiffs' requests for admissions, although the government was required to concede that the attorney general had a legal duty to enforce the Civil Rights Act and intended to do so. Finally, counsel for the McClungs requested an admission from government counsel as to whether the attorney general would enforce the public accommodations provisions against any place of public accommodation that discriminated on the basis of race. "If the plaintiffs are fearful or wonder whether the attorney general is going to desist from performing what appears to be his duty under the act because in his view the act is patently unconstitutional," St. John Barrett responded, "certainly I can relieve them of that fear."

"Is it your contention that the attorney general will enforce the law?" Judge Grooms asked.

"Yes, it is," Barrett replied.[37]

Ollie McClung Sr. was then sworn as a witness and, under questioning by Robert McDavid Smith, testified that his father had established the original restaurant in 1926 at Sixth Avenue South and Goldmire Street, but moved it to its present location on Seventh Avenue South in 1927. He became a junior partner with his father in 1937, McClung said, and when his father died in 1941, he had inherited the business. McClung Sr. had operated the restaurant alone until 1958, when his son, Ollie McClung Jr., became a partner in the business. McClung Sr. also testified that Ollie's Barbecue was located in a black residential and light industrial section of Birmingham, with several black schools and churches in the vicinity of the restaurant. He also confirmed the allegations in the complaint filed in the case that the restaurant was remote from any railway or bus station, airport, interstate highway, or state highway that would make it attractive as an eating place for interstate travelers. Ollie's Barbecue specialized in barbecue meats, homemade pies, and nonalcoholic drinks, the elder McClung also confirmed.[38]

"Have you in the almost forty years you have been in business there, have you at any time served Negroes?" Robert Smith asked.

"No, sir. Not on the premises," McClung responded.

"Do you—have you had the practice of selling them food to be taken away from the premises?" Smith inquired.

"Yes, sir," McClung said, "we continue to serve them take-out food." He testified that the restaurant would seat 220 people when totally full and that most of his customers arrived at the establishment by automobile. Among his duties, he said, were cooking, waiting on customers, and on occasion serving as cashier. Ollie's Barbecue did no advertising at all, McClung added, and made no attempt to attract transient customers, while in fact virtually all of the restaurant's customers were local people whom he knew on sight. In 1963, the restaurant's total gross sales were $350,000, based on serving over 500,000 meals, McClung said. The daily average of gross sales at the restaurant was $1,039, with a break-even point of $939. The amount the McClungs had invested in Ollie's Barbecue was $200,000, and the profit was $55,000 in 1963. He would not sell the business for less that $250,000 or $300,000, he said. It had purchased $150,000 worth of food in 1963, 55 percent of which consisted of meat. Eighty to 90 percent of the meat was purchased from Hormel, McClung testified, amounting to $69,683 in 1963. The Hormel salesman came to the restaurant and took the meat order in person and was paid directly by check.[39]

"Were you aware of the adoption of the Civil Rights Act of 1964 when it was signed by the president?" Robert Smith asked.

"I was aware of it," McClung responded. "I wasn't informed by anyone other than just common knowledge."

"You picked it up by the radio or television?" Smith asked.

"Yes, sir, and the restaurant association," McClung said.

Smith then inquired whether any blacks had requested service at Ollie's Barbecue since the Civil Rights Act had become law. McClung replied that blacks had requested service as early as July 3 when he was not present, but he had been present when blacks had requested service since the filing of the lawsuit challenging the act. "Have you declined to serve them?" Smith inquired.

"We declined to serve them, sir," McClung said. "Serve on the premises. Offered to serve them take-out service and when they refused we declined service."

"Were they declined service because they were Negroes?" Smith asked.

"Yes, sir, I would think so. Because we chose not to serve them," McClung affirmed.[40]

By this point in the testimony of Ollie McClung Sr., Robert McDavid Smith had established two important points relevant to the coverage of the Civil Rights Act. First, Ollie's Barbecue purchased meat from the Hormel Company that had moved in interstate commerce, and since almost half of the restaurant's budget for food was spent on meat from Hormel, it could be argued that a substantial portion of the food sold by the restaurant had moved in interstate commerce. Secondly, McClung had admitted that Ollie's Barbecue refused service to blacks because of their race after the effective date of the Civil Rights Act, and it thus also came within the act's prohibition of racial discrimination in restaurants that served food a substantial portion of which had moved in interstate commerce.

Smith then directed his questioning of McClung to elicit responses indicating the extent of the damage his business would suffer if he complied with the Civil Rights Act and served blacks. "Are you familiar with restaurants [in Birmingham] that have, since July 2 of this year, served Negroes?" he asked. "Are you familiar with whether that had any effect on their business?"

"Yes, sir, I think so," McClung responded.

"Tell the court what that effect has been," Smith directed.

"The Britling's downtown has lost 25 percent of their business," McClung said. "Several restaurants in Atlanta I have heard from have lost a good deal of the business and in Memphis, Tennessee, where I had some direct connection with people, I understand they lost a lot of business when they integrated."

"Do you have any judgment whether your restaurant would be affected more or less or about the same as the downtown cafeterias?" Smith inquired.

"I would think extremely more," McClung replied.

"For what reason?" Smith asked.

"Because of our location principally with some 1500 or 2000 high school [black students] passing there every day," McClung explained. "[A]nd with the churches that are close by and the number of Negro children that are connected with the church, of course. I am assuming it would damage my business 75 or 80 percent, sir."[41]

"If you were required to serve Negro customers, would you do so voluntarily?" Smith then inquired.

"No, sir," McClung responded.

"Is that your own judgment, Mr. McClung, or your own decision?" Smith persisted.

"Yes, sir," McClung said, "I would refuse to serve a drunken man or a profane man or a colored man or anyone I felt would damage my business and I run a good clean place there." Smith inquired if McClung had ever called the police to eject objectionable white people from his restaurant, and McClung affirmed that he had. Under further questioning by Smith, McClung testified that not only did Ollie's Barbecue not serve alcoholic beverages but that it also refused service to anyone who had been drinking. The establishment, he added, would not tolerate anyone who used profanity on the premises. Indeed, on each table in the restaurant there was a small sign saying, "No Profanity, Please. Ladies and Children are Usually Present. We Appreciate Your Cooperation."[42]

Robert Smith then elicited testimony from McClung that no official policy or action of the state influenced his decision to refuse service to blacks. "Mr. McClung, did you reach the decision after July 2 of this year not to serve Negroes as your own independent, voluntary decision, or were you influenced by any public officer?" Smith inquired.

"No," McClung replied, "we reached the decision before July 2nd. We reached it several days before on our own. We had no other influence."

"It is a fact that most of the restaurants in Birmingham, Alabama, have served Negroes since July 2 of this year?" Smith asked.

"Yes, sir, I think the large majority," McClung responded.

"And at any time in your restaurant have you been influenced in any way whatever in making this decision [not to serve blacks] by any state or local official?" Smith persisted.

"No, sir," McClung replied. By this line of questioning Smith thus established that the McClungs' restaurant was not covered under provisions of the Civil Rights Act prohibiting racial discrimination in places of public accommodation that was supported by state action within the meaning of the Fourteenth Amendment.[43]

"In making your determination or decision you would not comply with the Civil Rights Act after July 2nd," Smith then inquired of McClung, "did you take into consideration the responsibility to your customers?"

"Yes, sir," McClung responded, "very definitely."

"Explain that," Smith directed.

"We consider that we operate our business as a trust to our customers, we are a steward of it, and it is our feeling that they have a place to come in and eat where they will enjoy and where they will leave in a better frame of mind than when they came in, that they will get good food and good service," McClung explained. "If we fail to do that we feel like we have failed to fulfill our obligation and we don't deserve their business if we don't give them that kind of atmosphere. And to do that we feel like it is absolutely essential that we control our clientele."

"To some extent your restaurant has something of a religious atmosphere?" Smith asked.

"Yes, sir, we try to make it so," McClung said. He explained that he was a member of the Cumberland Presbyterian Church, had been a church elder, treasurer, Sunday school teacher, and had served on Presbyterian boards and Synodic boards as well as the Presbyterian Assembly board, and was considered by some to be a lay minister.[44]

Finally, Robert Smith elicited testimony from Ollie McClung Sr. regarding where Ollie's Barbecue obtained the remainder of the food it served, other than the meat purchased from the Hormel Company. McClung testified that the restaurant also purchased small amounts of meat from Swift and Company and Rath Packing Company. Most of the general groceries for the restaurant were purchased from the Wood-Fruitticher Grocery Company, while the produce used in the establishment was obtained from Carlisle Brothers Produce Company. The buns and bakery goods for the restaurant were purchased from a local baker, McClung said, Rutland Baking Company. "I believe that is all," Smith then announced.[45]

St. John Barrett then briefly cross-examined Ollie McClung Sr. and again elicited an acknowledgement from him that Ollie's Barbecue refused service to blacks on the premises of the restaurant on the ground of their race. And in response to Barrett's questions, McClung explained that blacks could obtain take-out service at the end of the counter in the restaurant, while whites could obtain that service at the other end of the counter near the cashier, indicating that even the take-out service was segregated. Asked if his employees ate on the premises, McClung said that most did, but the employees were also segregated when they ate. The white employees ate in the dining room, Mc-

Clung said, while the black employees ate in another room. "Mr. McClung, have you been contacted by any representative of the federal government in connection with compliance with the Civil Rights Act?" Barrett asked.

"No, sir," McClung answered.

"I have no further questions," Barrett then said.[46]

Ollie McClung Jr. was then called as a witness, and he testified regarding the first occasion on which blacks had requested service at Ollie's Barbecue after the passage of the Civil Rights Act. The incident occurred on July 3, he said in response to questions from Robert Smith, and at first a single, young black male had entered the restaurant and requested service at a seat at the counter. McClung testified that he had explained to him that it was the restaurant's policy not to serve blacks on the premises but only on a take-out basis, and the young man had then left. "Approximately 45 minutes later," he said,

> he came back this time with the young girl that I mentioned and four other colored people, older. They again—they didn't ask anything but rather came in and sat at the counter. Even though it was rather obvious he was aware what the policy was, they came in and sat at the counter and one white young person was sitting at the counter, a boy, and he got up and left the minute they sat down and I went over to them, the girl and boy were obviously part of the professional or paid civil rights agitators—

"You can't tell about that," Robert Smith interrupted. "Anything you saw or heard."

"They had a card and they wanted to know why we did not serve them and this sort of thing, and they filled out the card and wanted to know my name and address of the place," McClung continued.

"They were taking notes with pen and pencil?" Smith asked.

"Yes, sir," McClung replied. "And after a couple of minutes I told them that I was sorry that they would have to leave, that it wasn't our policy to serve them there and they got up and left."

"And there was no threatening on either side?" Smith inquired.

"That is correct," McClung answered, "they got up and left."[47]

Ollie McClung Sr. was then recalled as a witness by Robert Smith to testify regarding why the *McClung* suit had been filed. This was again an attempt by Smith to demonstrate that the McClungs feared irreparable injury to their business if the Civil Rights Act were enforced against their restaurant by the Department of Justice. "Mr. McClung, the records of this court show that this suit was filed on July 31, 1964, which I believe was a Friday. Is it your recollection this suit was filed on Friday?" Smith asked.

"Yes, sir," McClung replied.

"Did anything occur shortly before that date that in any way influenced your decision in bringing this suit?" Smith inquired.[48]

McClung replied that there "very definitely" had been such an occurrence, and it was the suit filed "by the attorney general against the group of restaurants in Tuscaloosa" on July 29. On the following day, McClung said, he contacted Robert Smith about filing suit for an injunction to prevent the enforcement of the Civil Rights Act against his restaurant. "Are you telling the court that the filing of that suit [against the Tuscaloosa restaurants] was one of the factors that influenced you to bring this suit?" Smith asked.

"It was the important factor, sir," McClung said, "because I felt like if I were grouped with Howard Johnsons and Holiday Inn and other restaurants of that nature that I would have no opportunity at all to present my case as a local restaurant." Although Robert Smith had never represented him as counsel previously, McClung said, he was acquainted with him and therefore retained him along with William Somerville to attack the constitutionality of the Civil Rights Act as applied to Ollie's Barbecue. And with that, the hearing before the three-judge court came to an end.[49]

Attorney General Robert Kennedy announced his resignation on September 3, two days following the hearing in the *McClung* case, with the result that he was dropped as a defendant in the case. Acting Attorney General Nicholas Katzenbach thus became the principal defendant in the case, and the case in the three-judge court became *McClung v. Katzenbach*, rather than *McClung v. Kennedy* as it had been since its initiation on July 31. The three-judge court announced its decision in *McClung v. Katzenbach* on September 17, holding the Civil Rights Act unconstitutional as applied to Ollie's Barbecue and issuing an injunction prohibiting the enforcement of the act by the Department of Justice against the restaurant.[50]

Addressing the government's motion to dismiss the *McClung* case, the court noted that the McClungs had admitted that they were refusing to serve blacks in their restaurant. The court also found as a matter of law that a substantial portion of the food the McClungs served at Ollie's Barbecue had moved in interstate commerce. It also noted that the initiation of the *McClung* suit had been prompted in large part because the Department of Justice had brought enforcement proceedings against many similar restaurants in Tuscaloosa and that those proceedings were based at least in part on the fact that some of the restaurants in Tuscaloosa had served food a substantial portion of which had moved in interstate commerce. "And plainly the attorney general has indicated an intention to enforce the provisions of Title II as against its violators," the court said. "We cannot say, in these circumstances, that enforcement against plaintiffs was not reasonably imminent when this action was commenced, and no case cited by defendants or found by us has held under comparable circumstances that for this reason an actual controversy did not exist." Indeed, the court pointed out, a threat of imminent enforcement of a law "has not been considered requisite to the existence of a justiciable controversy or the exercise by federal courts of equitable jurisdiction in similar suits seeking anticipatory relief from the operation and enforcement of the law." The court therefore overruled the government's motion to dismiss and proceeded to consider the merits of the case.[51]

A review of the legislative history of the Civil Rights Act of 1964 indicated that Title II could only be based on congressional power derived from the Commerce Clause or the Thirteenth and Fourteenth Amendments of the Constitution, the court said. The act, however, was not based on the Thirteenth Amendment, nor did that amendment prohibit the act, the court held, overruling the contention of counsel for the McClungs that the act imposed involuntary servitude. The act as applied to the McClungs' restaurant also was not based on the Fourteenth Amendment, the court additionally ruled, since "the State of Alabama, in none of its manifestations, has been involved in the private conduct of the plaintiffs in refusing to serve food to Negroes for consumption on the premises" of their restaurant. The validity of the application of the Civil Rights Act to Ollie's Barbecue, the court consequently concluded, depended on whether such an application could be sustained under the Commerce Clause.[52]

The court said:

In any discussion of the Commerce Clause as a grant of power to the national government to regulate activities commonly described as private and local we keep in mind the admitted fact that a majority of sincere and conscientious members of Congress believed this legislation to be in the national interest and necessary to end practices which they considered debasing to human dignity. Of course, we express no opinion as to the wisdom of the legislation and confine our consideration to the constitutionality of the provisions with which we are concerned.[53]

The court continued:

While we shall not attempt the impossible task of a precise delineation of the contours of the power to regulate interstate commerce granted to Congress or the Herculean labor of analyzing the multitudinous cases dealing with various aspects of what may be termed primary and implied power, we shall make an effort to distill from the decided cases a definitive statement of such power which may be applied in this case only. Some presuppositions are permissible; indeed they are required by the teaching of *Wickard* v. *Filburn*.

The power of Congress to regulate interstate commerce included not just the power to regulate interstate commerce itself, the court conceded, but also included the power to regulate local activities when their regulation was necessary for the effective regulation of commerce itself. The regulation of intrastate activities was justified, however, only when those activities bore such a close and substantial relation to interstate commerce that their regulation was essential to protect interstate commerce from burdens that obstruct the flow of commerce, the court said. Interstate commerce, the court nevertheless maintained, "unlike Tennyson's brook" did not run on forever: "At some time it must come to an end within the boundaries of some state."[54]

The Civil Rights Act regulated restaurants that served interstate travelers or that served food a substantial portion of which had moved in interstate commerce, the court pointed out. And it expressed the view that there was no precedent for Congress to regulate "the conduct of people on the local level because they may happen to trade sporadically with persons who may be traveling in interstate commerce." As for the interstate food test, which was also applicable to restaurants under the act, the court declared it to be a settled rule of constitutional law that "goods cease to constitute part of interstate commerce, and become a part of the general property in a state, and amenable to its laws, when they are sent into a state, either for the purpose of sale or in consequence of a sale." The court continued:

> The simple truth of the matter is that Congress has sought to put an end to racial discrimination in all restaurants wherever situated regardless of whether there is any demonstrable causal connection between the activity of the particular restaurant against which enforcement of the act is sought and interstate commerce.[55]

"If our premise is correct," the court maintained,

> Congress sought to achieve its end by the sophisticated means of first declaring a restaurant is a place of public accommodation if its operations affect commerce and by thereafter abandoning the "affect commerce" requirement by legislating what is tantamount to a conclusive presumption that the operations do affect commerce if it is proved either that it serves or offers to serve interstate travelers or that a substantial portion of the food which it serves has at some time, however remote, moved in commerce.

The courts would not sustain a presumption when there was no rational relation between the fact presumed and interstate commerce, the court said, if the relation "is arbitrary because of lack of connection between the two in common experience."[56]

"If Congress has the naked power to do what it has attempted in Title II of this act," the court declared,

> there is no facet of human behavior which it may not control by mere legislative *ipse dixit* that conduct "affects commerce" when in fact it does not do so at all, and rights of the individual to liberty and property are in dire peril. We conclude that Title II of the Civil Rights Act of 1964 as applied to the business operated by these plaintiffs, was beyond the competence of Congress to enact.

Its enforcement would deprive the plaintiffs of their liberty and property without due process of law in violation of the Fifth Amendment of the Constitution, the court held. "Accordingly they are entitled to the relief for which they pray." The court consequently issued a temporary injunction prohibiting the enforcement of the Civil Rights Act against Ollie's Barbecue.[57]

The decision of the three-judge court in *McClung v. Katzenbach* was the subject of a front-page banner headline in the *Birmingham News* on September 17. "Court Voids Part of Civil Rights Act," the headline announced. Ollie McClung Sr. heard the news of the court's decision on the radio and immediately telephoned his son to announce the news of their victory against the Civil Rights Act. "We are pleased with the decision," Ollie McClung Jr. announced to the press, "and think it is upholding the Constitution." Ollie McClung Sr. later said that the "Lord gives people a choice. And I feel that the people in this country should have the same choice and control over their businesses." Under the Civil Rights Act, he maintained, "I would become an agent of the government. It would be the people serving the government instead of the government serving the people."[58]

The victory of the McClungs was also editorially praised by the *Birmingham News*. "*The Birmingham News* long ago said that there was only the vaguest basis for any assumption the interstate commerce clause was intended to cover activities of local retail business," the editorial said. But the paper warned rather presciently that it did

> not entertain hope that a strict interpretation will be applied [by the U.S. Supreme Court to the Commerce Clause], although this newspaper believes it is logic both to laymen and lawyers to restrict such clause to that which is reasonable. Otherwise we shall have made of law a yard of rubber sheeting which can be stretched to cover anything.[59]

The *Montgomery Advertiser* also applauded the decision in the *McClung* case, although it noted that the decision was narrowly limited to the circumstances of Ollie's Barbecue only. "The dwindling sanctity of property rights took a powerful mauling from the public accommodations law," the *Advertiser* said. "The liberal hucksters have been allowed to make headway against property rights by urging that 'human rights' are paramount—as if the property right to a restaurant or home is not a human right second to none." The *McClung* decision was also welcomed by Alabama Governor George Wallace, who was on a speaking tour in Milwaukee, Wisconsin. Wallace predicted that many members of Congress would "bite the dust politically" for voting for the Civil Rights Act that "this country does not need." And he drew an enthusiastic response from a crowd when he declared, "I object and you object to the federal government telling a private businessman who he can and cannot serve. You more than any other people are going to be responsible for repealing the civil rights bill and the restoration of constitutional government."[60]

Following its defeat in the *McClung* case in Birmingham, the Department of Justice was faced with the decision of whether or not to appeal the case to the Supreme Court. While that decision was pending, the department submitted an application to Justice Hugo Black, in his capacity as circuit justice of the fifth circuit, for a stay of the three-judge court's injunction prohibiting the enforcement of the Civil Rights Act against Ollie's Barbecue.

Later in the fall, an ad appeared in the *Birmingham News* soliciting contributions from the public to support the McClungs' cause. "Ollie's freedom is your freedom!" the ad declared, and continued:

> Dollars are needed now to win this crucial fight! Who more than Alabamians value FREEDOM? Who more firmly believe in one's freedom to choose his own friends and associates? Who cherishes the right to operate his business without interference? Ollie McClung, Sr., and Jr., are willing to place their security, their financial resources, and their families in jeopardy to fight for freedom for you, your children, and their children.[61]

The "better restaurants" of Alabama were supporting the *McClung* case, the ad said. "You will want to join Ollie in his fight for freedom! Your dollars are needed now! Estimated overall cost is $25,000.00." Readers were urged to forward contributions to the Committee for Ollie McClung in care of the Exchange Security Bank in Birmingham.[62]

As the *Birmingham News* ad indicated, Ollie McClung Sr. had become something of a hero in segregationist circles and a symbol of resistance to the

Civil Rights Act. Unlike the grandstanding Lester Maddox in Atlanta, however, he was uncomfortable in the role he had acquired. A modest, self-effacing man, McClung appears to have been sincere in basing his opposition to the Civil Rights Act on his religious beliefs rather than the tenets of the more rabid racists. "Many Negroes," he maintained, "occupy a higher station in the eyes of God than whites do," but he said he was praying that the black community would support his stand against the Civil Rights Act. "I don't think that any Christian Negro would want to eat in this restaurant when he knows that it will hurt someone else," he said. McClung defended his resistance to the Civil Rights Act in a sermon he preached at the Crestline Presbyterian Church, basing the sermon on 1 Kings 21, which related the story of how Ahab, King of Israel, coveted the vineyard of Naboth. The vineyard, McClung said in his sermon, represented his restaurant, and Ahab represented the federal government.[63]

In his restaurant, Ollie McClung offered for sale six editions of the Bible in a display case near the cash register, and a plaque on a wall of the establishment quoted the Book of Psalms: "O taste and see that the Lord is good: blessed is the man that trusteth in Him." Another sign in the restaurant, however, informed the public, "We reserve the right to refuse service to anyone."[64]

On September 23, Justice Black announced his decision regarding the government's application for a stay. As he had said in the *Heart of Atlanta Motel* case, he pointed out, a temporary injunction against the enforcement of an act of Congress was in reality a suspension of the act, delaying the date selected by Congress to put its policies into effect. Black said:

> In recognition of this fact, it is an established rule that courts of equity will not exercise their power to enjoin the enforcement of an act of Congress except under the most imperative or exigent circumstances. Because of this policy I grant the application to stay the execution of the temporary restraining order and injunction of the District Court for the Northern District of Alabama.

The issues in the *McClung* case, like those in the *Heart of Atlanta Motel* case, he added, were important, and the final resolution of them should not be unnecessarily delayed.

> I have consulted with the five other members of the Court now in Washington and am authorized to say that the Court is prepared, if the parties desire, to set this case down for argument on all questions involved, immediately following the argument of the *Heart of Atlanta*

Motel case, which is already scheduled for argument on Monday, October 5, 1964.[65]

As he had in the *Heart of Atlanta Motel* case, Justice Black received correspondence from southerners regarding the *McClung* case. "I am writing you Judge because I feel that I should," one correspondent wrote.

> I am familiar with the location, and know the proprietors of the Ollie McClung Barbeque establishment, their clientele is exclusively that of the white race, and as you should realize, having resided in Alabama for many years of your life this institution would most certainly lose its clientele if Negroes undertook to integrate it, and if it did a great number of their own race would become unemployed as happened in Atlanta, what a loss to the economy in the South if the Negro undertook to do such a thing.

"I cannot realize anyone of the white race," he continued, "adhering to the 'public accommodation section' of the Civil Rights bill." Those provisions of the act, he predicted, would destroy the economy if the Court upheld them. And as a postscript, he added, "The proprietors of this establishment referred to above, are Christian men, and their employees are well paid."[66]

"Would it be possible for the Communists to blackmail the Supreme Court?" another of Black's correspondents asked. "They killed our President. As you weigh this decision, you will have our prayers for a correct answer."[67]

Another correspondent informed Black that he was writing as an "*amicus curiae,*" and said,

> The writer refers to the case of the legal harassment of Ollie McClung, of Ollie's Hamburger Joint, charged with refusing to serve an intruder in his restaurant, and as a corollary, of exercising his right as a free man, to serve who he pleases. . . . Any Negro entering a White restaurant in Birmingham *knows* he is an intruder.

"The act of intrusion is a rotten thing," he continued. "It is rotten whether performed by a stealthy intruder in the bedroom of a sleeping White woman, or whether performed by a hate-filled demonstrating racist into a restaurant where the many racist street demonstrators of ill-will of his group make him unwelcome to the opposite group." The writer declared that the "right of a man to defend his property being taken from him by racial intrusion is greater than the right of the racial intruder to force that restaurant owner to effect such racial mixture as will destroy part of his property."[68]

As Justice Black had indicated in his opinion granting a stay of the injunction in the *McClung* case, as well as his opinion denying a stay of the injunction in the *Heart of Atlanta Motel* case, the Supreme Court was receptive to accelerated appeals in both cases in order to settle promptly the issue of the constitutionality of the public accommodations provisions of the Civil Rights Act. As the *Heart of Atlanta Motel* and *McClung* cases reached the Supreme Court, the conduct of the litigation in the cases passed from the Civil Rights Division to Solicitor General Archibald Cox, whose office was responsible for filing the briefs and conducting the oral arguments in the cases on behalf of the government. On August 12, Solicitor General Cox wrote Moreton Rolleston his understanding of Rolleston's agreement to accelerate the appeal of the *Heart of Atlanta Motel* case to the Supreme Court. Rolleston was to file a jurisdictional statement in the case by September 21, Cox said, and the jurisdictional statement would "contain your full argument on the merits and will serve ultimately as your brief on the merits."* The government in turn agreed to file its response on or before September 28, Cox said, and its response "will set forth the government's argument in full and will serve as its brief on the merits." He added that the "parties will file a joint motion with the Court requesting expedition of the oral argument and suggesting that, if practicable, such argument be scheduled for a day certain during the week of October 5th."⁶⁹

By August 13, the joint motion for acceleration of the oral argument in the *Heart of Atlanta Motel* case had been prepared by the solicitor general's office, and with Rolleston having approved the motion, it was filed with the Court. On August 25, Chief Justice Earl Warren informed Cox that "it has been determined that the motion can be granted, provided the time schedule recommended to the Court in the motion, fixing September 21st as the date for the jurisdictional statement and September 28th for the response thereto, is met." Warren continued:

> In view of all of the circumstances in this case involving not only the interest of the parties themselves, but the public interest as well, the Court will hear oral argument in the [*Heart of Atlanta Motel*] case on October 5, 1964, provided the time schedule recited above is complied with. It

---

*Decisions of three-judge federal district courts, such as those involved in the *Heart of Atlanta Motel* and *McClung* cases, are appealed to the U.S. Supreme Court by "appeal" rather than by the filing of a petition for a writ of certiorari, the method by which virtually all other decisions of the lower courts are appealed to the Court. In an appeal case, the party seeking Supreme Court review of a decision of a three-judge court files a jurisdictional statement seeking review by the Court, rather than the more commonly utilized petition for a writ of certiorari, and the party that prevailed in the court below files a motion to dismiss or affirm.

must be understood that any issues as to jurisdiction are reserved for consideration at the time the case is presented on the merits.[70]

In his reply to Warren on August 28, Solicitor General Cox acknowledged that "I have your letter of August 25 informing me that the Court will hear oral argument in the [*Heart of Atlanta Motel*] case on October 5, 1964, provided the time schedule fixed in the joint motion is met. You may be sure that the government will take every step to meet the September 28 deadline."[71]

In *Katzenbach v. McClung*, as the *McClung* case was styled in the Supreme Court, on the other hand, counsel for the McClungs had yet to be notified that the *McClung* case was to be appealed to the Supreme Court. And they were concerned that the Department of Justice might establish the constitutionality of the public accommodations provisions in the *Heart of Atlanta Motel* case and delay dealing with the *McClung* case until later. Without having been notified of the appeal of the *McClung* case by the Justice Department, Robert McDavid Smith nevertheless learned from a source in Atlanta that the case was in fact being appealed to the Supreme Court. Smith telephoned the clerk of the Court, who confirmed that the appeal had been filed, and informed Smith that Solicitor General Cox and members of his staff were in Justice Black's office arranging for the appeal. The clerk connected Smith with Black's office, and Justice Black, in consultation with Smith and Solicitor General Cox, completed the arrangements for the appeal of the *McClung* case by telephone. As a result, the Court also granted a motion to accelerate the oral argument in the *McClung* case and scheduled the argument to occur immediately following the argument in the *Heart of Atlanta Motel* case on October 5. The battle over the constitutionality of the public accommodations provisions of the Civil Rights Act of 1964 thus shifted from Birmingham and Atlanta to the Supreme Court in Washington.[72]

4

THE *HEART OF ATLANTA MOTEL* CASE:
THE CLASH OF ARGUMENT

In his Supreme Court brief filed in the *Heart of Atlanta Motel* case, Moreton Rolleston continued to rely heavily on the *Civil Rights Cases* of 1883 as determinative of the constitutional validity of the public accommodations provisions of the Civil Rights Act of 1964. In the *Civil Rights Cases,* he argued, the Court had not only ruled the Civil Rights Act of 1875 to be beyond the valid scope of congressional power under section five of the Fourteenth Amendment, but had also indicated that Congress could not validly prohibit discrimination in public accommodations under the Commerce Clause. The Court had stated in the *Civil Rights Cases,* he pointed out, that no one would have contended that the Civil Rights Act of 1875 could have been validly enacted by Congress before the adoption of the Civil War Amendments to the Constitution, and this statement, Rolleston contended, clearly indicated that the Court had concluded that the 1875 act could not have been validly enacted under the Commerce Clause. And since the public accommodations provisions of the 1964 act were very similar to the provisions of the 1875 act, he maintained, the provisions of the 1964 act were as constitutionally invalid as those of the 1875 act had been.[1]

The Court's 1964 decision in *Bell v. Maryland* and its refusal to hold that the Fourteenth Amendment prohibited discrimination in places of public accommodation were essentially a reaffirmation of its ruling in the *Civil Rights Cases,* Rolleston argued, and he attacked the concurring opinion of Justice Douglas in the *Bell* case and its support for a holding that the Fourteenth Amendment required the desegregation of public accommodations. "If these arguments were used by a young law student on his bar examination to practice law," he observed, "counsel submits that he would never be granted a license."[2]

Rolleston also argued in his brief that the operations of motels and hotels were essentially local in nature and as such were beyond the valid reach of congressional power under the Commerce Clause. Congressional power to regulate commerce included the power to regulate the interstate exchange of goods and the sale and delivery of the products of agriculture and industry, he conceded, but, citing the Court's 1837 decision in *New York v. Miln,* he argued that the regulation of the interstate movement of people was not included under the commerce power. "People conduct commerce and engage in trade," he said, "but people are not part of commerce and trade."[3]

Finally, as he had in the lower court, Rolleston contended that the public accommodations provisions violated the Fifth, Tenth, and Thirteenth Amendments to the Constitution. The right of property ownership, he insisted, included the right of an owner of a business to select his own customers, and by depriving business owners of this right, the public accommodations provisions deprived them of their property without due process of law and took their property without compensation in violation of the Due Process and Just Compensation Clauses of the Fifth Amendment. The expansive and intrusive extension of congressional power under the Commerce Clause in the Civil Rights Act of 1964 was also an invasion of the powers reserved to the states under the Tenth Amendment, Rolleston contended. "If such an Act is upheld, the floodgates of federal power will be wide open and no one will ever again legally and peacefully be able to resist the onslaught of federal control by congressional legislation." By requiring business owners to serve customers they had chosen not to serve, he concluded, the public accommodations provisions in addition subjected business owners to involuntary servitude in violation of the Thirteenth Amendment.[4]

In the *Sit-in* cases, United States Solicitor General Archibald Cox had steadfastly resisted making the argument that the Fourteenth Amendment prohibited racial discrimination by private owners of places of public accommodation, or that the enforcement of trespass laws by the states against sit-in demonstrators was sufficient state action to trigger the Fourteenth Amendment. And in the public accommodations cases under the Civil Rights Act of 1964, Cox similarly eschewed any reliance on congressional power under section five of the Fourteenth Amendment as the constitutional basis of the public accommodations provisions. Consequently he neither attacked the continuing validity of the Court's ruling in the *Civil Rights Cases* of 1883 nor invited a reversal of that ruling. The government "has proceeded throughout this litigation upon the theory that the constitutionality of Title II, as applied to appellant, may be sustained under the Commerce Clause without reference to the additional power conferred by section 5 of the Fourteenth Amendment," Cox thus said in his brief in the *Heart of Atlanta Motel* case. "We stake our case here upon the same theory."[5]

In asking the Supreme Court to uphold the constitutionality of the public accommodations provisions, the solicitor general asserted, "we invoke no novel constitutional doctrine or seek no extension of existing principles." The validity of the public accommodations provisions was rather supported by "established rules" that were a "familiar part of our constitutional history." The decisions of the Court, beginning as early as *Gibbons v. Ogden* and *McCulloch v. Maryland* and including more recent decisions in *NLRB v. Jones and Laughlin Steel Corp., United States v. Darby,* and *Wickard v. Filburn,* had firmly established the principle, he maintained, that under the Commerce Clause and Necessary and Proper Clause, Congress could enact all appropriate legislation for the advancement and protection of interstate and foreign commerce. And the Court had additionally held that congressional power under the Commerce Clause, supplemented by the Necessary and Proper Clause, could be validly exercised to remove the burdens and adverse effects essentially local or intrastate activities might impose on commerce.[6]

That hotels and motels were within the scope of congressional power under the Commerce Clause had been established by the Court's decision in *Hotel Employees v. Leedom,*[7] holding that hotel labor relations came within the jurisdiction of the National Labor Relations Board since a strike by hotel employees would adversely affect commerce, Cox pointed out. Racial discrimination in hotels and motels like the Heart of Atlanta Motel, he continued, while concededly local in nature, nevertheless also imposed on interstate commerce substantial burdens that Congress had the valid power to remove or prohibit. As the evidence before Congress when it was considering the Civil Rights Act demonstrated, the most immediate adverse effect produced by discrimination in hotels and motels was its discouragement of interstate travel by blacks, he argued, with the attendant adverse economic impact on interstate commerce. Discrimination in hotels and motels also discouraged the convention trade in the communities where it was practiced, the solicitor general added, thus imposing an additional adverse effect on commerce. Protests and demonstrations against discrimination in facilities of public accommodation not only curtailed the business activities of the targets of such protests and demonstrations, he continued, but also reduced economic activity generally in the affected communities. Further, business and commercial enterprises were reluctant to locate in communities where racial unrest and protests occurred, thus producing yet another retardant effect on economic development in those communities and another burden on commerce. "The disputes and their impact on interstate commerce," Cox maintained, "do show that the problem is not only social and moral—but national and commercial."[8]

Economic regulation of business enterprise such as the public accommodations provisions did not constitute a taking of property for public purposes within the meaning of the Just Compensation Clause of the Fifth Amendment, Cox argued, nor did it deprive those affected of their property without due process of law. And since the Court's decision in *United States v. Darby* in 1941, he said, valid exercises of its power under the Commerce Clause by Congress had not been regarded as violative of the Tenth Amendment. To argue that an act of Congress prohibiting racial discrimination against blacks, itself a legacy of slavery, was violative of the Thirteenth Amendment, he added, "is nothing short of absurd."[9]

The public accommodations provisions of the Civil Rights Act of 1964 were based on congressional power under the Commerce Clause, the solicitor general noted, and consequently the Court's decision in the *Civil Rights Cases* of 1883, holding that Congress could not prohibit discrimination in places of public accommodation under section five of the Fourteenth Amendment, was not relevant to the question of the validity of the provisions of the 1964 act. The Court's comment that no one would have contended that Congress possessed the power to enact the Civil Rights Act of 1875 prior to the adoption of the Civil War Amendments, he also contended, was merely an acknowledgment that the 1875 act had not been based on the Commerce Clause. And this interpretation of the meaning of its comment in the *Civil Rights Cases* was confirmed by the Court when it refused to apply the 1875 act to a ship operating in interstate commerce in *Butts v. Merchants & Marine Transportation Co.* in 1913 on the ground that the 1875 act had not been based on the Commerce Clause.[10]

"So far as the power of Congress under the Commerce Clause is concerned," Cox argued,

> the decision upon the constitutionality [of the public accommodations provisions] turns upon a single, simple question—Is there a rational basis for the legislative determination that discrimination on grounds of race or color in places of public accommodation—in particular, by hotels and motels receiving transient guests—burdens or obstructs interstate commerce?

"The evidence before Congress," he concluded, "provides overwhelming support for an affirmative answer to that question."[11]

The *amicus curiae* brief is a method by which groups or parties that are not direct participants in litigation may nonetheless present to courts their views on the issues in pending cases that may affect their interests.[12] The *Heart of Atlanta Motel* case attracted five *amicus curiae* briefs, from the States of California, Florida, Massachusetts, New York, and Virginia. California Attorney General Thomas C. Lynch, Massachusetts Attorney General Edward W. Brooke, and New York Attorney General Louis J. Lefkowitz each pointed out that their states had enacted laws prohibiting racial discrimination in places of public accommodation that were similar to the Civil Rights Act of 1964. Such state laws, however, they said, did not protect black citizens of their states when traveling in other states. As New York Attorney

General Lefkowitz thus argued, black citizens of New York were "protected under the laws of this state against discrimination in places of public accommodation, but their ability to move freely in certain other parts of the country for pleasure or business has been impeded by discrimination and segregation because of their race or color."[13] The *amicus* briefs of California, Massachusetts, and New York therefore fully supported the constitutionality of the Civil Rights Act, but they did not add any arguments in support of the act not already contained in Solicitor General Cox's brief on behalf of the government in the *Heart of Atlanta Motel* case.

Florida Attorney General James W. Kynes and Virginia Attorney General Robert Y. Button, not unexpectedly, argued against the constitutionality of the 1964 Civil Rights Act in the *amicus curiae* briefs filed on behalf of their states. As Button argued, the "issue before the Court is not whether it is morally proper for one man to discriminate against another on the basis of race. The issue is one of constitutional law. Did Congress have the power to act?" "The *Civil Rights Cases* [of 1883] . . . dispose of the Fourteenth Amendment argument—history disposes of the Commerce Clause," Button contended. "Even though such a decision may offend the judgment of members of this Court as to what the law should be, their decision as judges must be predicated on what the law is."[14] The *amicus* briefs on behalf of Florida and Virginia, however, did not advance any arguments that had not been raised by Moreton Rolleston in his attack on the 1964 act.

In addition to the constitutional arguments and factual information presented to the Court by the briefs of Solicitor General Cox and Moreton Rolleston, and those of the *amici curiae*, the law clerks of the various justices were also busy preparing memoranda detailing the facts and issues involved in the *Heart of Atlanta Motel* case in order that the justices would be fully prepared for the oral argument of the case scheduled for October 5. And the memoranda of the clerks of Chief Justice Warren and Justices Douglas, Brennan, and Harlan furnish insight regarding how the issues in the case were being perceived in the chambers of the Court's liberals as well as its most conservative justice.

On October 4, one of Justice Douglas's clerks submitted to him a memo summarizing the facts and issues in the *Heart of Atlanta Motel* case as well as the principal arguments relied on by both sides. And Douglas's clerk also did not overlook the attack on Douglas's concurring opinion in *Bell v. Maryland* that was contained in Moreton Rolleston's brief on behalf of the Heart of Atlanta Motel. "Appellant in its brief . . . deals critically and at length with your concurring opinion in *Bell v. Maryland*," the clerk informed Douglas. And "counsel seemed to go a bit beyond the 'utmost respect' which he professes in the last sentence of the only full paragraph on p. 17."[15]

Similarly, one of Chief Justice Warren's clerks submitted to him on Septem-

ber 30 a very thorough memorandum regarding the *Heart of Atlanta Motel*
case. The memo summarized the proceedings in the court below as well as the
arguments of Solicitor General Cox and Moreton Rolleston. "The SG's brief,"
the clerk noted, "deals only with congressional power under the Commerce
Clause." This was undoubtedly due to the fact that Congress had relied almost
exclusively on the Commerce Clause as the constitutional basis of the public
accommodations provisions of the 1964 act, the clerk said, because of its doubt
regarding whether those provisions could be validly based on section five of the
Fourteenth Amendment. "I am of the opinion that the enactment of the public accommodations sections could be sustained as a proper exercise of the congressional power to regulate commerce among the states," Warren's clerk
advised. The Civil Rights Act, he pointed out, was similar to previous exercises
of congressional power under the Commerce Clause, such as the Sherman
Anti-Trust Act, the Fair Labor Standards Act, the National Labor Relations
Act, and other measures. "It seems to be well established," he added, "that Congress, in the exercise of its power over interstate commerce, may regulate commerce or that which affects it for other than purely economic goals."[16]

The clerk continued:

The events of the past year make clear, I think, the impact of discriminatory practices in places of public accommodation upon interstate
commerce. The *Congressional Record* is replete with evidence of the impact upon commerce: the extensive amount of traveling by the American citizen, the inadequacy of public accommodations for the Negro, the
ramifications of civil strife engendered by discriminatory practices, etc.

Congress could validly remove these burdens imposed on commerce by discrimination in public accommodations through an exercise of its power under
the Commerce Clause, he advised Warren, and the "appellant's contention that
the *Civil Rights Cases* implicitly decided that Congress lacked the power under
the Commerce Clause to enact such legislation is not too persuasive."[17]

Despite his conviction that the public accommodations provisions could be
upheld as a valid exercise of the commerce power, Warren's clerk leaned toward
section five of the Fourteenth Amendment as the constitutional basis upon
which the Court should sustain the act. "Mr. Justice Goldberg's concurring
opinion in *Bell v. Maryland,* which you joined, provides one clear vehicle for
upholding the present legislation as a proper exercise of congressional power
under sec. 5 of the 14th Amendment," he said. He nevertheless expressed
some difficulty in accepting Goldberg's view that the Fourteenth Amendment itself guaranteed equal access to places of public accommodation and
prohibited the states from enforcing their trespass laws against sit-in demon-

strators. "Historically, I feel that this conclusion is somewhat tenuous," he admitted. "I am not convinced that the 'neutral' enforcement of trespass laws, giving effect to any type of discriminatory motive, constitutes 'state action' which is proscribed by the 14th [Amendment] in and of itself."[18]

The chief justice's clerk continued:

> One consideration which perhaps militates against the invocation of Justice Goldberg's view to uphold the present legislation lies in the lack of consensus among the members of the Court as to the self-executing effect of the 14th [Amendment] as indicated by the positions taken in *Bell v. Maryland.* The Goldberg view seems to be unacceptable to at least the three dissenters in that case, even though they indicated in their dissent the possibility that civil rights legislation pursuant to sec. 5 might not be subject to the state action limitations of sec. 1.[19]

Despite these misgivings, however, the clerk recommended that the Court base its decision in the *Heart of Atlanta Motel* case on the Fourteenth Amendment: "Although I feel that the public accommodations sections of the 1964 Civil Rights Act fall within the scope of the commerce power as defined by this Court, I recommend that the legislation be upheld as a proper exercise of congressional power under section 5 of the Fourteenth Amendment." Still expressing some hesitation on this point, he noted that all of the parties had relied on the Commerce Clause throughout the litigation. He nevertheless urged that the legislation be sustained under the Fourteenth Amendment on the theory that the states had sanctioned discrimination in public accommodations by fostering and permitting it. The Court should therefore note probable jurisdiction in the *Heart of Atlanta Motel* case, Warren's clerk concluded, and affirm the decision of the three-judge court sustaining the act.[20]

Like Chief Justice Warren, Justice Douglas, and the other members of the Court whose clerks were assisting in the preparation of the justices for the oral argument, Justice Brennan also received from one of his clerks a lengthy memorandum analyzing the facts and issues in the *Heart of Atlanta Motel* case. The clerk noted that Congress had not included in the 1964 act any findings of fact indicating its conclusions on the question of the relationship between racial discrimination in public accommodations and its resultant effects or burdens on interstate commerce. The public accommodations provisions of the act were nevertheless primarily based on congressional power under the Commerce Clause, he said, since Attorney General Kennedy in his testimony before the Judiciary Committee of the House of Representatives had made it "quite clear that the bill was no broader than the *Sit-in* cases" on the question of the scope of congressional power under section five of the Fourteenth Amendment.[21]

Addressing the issues in the *Heart of Atlanta Motel* case, Brennan's clerk recommended that for "obvious reasons, the judgment below should be affirmed. The only question is one of the reasoning to be employed." He suggested that the Court should not reach the question of the act's validity as it applied to motels serving only intrastate transients. "To avoid groping for too much at once, I would suggest that that step not be taken in the *Heart of Atlanta* case." On the other hand, the act could be sustained as it applied to motels serving only intrastate travelers on the ground that the act would not be administratively feasible otherwise and on the principle that Congress could regulate purely intrastate activities if their regulation was necessary for the effective regulation of interstate commerce itself. "And the aftermath of *Brown* [*v. Board of Education*]," he added, "may indicate the necessity of clear standards where massive resistance is likely."[22]

The clerk observed that the "Thirteenth Amendment objection, that the statute subjects proprietors of places of public accommodation to involuntary servitude, can properly be laughed out of court," and he noted that no such objection had ever been made to statutes requiring segregation in such establishments. "The Fifth Amendment argument is similarly without merit," he said. "So long as the commerce power is validly exercised, the Fifth Amendment should create no difficulties."[23]

Summarizing his recommendations to Justice Brennan, the clerk concluded:

In *Heart of Atlanta,* affirm. Do not rule on the constitutionality of applying the statute to motels serving only intrastate transients. Point out that very few interstate transients are necessary to uphold the statute, without the necessity of relying on any congressional power to cover purely intrastate motels.[24]

The favorable recommendations regarding the validity of the public accommodations provisions by the clerks of the Court's more liberal justices were echoed in the responses of Justice Harlan's clerks as well. "Although the Civil Rights Act contains no factual recitals as enacted, I think there is ample support for the statutory statement in Title II that the covered establishments 'affect commerce,'" one of Harlan's clerks reported to him. "Thus the only remaining question is whether Congress can constitutionally reach these activities under the Commerce Clause." The clerk continued:

The coverage of the Act as it attempts to guarantee freedom from discrimination to interstate travelers seems reasonable and within the scope of the federal commerce power. This is enough to decide the *Heart of Atlanta* case, which involves a motel principally serving interstate guests. The *Civil Rights Cases* . . . probably would not be a bar to the constitutionality of the Act. Although Justice Bradley [the author of the majority opinion in the *Civil Rights Cases*] stated that no one would contend that a civil rights act could have been passed prior to the enactment of the 13th, 14th, and 15th Amendments . . . , he later conceded that Congress had not invoked the Commerce Clause in passing [the Civil Rights Act of 1875].[25]

Another of Harlan's clerks submitted to him a memorandum regarding section five of the Fourteenth Amendment as a possible source of congressional power to enact the public accommodations provisions. A decision of the Court upholding the public accommodations provisions under section five, the clerk pointed out, "would require an about-face from your position in the recent sit-in cases, and a substantial modification in the underlying theory of all previous state-action cases decided by the Court with the possible exception of *Shelley v. Kraemer*."[26] A ruling by the Court that the 1964 act's public accommodations provisions were supported by section five only insofar as discrimination in places of public accommodation was supported or required by state action, the clerk noted on the other hand, would result in "leaving a lion's share of the Act's accomplishments in the civil rights field to be pinned on the Commerce Clause."[27]

A third alternative basis of the Court's decision in the public accommodations cases, the clerk continued, would be to rely on the Commerce Clause exclusively as the source of congressional power to enact the public accommodations provisions. "Granting that Congress has virtually unlimited power to regulate commerce, and granting that it has been upheld in using that power to achieve non-commercial ends in the past, it is nonetheless unfortunate that major or sole reliance must be placed on the commerce power if the Act is to be sustained," the clerk argued.

> The Constitution has sections specifically directed to the protection of civil rights. To hold that the civil rights amendments do not empower Congress to enact civil rights legislation, but that the Commerce Clause does, smacks of the devious legalisms which serve to base judicial pronouncements in power (or perhaps the lack of it) rather than reason.[28]

While the Court was bound by its previous definitions of state action, Congress was not, and it could find that discrimination in public accommodations had been supported and encouraged by the states and that congressional legislation based on section five of the Fourteenth Amendment could require the expunging of the resulting discriminatory system, the clerk suggested. Congress, he conceded, had nevertheless defined state action in the 1964 act as the Court had traditionally defined it and had not attempted to base the act on the Fourteenth Amendment any further than the Court's state action doctrine would support. "The Fourteenth Amendment arguments need not be reached at all in *Heart of Atlanta*," the clerk reluctantly concluded. "The government is placing complete reliance on the Commerce Clause. It is not arguing equal protection, no record was made below on any questions of state action, and no allegations of state-supported discrimination appear in the government's complaint."[29]

The term of the United States Supreme Court begins on the first Monday in October, and the proceedings on the Court's opening day are usually ceremonial, consisting only of the formal announcement of the Court's new term, the admission of attorneys to the practice of law before the Court, and on occasion the acknowledgment of anniversaries in the Court's history, the retirements or deaths of members of the Court, or the appointment of new members. October 5, 1964, the opening day of the Court's 1964 term, was not characterized by the usual opening day proceedings, however, since after some ceremonial preliminaries, the Court proceeded to hear four hours of argument in *Heart of Atlanta Motel v. United States* and *Katzenbach v. McClung*.

Chief Justice Warren announced the first case, Number 515: "Heart of Atlanta Motel, Incorporated, appellant, versus the United States, et al. In this case probable jurisdiction is noted, the joint motion for acceleration of oral argument is granted, and the case is set for argument on Monday, October 5th, 1964," Warren said. "We will proceed. Mr. Rolleston." Moreton Rolleston then opened the argument on behalf of the appellant in the *Heart of Atlanta Motel* case.[30]

Rolleston described the proceedings in the three-judge court and then the Heart of Atlanta Motel's location in downtown Atlanta, fronting an interstate highway and offering to serve interstate travelers in its 216 rooms. The restaurant in the motel was operated by a lessee that was complying with the 1964 act, he pointed out, and was therefore not an issue in the case. Given its location and interstate clientele, he admitted, the Heart of Atlanta Motel was "squarely under the law," but the public accommodations provisions were unconstitutional as applied to the motel because the 1964 act provided that "every motel in the United States, all sixty thousand of them, affect interstate commerce."

"This case has gotten here in a hurry," Rolleston noted; he was unsure whether the members of the Court had had time to familiarize themselves with the briefs filed in the case, and he therefore assured the Court that he would attempt to cover the issues in the case as thoroughly as possible in the time allotted to him. He was relying on five theories to demonstrate that the public accommodations provisions were unconstitutional, he informed the Court. First, the 1964 act was unconstitutional under the Fourteenth Amendment and the Court's decision in the *Civil Rights Cases* of 1883; second, neither the Fourteenth Amendment nor any other provision of the Constitution authorized Congress to prohibit racial discrimination by a private individual unsupported or unauthorized by state action; third, the act was additionally an invalid exercise of the commerce power; fourth, the act violated the Fifth Amendment by depriving persons of property rights without due process of law and by taking private property without just compensation; and finally, the law violated the Thirteenth Amendment by imposing involuntary servitude on owners of places of public accommodation. "We submit, gentlemen, that if we can prevail on any theory, any one of those five theories, then this act's got to fall," Rolleston said.

"Any lawyer," he continued, "is delighted to have a white horse case that says what the law of the land is, if it's true, . . . [and] that is the decision in the *Civil Rights Cases*,[31] which was upheld by this Court in 1883." Justice Goldberg interrupted to inquire what a "white horse case" was. "A white horse case is one that just fits your case exactly," Rolleston answered. "[I]t doesn't have a red head or a black tail, it's all white and fits the whole case precisely."

"We used to call that a blue bottle case up in Ohio," Justice Stewart remarked.

"We know what we're talking about," Rolleston responded.

> The fundamental question, I submit, is whether or not Congress has the power to take away the liberty of an individual to run his business as he sees fit in the selection and choice of his customers. This is the real important issue. And the fact . . . [that the] alleged civil rights of the Negroes are involved is purely incidental, because if Congress can exercise these controls over rights of individuals, it is plausible that there's no limit to Congress's power to appropriate property and liberty.

The Civil Rights Act of 1875 that was invalidated by the Court in the *Civil Rights Cases,* Rolleston argued, was "almost identical" to the public accommodations provisions of the 1964 act, and in the *Civil Rights Cases* the Court had held that Congress could not regulate racial discrimination by private owners of places of public accommodation absent state action supporting such discrimination. "And let me hasten to say that there's no state action in any way in this case. This case was brought two hours after the

President signed the bill. The state had nothing to do with it. They did not file even a friend of the court brief as did five other states." Justice Goldberg inquired whether Georgia had a trespass law, and Rolleston replied that Georgia's trespass law was the same as the Maryland law that was involved in *Bell v. Maryland.*32 Neither the State of Georgia nor the City of Atlanta, however, would initiate the enforcement of the trespass law, he pointed out, but rather private property owners had to initiate enforcement of the law themselves by swearing out warrants.

Reverting to his argument based on the *Civil Rights Cases*, Rolleston noted that under "the 1883 decision, which under the American jurisprudence, is the law of the land until this Court overturns it, they held that this similar act was unconstitutional." He conceded that the Court had held in the *Butts* case in 1913 that the Commerce Clause was not the basis of the 1875 act.

> But I don't see how you can get around the language of the Court in . . . [the *Civil Rights Cases*], where it said that of course no one would contend that the power to pass this act, the Civil Rights Act [of 1875], was contained in the Constitution before the adoption of the Fourteenth Amendment. They start off the opinion that way, so there wasn't no doubt about it, that before we got the Fourteenth Amendment, you couldn't pass such an act to restrain an individual or prohibit him from exercising racial discrimination as long as the state wasn't involved.

"And in the *Civil Rights Cases*, it is my contention that the Court at that time knew that the Commerce Clause was sitting there in the Constitution, it had been there almost one hundred years," and yet the Court had said that the power to pass the 1875 act was not in the Constitution before the passage of the Civil War Amendments.

"Didn't the Court put the Commerce Clause expressly aside in connection to one of the defendants—one of the parties [in the *Civil Rights Cases*]?" Justice White asked, but Rolleston answered that in his opinion the Court simply held that the Commerce Clause had not been relied on by Congress in enacting the 1875 act.

Justices Goldberg and White then asked to what extent the 1964 act was based on congressional power to enforce the Fourteenth Amendment and whether the Court could rely on the Fourteenth Amendment in considering the validity of the 1964 act. Rolleston replied that in his view the Court could rely on any provision of the Constitution in its decision regardless of the arguments of the parties in the case. Justice Black then asked whether, assuming Congress relied exclusively on the Commerce Clause in enacting a law, the Court was bound to pass on the validity of the act only under the

Commerce Clause. Rolleston again said that the Court could rely on any provision of the Constitution. If Congress passed a law denying a person a jury trial, he said, the Court could invalidate such a law under provisions of the Constitution not relied on by Congress in passing such a law.

"Do you think that is an analogous argument?" Justice Black asked.

"It may not be, but I hoped to make it that," Rolleston responded amid laughter in the courtroom.

Justices Brennan and Goldberg continued questioning Rolleston on what provision of the Constitution the Court could rely on in the *Heart of Atlanta Motel* case, given the government's exclusive reliance on the Commerce Clause as the constitutional basis of the public accommodations provisions. But Justice Harlan, his voice indicating exasperation at what he considered the diversionary questions of his colleagues, finally interrupted that line of questioning:

> Whatever the Congress intended to do beyond the Commerce Clause, it certainly intended to exercise the Commerce Clause power. And it is perfectly clear that the government is arguing only that this act in this case, is saying only that this act is constitutional, is a constitutional exercise of the Commerce Clause power, and that's all we've got; this other debate may be interesting but [it] hasn't anything to do with this lawsuit.

Justice Goldberg persisted, however, and asked if it was Rolleston's argument that the Court had held in the *Civil Rights Cases* that Congress could not enact a public accommodations law under the Commerce Clause. "That is my position, Mr. Justice Goldberg," Rolleston answered.

He then discussed the dissenting opinion of Justices Black, White, and Harlan in *Bell v. Maryland* and argued that the opinion had denied that the Fourteenth Amendment prohibited private racial discrimination unsupported by state action. Justice Harlan again interrupted, however, and pointed out that since the *Bell* case, Congress had enacted the 1964 law. He urged Rolleston to focus on whether the act was a reasonable or unreasonable regulation of owners of private property under the Commerce Clause. Rolleston nevertheless persisted in his argument that the dissenting opinion in the *Bell* case had held that private individuals could discriminate under the Fourteenth Amendment. In response, however, Justice Black pointed out that the *Bell* dissent "did not refer at all, did it, to what Congress could do under the fifth section of the Fourteenth Amendment and under the Necessary and Proper Clause?"

"Mr. Justice Black, you made that very clear," Rolleston replied.

Chief Justice Warren then rather pointedly urged Rolleston to focus his argument on the Commerce Clause issue:

> Mr. Rolleston, you've indicated that you don't intend to get to your argument on the Commerce Clause until . . . rebuttal. Don't you think that inasmuch as you both agree that the thrust of this case is under . . . the Commerce Clause, and that inasmuch as you are the top side of the case, that we ought to hear your argument on the Commerce Clause before we hear from the solicitor general?

"Mr. Chief Justice, I will be glad to accede to the wishes of the Court," Rolleston responded, but indicated he first wanted to address the Thirteenth Amendment issue.

"Yes, of course," Warren said, and Rolleston then briefly argued that the 1964 act imposed involuntary servitude on owners of public accommodations. Involuntary servitude under the Thirteenth Amendment, he argued, included "compelling service of one to another" or compelling someone to serve another "against his will," and that was essentially what the Civil Rights Act required of operators of places of public accommodation.

"Now, may it please the Court, as to the Commerce Clause," he then said. Justice Goldberg, in his concurring opinion in *Bell v. Maryland,* had made "probably one of the most profound statements about the Constitution that I have ever read," he declared, and quoted Goldberg's statement that in construing the Constitution "we read it to effectuate the intent and purpose of the Framers."[33] This meant, Rolleston argued, that it was the Court's duty to interpret the Constitution in light of what the Framers intended in 1787. "If that theory is not so, then the Constitution is just like any other law, and can be changed from day to day by the Congress and the courts." He maintained that "our Constitution is still the same Constitution it was in 1787, except the amendments that the people . . . have decided should be added to it."

The Commerce Clause of the Constitution had been adopted in response to the financial crisis confronting the country during the Articles of Confederation period, he said, and it was intended to cover commerce among businesses and the transportation related thereto, but "commerce has got to end somewhere. It cannot go on forever. It is true that Congress and decisions of the Supreme Court have enlarged the commerce power beyond which, I submit, the Framers never intended, and never thought it could be," he continued. In the fields of anti-trust, labor relations, and wages and hours, which were regulated by Congress under the Commerce Clause, Rolleston contended, standards were enacted by Congress under which it could be determined whether individual businesses affected commerce or not, but this was not the case under the Civil Rights Act of 1964.

"We're talking here about, aren't we, about a person moving in interstate commerce?" Justice Douglas asked. "Driving from Virginia to Atlanta, and asking [for] accommodations for the night. Now that is interstate commerce, that person is moving in interstate commerce. You don't treat in your brief that point precisely, as I read your brief. . . . You say people are not commerce. True?"

Rolleston replied that "there is a holding of the United States Supreme Court that says people are not commerce. People engage in commerce, people take part in commerce, but people themselves are not commerce. And it's so been held by this Court, and never been overruled."

Justice Black commented, "That is not a good case to rely on. Which case are you referring to?"

Rolleston answered that he was relying on the Court's 1837 decision in *New York v. Miln*.[34] "And certainly the Framers in putting that one clause in the Constitution didn't include or intend to include people at that time."

Rolleston argued that the Court's ruling in *Hotel Employees v. Leedom*[35] was distinguishable from the *Heart of Atlanta Motel* case, since in the *Leedom* case the Court had merely ruled that the National Labor Relations Board could not exclude hotel and motel employees as a class from its jurisdiction, but left the question of whether labor disputes in hotels and motels affected commerce to be determined on a case by case basis. "So we say that in this case, the means adopted, the Commerce Clause if you have it, to the end, and the end desired, have no rational relation," he contended. "They have simply, after being advised of the *Civil Rights Cases* in 1883, it seems like, have said well we can't find anything else in the Constitution to put . . . [the Civil Rights Act of 1964] on, let's do put it on the Commerce Clause, we've been able to get away with so much else with the Commerce Clause already."

Justice Goldberg asked, "Mr. Rolleston, what do you do with *Wickard v. Filburn?*"[36] The case involving the validity of the Agricultural Adjustment Act of 1938? Rolleston inquired. "Yes," Justice Goldberg said. "If the Court were to decide in your favor in this case, would we have to overrule that case?"

Rolleston replied that in the *Filburn* case the Court had held that while the wheat production of one farmer might not affect commerce, the production of wheat by all similarly situated farmers would affect commerce. "And therefore if you carry it to the extreme, then Congress can cover every activity, every facet of life . . . ," he maintained; "it gets to a ridiculous situation where Congress then can do anything; and that gets me to another point that I want to make before I stop for rebuttal."

"This Constitution set up powers between the states and federal government and enumerated them," Rolleston declared, his voice rising almost to a shout as he pounded the lectern.

And in the Tenth Amendment it reserved to the states all powers not set forth therein to the states or the people. And the only reason for the existence of this Supreme Court, may it please the Court, is to maintain the balance of powers between those different governments. And if this Court will let Congress do anything it wants under the Commerce Clause, that's what that argument [in *Wickard v. Filburn*] means, if this Court will let them do anything, then this Court has abdicated, and there's no reason for the existence of the Supreme Court to adjust and maintain the balance of powers between the various governments in this country. That is the function of the Supreme Court. That is the very reason for it [to be] set up in the Constitution. . . . And if you abdicate that power, there will be no reason for the Supreme Court, because Congress can then do anything it wants in any facet of our lives. I'll pose the question which I'll try to answer in rebuttal, the real question in this case, how far can Congress go? What limit is it beyond which Congress cannot go? Is there any limit? Does Tennyson's brook run on forever too? What limit is it that Congress cannot overstep and pass?

It was apparent that Rolleston planned to end his opening argument at this point, reserving the remainder of his time for rebuttal, but Justice Black was not prepared to allow Rolleston to sit down at this point in his argument. "You haven't discussed at all the thing it seems to me the most important on both sides," Black said.

That is the series of cases which started, generally started, in *Gibbons* and *Ogden*,[37] carried on by Mr. Chief Justice Hughes before he became chief justice in the *Shreveport Case*,[38] and various other cases, that Congress has not only the right to regulate interstate commerce itself, it has the right to regulate local activities, wholly local, within a state, purely intrastate, if Congress concludes, or if it is concluded, that those would adversely affect interstate commerce or that they would fail to give it the protection and fostering care which Congress is supposed to give it.

Black added that "it seems to me that you have not touched on that yet, and that to me is a very important part of this case."

Rolleston responded by citing the Court's decision in *United States v. Yellow Cab Co.*,[39] in which the Court held that the transportation of passengers

by taxicab to and from interstate railroad stations in Chicago was not a part
of interstate commerce within the meaning of the Sherman Anti-Trust Act.

"That's right. It was not engaged in interstate commerce, and for one reason or another that case was decided as it was," Justice Black replied.

> But it does not have to be actually engaged in interstate commerce
> under the line of cases beginning with *Gibbons* and *Ogden,* which
> have said Congress has the right to take care of interstate commerce,
> to foster it, to care for it, and to see that it is not adversely affected
> in any way, even going so far as to regulate the purely intrastate rail-
> road rates in every state in the Union, and various other activities of
> that kind.

In *United States v. Sullivan,*[40] Black pointed out as an example, the Court
had sustained under the Commerce Clause the federal food and drug act's
labeling requirements as applied to pills offered for sale at retail by a local
druggist. "Why wouldn't that apply here? That seems to me to be your problem," he said.

Obviously attempting to buy time, Rolleston responded, "I recognize,
your honor, there is a long line of cases that . . . Congress can regulate under the commerce power intrastate activities, purely local activities, if Congress thinks that they place a burden on interstate commerce. I'll try to get
to that in rebuttal."

"You will take that up later," Black said, acquiescing in the evasion.

"Mr. Solicitor General," Chief Justice Warren then announced. Solicitor
General Archibald Cox was sometimes said by observers to appear to be lecturing the Court in his distinctly professorial manner, but on this day, in his
opening argument on behalf of the government in the *Heart of Atlanta Motel* case, Cox's words approached the poetic. "Mr. Chief Justice, may it please
the Court," he began.

> The fact that the Court is sitting to hear argument on the day that usu-
> ally marked only an opening ceremonial occasion, testifies more
> forcibly than any words of mine can do to the importance of the issues
> being presented today. The Civil Rights Act of 1964 is surely the most
> important legislation enacted in recent decades. It's one of the half
> dozen most important laws, I think, enacted in the last century. No leg-
> islation, within my memory, has been debated as widely, as long, or as
> thoroughly. Certainly, none has been considered more conscien-
> tiously. . . . Title II, as I will show, is addressed to a commercial prob-
> lem of grave national significance.

Only a commercial problem, Justice Goldberg interrupted, and not a moral problem?

"I wish to emphasize, and will emphasize repeatedly in my argument that Title II was addressed to a grave commercial problem, grave at the time the act was enacted and plainly growing," Cox continued.

Nor should we forget, Mr. Justice Goldberg, that Congress in addressing itself to that commercial problem was also keeping faith with the promise declared by the Continental Congress that all men are created equal. The failure to keep that promise lay heavily on the conscience of the entire nation, North as well as South, East as well as West. Nor do I overlook the difficulties of adjustment that accommodation to this act may require, difficulties that may bear heavier on some regions than upon others. Nor do I overlook the need for a spirit of cooperation and mutual understanding in facing those difficulties. We shall solve the problem as one people, and thus escape the consequences of the sins of the past, only if we act in the spirit of Lincoln's second inaugural, without malice, with charity, and perhaps above all without the spirit of false self-righteousness that enables men who are not themselves without fault to point the finger at their fellows.

The solicitor general continued:

Happily, the difficulty of the constitutional issues here is not equal to their importance. Title II, as we see it, rests upon the powers delegated to Congress by Article I, section 8, . . . clause 3, of the Constitution to regulate commerce among the several states, and upon the power delegated by clause 17 of the same article to enact laws that are necessary and proper to effectuate the commerce power. The constitutionality of Title II under these provisions is sustained by principles that are so familiar because they have been enacted over and over again, applied indeed throughout our entire history, going back, as Mr. Justice Black pointed out a moment ago, to the opinion of Chief Justice John Marshall in *Gibbons* and *Ogden*. We do not seek the extension of any existing principles, *a fortiori,* we invoke no new doctrine.

"I think it is somewhat new, at least as I read the cases," Justice Douglas said, "to the extent that . . . [the 1964 act] covers the requirement that this motel . . . serve a local person who hasn't moved in interstate commerce."

Cox responded by citing the Safety Appliance Act and similar measures in which Congress had regulated local activities when their regulation was essential to the protection or regulation of interstate commerce itself. He then began an exposition of the provisions of Title II of the act and noted that one section of the Title prohibited racial discrimination when supported by state action. "The government did not proceed in either case in the lower court and does not proceed here on the theory that this discrimination is supported by state action within the meaning of the statutory provisions, which may or may not be as broad as the meaning of state action under the Fourteenth Amendment," Cox pointed out.

"General," Justice Goldberg interrupted, "where does that leave the Court? Are we free at this point to consider the statute and the state action concept as set forth in the statute? You made no argument about it. Does that mean that the government loses the day in this Court if this Court decides that your position on commerce is not to be sustained?"

"Well, frankly," Cox replied, "I find that alternative so unlikely, that if we were to lose on that [Commerce Clause] ground I might despair of persuading the Court on the other ground, because I think that is so much stronger." When Goldberg persisted in questioning why the government completely ignored the Fourteenth Amendment as a possible source of congressional power to enact the 1964 law, the solicitor general responded that:

We have thought it quite unnecessary, in performing our duty to the Court, to discuss that issue. But theoretically I think the Court is free, Mr. Justice, to go ahead and consider that issue, [but] if it should reach it, we would feel remiss in our duties as counselors not to have discussed it, but in our judgment it was unnecessary to be considered.

"Well, for the purpose of this case, therefore," Goldberg persisted, "you are really saying to us that we stand or fall on the Commerce Clause?"

"You've said that specifically in your brief," Justice Harlan interjected, again indicating some irritation at questions from the bench that he regarded as beside the point. "'We stake our case,' your language, 'we stake our case on the Commerce Clause.' The Civil Rights Cases aside, the meaning of state action aside, you do not reach any of that?" Harlan asked.

"That's correct," Cox replied. Justice Brennan then pointed out that before an argument based on the Fourteenth Amendment or regarding state action would be relevant, there would have to be facts in the case raising those issues, and in this case there were none. "There was no need to traverse that path," the solicitor general agreed.

The solicitor general continued his exposition of the provisions of Title II, and in response to questions from Justices Brennan, Douglas, and White, he argued that the act applied to even those motels whose guests were intrastate

travelers if they offered service to transients, but added, "I have in this application a much easier case." Cox pointed out that the "only question on
the merits" in both of the cases before the Court was the constitutionality of
the public accommodations provisions as they applied to motels offering to
serve transient guests and restaurants offering to serve interstate travelers or
serving food a substantial portion of which has moved in interstate commerce. "The major premise of our argument," Cox said, emphasizing a point
made in the government's brief,

> is the familiar rule that the powers delegated to Congress by the Com-
> merce and Necessary and Proper Clauses authorize Congress to regu-
> late local activities, at least activities that are local when separately
> considered, even though they are not themselves interstate commerce,
> if they have such a close and substantial relation to commerce that their
> regulation may be deemed appropriate or useful to foster and promote
> such commerce, or to relieve it of burdens and obstructions.

And, he continued,

> Our minor premise is that Congress, to which the economic question
> thus raised is primarily committed, had ample basis from which to find
> that racial discrimination in inns in one case, inns and motels in the
> one case, restaurants in the other, does in fact constitute a source of
> burden or obstruction to interstate commerce. And of course from
> those premises, the conclusion would follow that this is a legitimate ex-
> ercise of power under the Constitution.

"You are not arguing, I take it, from what you just said," Justice Harlan
asked, "that Congress by definition in effect precluded this Court from taking a look at the record, the legislative record, to see whether in fact Congress
had sufficient basis for the exercise of the commerce power before it acted?"

No, the solicitor general replied, but he insisted that the party attacking
the validity of the act had to shoulder the burden of demonstrating that
there was no rational relation between the activity regulated and interstate
commerce, or that the activity regulated did not in fact affect commerce, and
if that could be done, then the Court should invalidate the act. The Court
should, he added, look not only to the legislative record in determining if
such a rational relationship existed but also at facts that might exist outside
the legislative record.

"As a matter of fact, I presume most legislation in the country has been
passed, both state and national, without findings [of fact] by Congress, and

without hearings frequently," Justice Black said. "It's a question of whether they had power under the Constitution to pass the law, not whether they made findings." Cox agreed, and cited the Court's 1938 holding in *United States v. Carolene Products Co.*[41] that findings of fact in legislation enacted by Congress were unnecessary.

"But of course it is also true, I think," Justice Harlan interjected, "that when the Congress has exercised its power under the Commerce Clause, particularly you might call it, extensions of preconceived notions of the commerce power, [it] has been at pains not only to make a substantial legislative record, evidentiary record, but to include in the statute elaborate findings—"

To which Cox replied, "It's quite clear the record was made here, Mr. Justice Harlan."

Justice Goldberg inquired whether the solicitor general believed that Congress could have enacted a public accommodations statute based on the Commerce Clause during the nineteenth century. "I think it is very dangerous to say that anything Congress can do under the Commerce Clause today, that is, a regulation of any specific person or local activity, that it may reach today, it could have reached in 1789, and conversely that anything it couldn't reach in 1789, it can't reach today," Cox responded. While the principles of the Constitution were constant, he argued, the facts and conditions in the country changed, with the result that activities that might affect commerce today might not have affected commerce earlier in our history.

Quoting *McCulloch v. Maryland*[42] and the Necessary and Proper Clause, Justice Black then said that if the end was legitimate, the means that were reasonably adapted to reach that end were also legitimate and constitutional, and "it cannot be said that it is an illegitimate end to try to carry out a policy [of prohibiting racial discrimination] that the Constitution commands."

At that point, the Court took its noon recess, and when the argument resumed at 12:30 P.M., Justice Harlan put to Solicitor General Cox a long question, which in substance asked whether the limitation of the power of Congress to enforce the Fourteenth Amendment as to state action violative of the amendment implied a similar limitation on other powers of Congress such as the commerce power. Cox responded in the negative, and argued that the fact that Congress could reach state action supporting racial discrimination only under its Fourteenth Amendment power did not mean that it could not regulate racial discrimination unsupported by state action under its other delegated powers, including the power delegated to it under the Commerce Clause. Justice Douglas then through questions again attempted to elicit from the solicitor general an argument on the Fourteenth Amendment as a possible constitutional basis of the Civil Rights Act, but Justice Brennan intervened and pointed out that there was convincing evidence before Congress demonstrating that there were substantial burdens being imposed on interstate commerce because of racial discrimination in places of public accommodation.

Cox agreed, and argued that the legislative record included overwhelming evidence that there was "a very real, national commercial problem" caused by racial discrimination in facilities of public accommodation. And, he pointed out, the regulation of hotels, motels, and restaurants under the commerce power was not a novel exercise of that power, since those businesses had been subjected to regulation under the anti-trust laws, the Federal Trade Commission Act, and the National Labor Relations Act, all of which were enacted under the Commerce Clause. Cox continued,

> Now Congress started with the outstanding fact, I think, of national life during the past decade, perhaps longer, the thrust toward the realization for Negroes and in some instances other minorities, of the promise that all men are created equal. We are concerned here with the commercial consequences, which were of nationwide scope and almost incredible proportions.

The thrust toward equality had resulted in demonstrations directed to a substantial degree against racial discrimination in places of public accommodation, he argued, and these demonstrations had had a "dramatic" effect on commerce and business conditions generally. Such demonstrations in Birmingham, Alabama, Cox pointed out, had resulted in a 15 percent reduction in sales by department stores there, while other downtown businesses reported that their sales dropped by 40 to 50 percent, and business failures were greater than during the Depression. Any reduction of retail sales, he argued, necessarily affected commerce, since reductions in purchases of goods in commerce inevitably resulted from reductions in retail sales. Racial unrest and demonstrations also discouraged the flow of investment into areas affected by such occurrences, and businesses were reluctant to relocate in cities and areas where racial unrest occurred, again producing an adverse effect on commerce. When racial disputes were occurring in Little Rock, Arkansas, the solicitor general pointed out as an example, relocations of businesses and investments in that community plummeted, and economic growth there stagnated.

In addition, Cox argued, there was "literally overwhelming evidence" before Congress when it enacted the Civil Rights Act that racial discrimination in facilities of public accommodation discouraged interstate travel by blacks, and he cited the distances black families had to travel in the South before reaching public accommodations that would serve them. Segregation also discouraged the convention trade in the areas where it was practiced, he added, because organizations would not schedule conventions in cities where their members would not be served on a nondiscriminatory basis. When Atlanta's fourteen major hotels had recently agreed voluntarily to desegregate, Cox pointed out, after only one day those hotels had received commitments from organizations with three thousand members to hold conventions in Atlanta. In other fields of commercial and business activity, as with the convention trade, he argued, racial discrimination in public accommodations diverted commerce from the channels into which it otherwise would normally flow.

There could be no doubt that Congress could prohibit discrimination against people under the Commerce Clause, Cox argued. "I suggest that there is no possible doubt since the *Edwards [v. California]* case[43] or before the *Edwards* case that interstate travel by men and women is interstate commerce." In the *Edwards* case the Court invalidated a California statute making it a criminal offense for anyone to knowingly bring any nonresident into the state who was indigent. Commonly known as California's "anti-Okie" law, the statute was the California legislature's response to the influx of indigent individuals into the state during the Depression years, an influx that had dramatically increased the state's costs for public assistance and welfare. In reversing Edwards's conviction under the statute, the Court ruled that the statute was an unconstitutional state regulation of interstate commerce and thus violative of the Commerce Clause.

Responding to Solicitor General Cox's reference to the *Edwards* case, Justice Clark inquired, "Do you say that people are commerce?" People themselves were not commerce, but people traveling in interstate commerce were involved in commerce, the solicitor general responded.

"Certainly that's what *Edwards v. California* squarely holds," Justice Stewart interjected. Cox agreed and pointed out that *New York v. Miln,* which was relied on by Moreton Rolleston, had been overruled as early as the *Passenger Cases* in 1849.[44]

"I thought *Edwards* distinguished *Miln.* Is that right?" Justice Black asked. Cox replied that the *Miln* case had been reversed earlier, but the *Edwards* case squarely held that people moving in commerce was interstate commerce.

"But they were certain types of people [in *Edwards*], they were Okies and —" Justice Clark said.

"Yes," the solicitor general replied, "but I take it that if Okies are commerce, so are other people traveling across state lines." [Laughter.]

There was ample evidence, Cox continued, from which Congress could have rationally concluded that racial discrimination in hotels and motels burdened interstate commerce and that the Civil Rights Act was a reasonable means by which to relieve commerce of that burden. The fact that Congress had prohibited hotels and motels from discriminating against all guests, whether traveling in interstate commerce or not, did not invalidate the act, he argued. To require a traveler to carry papers proving his status as an interstate traveler would itself impose a burden on commerce, he said, and to require blacks to prove their interstate status as travelers would be a form of invidious discrimination almost equal to that which the act sought to prohibit. Justice Harlan interrupted this argument, however, and pointed out that in the *Heart of Atlanta Motel* case that issue was not presented, since it was stipulated that 75 percent of the guests of that motel were interstate travelers.

By this time, the red light on the lectern at which lawyers argue before the Court had come on, indicating to the solicitor general that his time had expired. Cox requested that Chief Justice Warren allow him to borrow some of his time from the *McClung* argument, and Warren granted him five additional minutes. The solicitor general then addressed the Tenth Amendment, the Fifth Amendment, and the Thirteenth Amendment objections to the Civil Rights Act. Since the decisions in *McCulloch v. Maryland* and *United States v. Darby*,[45] he argued, it had been established that neither the Ninth nor Tenth Amendment imposed limitations on the delegated powers of Congress. The Fifth Amendment objections to the act had "equally little merit," he said, since the regulation of property was not a taking of private property for public uses requiring just compensation. Nor did the act violate the Fifth Amendment's Due Process Clause, he continued.

> Appellants say that they will lose profits as a result of this regulation. Experience rather indicates the contrary, but assuming that that is true, it still has clearly been held that subjecting a man to regulation, otherwise proper, along with all other similar businesses, does not violate the Fifth Amendment, simply because he loses money.

State statutes prohibiting racial discrimination in places of public accommodation, he pointed out, had also been held by the Court not to violate due process in *Bob-Lo Excursion Co. v. Michigan*[46] and *Colorado Anti-Discrimination Commission v. Continental Airlines*.[47]

Regarding the Thirteenth Amendment objection to the act, Cox asserted that

> surely it would turn the world quite upside down for anyone to seriously suggest that the Thirteenth Amendment was intended to prohibit either Congress or the state governments from guaranteeing Negroes equality of treatment in places of public accommodation. And Alice, I think, even at the end of her long journey through the looking glass, would have been surprised to be told that the restaurants and other

places of public accommodation in thirty-three states [that had public accommodations laws prohibiting racial discrimination] in the year 1964 are held in involuntary servitude and that the Anglo-Saxon common law for centuries has subjected to slavery innkeepers, hackmen, wharfingers, . . . [and] all kinds of other people holding themselves out to serve the public.

The Heart of Atlanta Motel could escape the provisions of the 1964 act by simply ceasing to hold itself out as a motel providing services to the general public, Cox added, and "as long as one is free to stop then there is no forced labor and no violation of the Thirteenth Amendment."

Finally, the solicitor general addressed the *Civil Rights Cases* of 1883 and the Court's ruling that the Civil Rights Act of 1875 was unconstitutional under the Fourteenth Amendment. The public accommodations provisions of the Civil Rights Act of 1964, he pointed out, were based on the Commerce Clause, and the 1883 cases were therefore irrelevant to the present case. The 1875 act had also applied to many businesses that probably did not affect commerce "in that day," he said. In contrast the 1964 act as an exercise of the commerce power applied to discrimination in places of public accommodation that under contemporary conditions plainly affected interstate commerce, Cox argued. "That's why I suggest very sincerely," the solicitor general concluded, "that the case here falls within the principle laid down by Chief Justice John Marshall in *Gibbons* and *Ogden* and that is virtually as old as the Constitution itself."

Chief Justice Warren then called upon Moreton Rolleston, who began his rebuttal argument. In *Bell v. Maryland,* he pointed out, Solicitor General Cox had argued that the Constitution permitted a sphere of private choice with regard to racial discrimination, but now the solicitor general was contending that the Civil Rights Act validly prohibited discrimination by owners of places of public accommodation because such discrimination affected interstate commerce. The solicitor general had also argued that the desegregation of fourteen of Atlanta's leading hotels, and the consequent mushrooming of the convention trade there, demonstrated the effects on commerce of discrimination in hotels and motels, Rolleston said. "And the truth of the matter is that the Heart of Atlanta Motel is the only . . . [hotel or motel] in Atlanta that hasn't desegregated voluntarily." Since all other motels and hotels there had desegregated, he argued, how much of a real effect on commerce could there be if the Heart of Atlanta Motel continued to be segregated? In fact, he added, desegregation in public accommodations had occurred throughout much of the South prior to the passage of the Civil Rights Act, and "there is no mention of the riots in the streets in New York and Rochester and Philadelphia, has the act accomplished anything?" No state action or compulsion required the Heart of Atlanta Motel to discriminate, Rolleston asserted, and given that fact could Congress "pass regulations and a code of laws that affect the personal conduct of individuals?"

Justice Goldberg interrupted to inquire regarding the Commerce Clause as the constitutional basis of the 1964 act. "Your honor, I intend to answer absolutely as truthfully as I should," Rolleston responded. "In my opinion, the argument of counsel and of the government that this is done to relieve a burden on interstate commerce is so much hogwash; that the purpose of Congress was to pass a law [by] which some way or another they could control discrimination by individuals in the whole United States." When Goldberg persisted in his questioning, Rolleston declared that this "is a Court of law to decide whether Congress had the right under the Constitution, the legal right, not whether it was a good thing to do, or whether it was the humane thing to do, or the kind thing, or the moral thing."

Justice Goldberg nevertheless continued to press Rolleston regarding the Commerce Clause basis of the act. Rolleston then replied that the

> government just quoted the school boy familiar quote that all of us know but none of us much understands, I think, that all men are created equal. It's in the Declaration of Independence; I don't believe it's in the Constitution. But Chief Justice Duckworth of our Georgia Supreme Court has said in one sentence something that is as clear to me as anything I've ever heard on the subject of all men being equal: "Liberty stops where to extend it invades the liberty of another."

Rolleston then rather frankly admitted in his argument that his objections to the Civil Rights Act were based more on ideological principle than on judicial precedents construing the Constitution.

> I didn't come here to talk about commerce. I didn't come here to argue the question of whether or not this motel has an effect on commerce. Certainly everything that happens in this country has an effect on commerce. But I did perceive I hope in the writings of members of this Court [that] there is still a great facet of personal liberty that this Court stands for.

He continued:

> This Court under the Constitution is the last bulwark of individual liberty. Where else can a man go to defend personal liberty? So if you get

to the questions that you ask, the answer is that commerce has got to stop somewhere . . . , and that the power of the Commerce Clause under the Constitution does not go to people. If you don't accept that fundamental, I'm lost.

Unless the Court "says that commerce stops with personal liberty," he added, "then there is no end to it."

Justice Black then asked about blacks traveling along a highway who had no place to stay—why did not that affect commerce? Black said,

So far as I am concerned, that is the crucial issue here, as to whether in this case that Congress was wrong in thinking that depriving a large segment of people of the right to stop anywhere at night when they are traveling in interstate commerce, whether they had a right rationally to say that that put a burden on commerce that Congress had a right to lift. I have read the facts in your case. You have a motel right along the highway that I'm reasonably familiar with, people go up and down all over the country traveling down that highway and your motel is there—I understand your position, you believe it would injure your business [to serve blacks]—but you have a highway there where 75 percent of the people who come there come from outside the state, one way or another, and you have advertisements asking them to come. So your problem in this case as I see it under our former opinions going back to the very beginning of the century, the nineteenth century, is whether or not we've got a right in saying that if these people are deprived of a right to spend the night on their trips that was likely to create a burden on commerce.

Rolleston responded that he knew more about "the travel of the Negro race than any white man in this room" because his corporation for ten years also operated a motel in Atlanta exclusively for blacks. The motel was well maintained, well run, and well appointed, he said, yet it was rarely fully occupied even though it had only twenty rooms, indicating that there was little travel by blacks and thus little effect on commerce resulting from discrimination in motels and hotels.

"Have you ever traveled with any colored people from the southern part of this country back up to Washington?" Black asked.

Rolleston answered that he had not, but that he was aware that the Holiday Inns and Howard Johnson motels had now desegregated, so there was not in fact a scarcity of facilities available to traveling blacks. The Heart of Atlanta Motel had not desegregated on principle, he declared, because he felt

No," Rolleston responded, "but this is different, because it makes people
omething."

You are asking in effect that *Hammer v. Dagenhart,*[48] and the doctrine
ual federalism that local business enterprises were constitutionally be-
d the reach of Congress under the Commerce Clause, should be rein-
d, Black pointed out, although *Hammer v. Dagenhart* and the doctrine
ual federalism had been repudiated by the Court twenty-five years pre-
sly.

If this means putting back in the Constitution that liberty of an individ-
is more important than interstate commerce," Rolleston replied, "then
's what I'm asking."

olleston concluded:

rom this point on in history, because of the issue I'm raising about
eople, the people of this country will know whether the government
xists for the purpose of the preservation of the liberty of the people, or
xists for the purpose of allowing Congress to concentrate power in
Congress and in the national government. And it's as simple as that.
Under the Constitution, the decision is yours. You are not responsible
or the consequences of the decision. But I submit that you are re-
ponsible that the decision be just.

Thus ended the oral argument in *Heart of Atlanta Motel v. United States*
:35 P.M. As Justice Black's final questions had indicated, Moreton Rolle-
n did not lose his case on October 5, 1964. Rather, he had lost it in the
ing of 1937, and during the decades of Commerce Clause decisions by
Court that had followed.

Congress lacked the constitutional power to require it t
principle," he said. "We started this case two hours afte
on principle because Congress didn't have the right to
Justice White then asked whether Rolleston would co
act was a valid regulation of interstate commerce if the
sufficient number of hotels and motels willing to serve
commerce. Rolleston replied that he would not concede
der those circumstances, since the act would still impos
tude under the Thirteenth Amendment. Justice Clark the
"been the experience of the Heart of Atlanta [Motel] si
was issued requiring it to serve blacks. "That's a good q
replied. "Just to show what a great market there is for Ne
in interstate commerce, we've had three requests [for serv
two months," and the motel had served two of them, but
when the motel had been fully occupied. He had also do
white customers, he added, and 90 percent had responde
not use the recreational facilities of the motel if they were al
Solicitor General Cox had seemed to indicate that the
had been enacted to benefit the South by ending the harm
protests and demonstrations had had on the southern eco
said. He continued:

> Counsel seems to think that the act was passed for the
> people in Birmingham and Little Rock and other people
> rienced racial demonstrations in the South. There are 43
> people in the South, and I will say for all of them so loud
> can hear, "Please don't do us any more favors if it's for us."
> says, with friends like this, who needs enemies. [Laughter.]

"Congress can do anything, if this Court does not stop th
reiterated.

Justice Black then again inquired whether it was rational f
conclude that discrimination in hotels and motels affected i
merce. "Is Congress denied the power to protect commerce
fact that it relates to people?" he asked.

"The Court it seems to me has got to decide whether or n
includes individuals," Rolleston replied. "It's that simple. If it
act is constitutional. If they don't have the right to fetter an
man's liberty to run his business, then the act is unconstitution

"Can you think of any law regulating commerce that doesn
viduals?" Black persisted.

5

OF BARBECUE AND COMMERCE:
THE ARGUMENT IN THE *McCLUNG* CASE

Since the government had lost *Katzenbach v. McClung* in the three-judge court in Birmingham, Solicitor General Archibald Cox represented the United States as the appellant before the Supreme Court. The solicitor general's brief on behalf of the government in the *McClung* case relied on much of the same argument on the Commerce Clause as his brief in the *Heart of Atlanta Motel* case. At the outset of his *McClung* brief, however, Cox argued strenuously that the issuance of the injunction by the lower court prohibiting the enforcement of the 1964 act against Ollie's Barbecue was improper and an abuse of equitable discretion by the lower court. The McClungs, he asserted, had not suffered nor were they about to suffer any irreparable injury justifying their protection by injunctive relief. The decision of the lower court, the solicitor general therefore argued,

> sustaining the power of a district court to render an opinion upon the constitutionality of a federal statute upon the bare request of any person who alleges he is subject to the act, without any showing of irreparable injury, threatens such serious interference with the normal operations of the government as to require us to insist upon the jurisdictional objection in addition to arguing the merits.[1]

There were 115,000 restaurants, lunch counters, and gasoline stations in the southern and border states that were arguably subject to the public accommodations provisions of the 1964 act, Cox pointed out, and there were 20,000 hotels and motels and 6,000 motion picture theaters in those states also subject to the act. The Civil Rights Division of the Department of Justice, on the other hand, had only 55 lawyers to enforce not only the 1964 act but also all other civil rights laws. "It is hardly necessary to point out the impact of these facts," the solicitor general continued. "The Department of Justice can only perform its functions under these statutes if it is free to select carefully the cases it will bring so as to use its limited manpower in the most effective way. The decision as to which cases will be litigated, and where and when, cannot be left to the private parties subject to the public accommodations provisions of the 1964 act."[2]

Despite these objections to the issuance of the injunction by the lower court on jurisdictional grounds, Solicitor General Cox conceded that from "the standpoint of the immediate administration of the Civil Rights Act we would welcome a decision upon the constitutionality of Title II as applied to establishments like appellees' restaurant." And turning to the merits, he noted that the major premise of the government's argument in the *McClung* case was that Congress possessed the power, under the Commerce Clause and the Necessary and Proper Clause, to regulate local activities that had such a close and substantial relation to interstate commerce that their regulation was necessary to foster and protect commerce itself. From that premise, he said, the government further argued that Congress could have reasonably determined that racial discrimination in restaurants that served food received from interstate commerce did in fact produce substantial burdens on interstate commerce that Congress had the power to remove.[3]

The burdens or effects on commerce produced by discrimination in restaurants serving food a substantial portion of which had moved in interstate commerce, Cox argued, were three in kind. First, racial discrimination in such establishments tended to produce disturbances and protests against the discrimination being practiced by them, and these disputes tended to interrupt the operations of those restaurants with a resulting reduction in the use by them of food or other goods they would otherwise have obtained in interstate commerce. "Where a restaurant serves food received from interstate commerce, either directly or indirectly," the solicitor general argued, "any dispute involving the establishment which causes it to close or reduces its patronage will curtail its purchases and thus diminish the flow of goods in interstate commerce." He pointed out that the effects of disputes engendered by racial discrimination were not, however, limited to the targets of such disputes, since the disputes also tended to disrupt business generally in the areas where they occurred, with the resultant diminution of purchases in interstate commerce by business generally. "Current history," he said, "makes plain the tendency of the practice of racial discrimination to produce such disputes with the consequent interruption in the flow of goods from other states."[4]

Racial discrimination in restaurants serving interstate food, Cox additionally argued, artificially narrowed the market for interstate food and other products, since absent this practice the patronage of such restaurants would increase, with a concomitant increase in their use of interstate food and other goods. This conclusion, he contended, was

> simply a truism. Not only do established businesses sell less but many new businesses are not opened, because of the narrowed market resulting from the exclusionary practices. This restriction on the market, in

turn, retards the flow of goods in interstate commerce channels. To avoid that result Congress may go to the cause.[5]

Finally, Cox asserted, the discrimination practiced by Ollie's Barbecue in Birmingham itself had an adverse effect on interstate commerce, since absent the practice of discrimination, the McClungs' restaurant would not only sell more interstate food but would also purchase more food in interstate commerce. "It is obvious, of course, that the volume of goods purchased by any restaurant, viewed in isolation, has scant effect upon the total volume of goods moving in interstate commerce," he conceded. "Here, appellees were receiving annually about $70,000 worth of meat from out-of-state sources." But citing *Wickard v. Filburn,* he argued that "the size and volume of purchases of the individual establishment are not conclusive," since Congress was entitled to consider the adverse effect on commerce produced by the reduction of interstate food purchases resulting from the practice of discrimination by all similarly situated restaurants in the nation as a whole.[6]

Solicitor General Cox concluded:

> Although we contend that Congress has, and has exercised, the power to prohibit racial discrimination in places of public accommodation . . . because the discrimination is a prolific source of burdens and obstructions to interstate commerce, we do not suggest that Congress was uninfluenced by the conviction that racial discrimination in public places is a grave moral wrong, lying heavy on the conscience of the entire Nation, which belies the ideals of America. Faced with the need for meeting the commercial problem, Congress was free to choose the remedy most conducive to the public welfare, and most consistent with the promise of America to all sorts and conditions of men.[7]

Robert McDavid Smith continued to be the lead counsel on behalf of the McClungs in the Supreme Court as he had in the proceedings in the three-judge court, although he was joined on the brief in *Katzenbach v. McClung* by James H. Faulkner and William G. Somerville. In contrast to the blunderbuss nature of the attack on the validity of the 1964 act that Moreton Rolleston had launched in the *Heart of Atlanta Motel* case, Robert Smith's argument in the *McClung* case was more comparable to a rifle as he made clear at the outset that he was attacking the validity of the public accommodations provisions only as they applied to Ollie's Barbecue in Birmingham. Smith therefore did not deny the breadth of congressional power under the Commerce Clause, nor did he deny that under the commerce power Congress could prohibit racial discrimination in some restaurants, particularly those serving interstate travelers. Ollie's Barbecue, however, was not included in the latter category of restaurants, Smith pointed out, given its remoteness from interstate highways, bus stations, or airports and its lack of advertising for the purpose of attracting interstate travelers. The 1964 act applied to the McClungs' restaurant only because a substantial portion of the food it served had moved in interstate commerce and it practiced racial discrimination in its operations.[8]

There was no evidence in the legislative record of the Civil Rights Act of 1964 that racial discrimination by a restaurant serving food that had moved in interstate commerce actually resulted in an adverse effect on commerce, Smith argued. When Congress had regulated local activities under the Commerce Clause in other legislation, such as the National Labor Relations Act, it had provided administrative machinery by which it could be determined whether the local activity being regulated in fact adversely affected or burdened interstate commerce, he continued. But in the Civil Rights Act Congress had provided for no such administrative machinery through which it could be determined on a case by case basis whether racial discrimination in restaurants serving interstate food adversely affected commerce. Instead, Smith maintained, Congress had simply embodied in the 1964 act a legislative presumption that racial discrimination in restaurants serving food that had moved in interstate commerce, like Ollie's Barbecue, adversely affected or burdened interstate commerce, without any factual basis for such a presumption. Congress had consequently in the 1964 act invalidly overextended its power under the Commerce Clause by prohibiting discrimination in restaurants serving interstate food, he argued, and the public accommodations provisions as applied to Ollie's Barbecue should therefore be invalidated by the Court.[9]

Smith conceded that the Civil Rights Act of 1964 had been supported in Congress by "sincere and conscientious Americans," but "if Congress under the pretext of exercising its commerce power can effectuate social changes by this sophisticated means, where does its power stop?" he asked. "If all that is necessary is to find that a restaurant's operations 'affect commerce,' and then the way is open to carry out any purpose thought desirable by a congressional majority, no matter how remote from commercial affairs as normally considered, then our federal system has undergone an alarming change."[10]

Smith noted that he had not relied on the *Civil Rights Cases* of 1883 "as primary authority for . . . [his] position in this case," but he noted that the Court's comment that Congress could not have passed the Civil Rights Act of 1875 prior to the Civil War Amendments did support his contention that the 1964 act was invalid under the Commerce Clause. In addition, he argued that the act violated the Fifth Amendment by depriving owners of private property of their right to use their property as they chose. "It has long been assumed that a businessman," he asserted, "as an incident of the right to use and control his property as he wishes, may deal or refuse to deal with whomever he pleases."[11]

Concluding his brief, Smith again emphasized that the appellees did not

> contend Congress does not have broad power under the Commerce Clause. Admittedly it has. Nor are they unmindful of the presumption in favor of the constitutionality of a statute. On the other hand, many statutes have been declared unconstitutional by this Court. The powers of Congress under the Commerce Clause have not expanded. For the better part of two centuries this Court has stood as the ultimate citadel in the protection of individual liberty and private property. It is not with the slightest degree of reluctance that the appellees urge this Court to hold that Title II of the Civil Rights Act of 1964 is unconstitutional as to them and as to restaurants generally.[12]

In addition to the briefs on behalf of the McClungs and the United States, the *McClung* case attracted *amicus curiae* briefs on behalf of the State of North Carolina and the National Association for the Advancement of Colored People (NAACP). The North Carolina *amicus* brief attacked the Civil Rights Act of 1964 in ideological terms similar to Moreton Rolleston's brief on behalf of the Heart of Atlanta Motel. North Carolina's attorney general, T. W. Bruton, argued that the Court was being asked in the *McClung* case to expand the reach of the Commerce Clause "beyond any point or limit as explained and developed in all previous decisions of this Court." This request was being made, he said, not because there were any actual burdens on or obstructions to interstate commerce requiring congressional action to remove, "but rather because a predesigned social objective is sought and those seeking to establish this leveling process look everywhere in the Constitution to find some basis for their preconstructed theory." The interpretation of the Commerce Clause the Court was being asked to embrace in the *McClung* case, the North Carolina attorney general asserted, was like that advocated by the Socialist Labor Party and its theoretician Daniel DeLeon. "Thus we have seen the prophecy and socialist vision made by this Marxist DeLeon in 1913 come to fruition and maturity by the Civil Rights Act of 1964."[13]

The NAACP *amicus* brief, in contrast, contended that the Civil Rights Act was fully supported by well-established precedent under the Commerce Clause. The appellees in the *McClung* case, it was argued, "with extraordinary intrepidity, have summoned arguments rejected by Congress and have persuaded a Court of the United States that the public accommodations law is an exercise of 'naked power' by the Congress unsanctioned by the Constitution." The NAACP emphasized that

> the importance of such a case is manifest. The desirability of promptly determining this issue has been recognized. We submit . . . .that congressional power to enact this law under the power to "regulate commerce . . . among the several states" can be sustained by settled and conventional constitutional doctrine reflected in decisions as old as *Gibbons v. Ogden*. . . . Indeed, in light of the precedents, the commerce issue cannot be regarded as difficult or close.[14]

As in the *Heart of Atlanta Motel* case, the clerks of the justices submitted to them memoranda discussing the facts and issues in the *McClung* case, with recommendations regarding how the case could be decided. In his memorandum regarding *Katzenbach v. McClung*, for example, Chief Justice Warren's clerk agreed with Solicitor General Cox's criticism of the exercise of jurisdiction and the issuance of the injunction by the three-judge court. There were no penalties, either civil or criminal, for violations of the Civil Rights Act, he pointed out, and the act was enforced only through injunctions against those who violated the public accommodations provisions. The McClungs were therefore in no danger of suffering irreparable injury justifying the issuance of an injunction in their behalf. The Department of Justice was not even threatening to enforce the 1964 act against Ollie's Barbecue, since it had never heard of that restaurant before the McClungs filed suit in the lower court. "In short," he said, "this is a suit seeking to enjoin a possible lawsuit for an injunction not even threatened. There is no precedent for adjudicating constitutional issues in such an action."[15]

Although the solicitor general's objection to the lower court's exercise of equity jurisdiction appeared "well taken," Warren's clerk nonetheless said, "I do not feel, however, that this precludes the Court from reaching the merits in this case." The Court could hold that the lower court could properly have afforded the McClungs declaratory relief, he suggested, and consequently the Court could treat the case as an appeal from a declaratory judgment. "Although each of these procedures seems to violate the principle that constitutional questions should not be decided unless necessary," he conceded, "the question is important enough, I think, to justify a minor departure from that principle in the case at hand."[16]

Turning to the merits in the *McClung* case, Warren's clerk argued that the public accommodations provisions as applied to the McClungs' restaurant were a valid exercise of congressional power under the Commerce Clause under "a wealth of decisions in this Court extending back to *Gibbons v. Ogden*," holding that Congress could regulate local activities if their regulation were necessary to protect interstate commerce. "The critical inquiry in the present case, therefore," he pointed out, "is whether racial discrimination in a local restaurant, as a matter of fact, burdens or obstructs the movement of goods in interstate commerce." That inquiry was primarily one for Congress to make, and its conclusion on the point should be binding on the Court unless "it appears to have no reasonable relation to the authorized end."[17]

He was assuming, he admitted, that the Court would sustain the 1964 act as applied to the McClungs' restaurant. "Should that assumption be erroneous, I would recommend that the case be reversed for want of equity jurisdiction without expressing any views on the merits." His discussion of the applicable constitutional principles in his *Heart of Atlanta Motel* memo was equally applicable to the *McClung* case, the clerk pointed out. "Although this is a more difficult case, I recommend that the legislation be sustained as a proper exercise of congressional power under sec. 5 of the 14th Amendment." He further advised that if "a consensus cannot be reached on that ground, I feel that the legislation can be upheld as a proper exercise of the commerce power." The Court should note probable jurisdiction in the *McClung* case, Warren's clerk concluded, and reverse the decision of the three-judge court holding unconstitutional the public accommodations provisions as applied to Ollie's Barbecue.[18]

As he had in the *Heart of Atlanta Motel* case, Justice Brennan also received from one of his clerks a memorandum analyzing the facts and issues in the *McClung* case. Taking a position similar to that taken by the chief justice's clerk regarding the *McClung* case, Brennan's clerk pointed out that the decision "can properly be reversed on the quite narrow ground of an improper assumption of equity jurisdiction" by the three-judge court, although "the great public importance of the issue may still justify a reversal on the merits as well." If the Court chose to reach the merits in the *McClung* case, the clerk said, it should be noted that the lower court conducted its own inquiry regarding the relation of the 1964 act's provisions regulating restaurants to interstate commerce, and while "its result may be a tenable or even a respectable one, its reasoning is not."[19]

Brennan's clerk continued:

Some of the applications of the statute, and some of the sections, can be upheld without too much difficulty; they will be close to orthodox applications of the Commerce Clause. This will be the case, for example, for restaurants which serve substantial numbers of interstate travelers. The main difficulty will be in articulating links to interstate commerce where the link spelled out by Congress might not on its face justify regulation, as in the interstate food section, or the motel-for-transients provision, to the extent that [this] applies to intrastate transients only.[20]

The *McClung* case, Brennan's clerk advised, "cannot come under that branch of the statute which covers restaurants dealing with interstate travelers," since the McClungs' restaurant did not fall in that category. "The statute must be upheld, if at all, either because the fact of serving interstate food is itself sufficient (and the fact that the food has stopped at a Birmingham wholesaler constitutionally irrelevant) or because some other ground emerges for upholding the statute." He suggested such a ground might be that sit-in demonstrations and protests against racial discrimination in restaurants serving interstate food affected commerce by reducing the demand for food supplies from commerce, or that Congress could regulate discrimination in restaurants that did not otherwise affect commerce on the ground that it could protect those restaurants it could regulate under the Commerce Clause from unfair competition by restaurants not so regulated. The clerk warned, however, that this competitive theory should be used with caution, since it would make congressional power virtually limitless.[21]

As he had in his discussion of the *Heart of Atlanta Motel* case, Brennan's clerk emphasized the point that Congress did not in the 1964 act seek to expand its power under section five of the Fourteenth Amendment beyond the Court's traditional definition of state action. And there was no state action requiring or sanctioning racial discrimination in the *McClung* case, he pointed out, not even any arrests by police. In its consideration of the 1964 act, he noted, Congress had also rejected the proposition that the licensing of places of public accommodation by the states was sufficient state action to trigger the Fourteenth Amendment.[22]

"In *McClung* reverse," Brennan's clerk recommended in summary. "After independent examination, accept Senate committee findings of unrest and distortion of consumer purchasing patterns, and use [National Labor Relations Act] analogy." The Court should make it clear that Congress could not in all cases regulate under the Commerce Clause businesses or individuals merely because they at some time used interstate goods, he suggested. "But make it equally clear that, to the extent use of interstate goods is relevant, it does not matter whether the goods happen to have been purchased inside or outside the state. Do not use the competitive argument, or at least do not rely on it heavily." He also proposed that the Court should also note "in passing that the district court's assumption of equity jurisdiction in *McClung* is somewhat questionable; this is not an Article III difficulty, but one of equitable discretion, and in view of the great public importance of the questions, the Court will rule on the merits anyway."[23]

In the *McClung* case, the Court consequently had to determine first whether it would decide on the merits or reverse the decision of the three-judge court on the narrow jurisdictional issue that the issuance of the injunction prohibiting the enforcement of the 1964 act against the McClungs had been an abuse of equitable discretion. The Court was aware from the briefs of Solicitor General Cox and Robert McDavid Smith, as well as the clerks' memoranda, that were it to reach the merits in the case, the issue under the Commerce Clause in the *McClung* case would be much more problematic than it was in the *Heart of Atlanta Motel* case. These considerations were undoubtedly on the minds of the justices as the argument in the *Heart of Atlanta Motel* case came to an end, and the argument of the *McClung* case began.

Since he was representing the United States as the appellant in *Katzenbach v. McClung,* Solicitor General Archibald Cox opened the argument in that case, and he began by discussing the facts in the case, which, he said, were "simple, and for the purposes of this appeal, undisputed." The McClungs operated a restaurant that during the previous year had served about $70,000 worth of meat that had moved in interstate commerce, he pointed out. The McClungs admitted that they refused service to blacks in their restaurant and had initiated the injunction proceedings in the lower court. The government had denied that the three-judge court possessed equity jurisdiction because there had been no intention of enforcing the Civil Rights Act against Ollie's Barbecue, Cox explained, but on the merits the government had argued that the act as applied to the McClungs' restaurant was constitutional. The lower court had overruled the government both on the jurisdictional issue and on the merits, and had issued an injunction prohibiting the enforcement of the act against Ollie's Barbecue, but Justice Black as circuit justice had stayed the injunction.[24]

"Prior to July 31, 1964, the Department of Justice had never heard of the appellees or of their restaurant," Cox said. "There's been no investigation and no specific threat to enforce compliance on the part of their restaurant." He conceded that while "we would welcome a broad ruling on the constitutionality of Title II as applied to appellees' restaurant or any other restaurant," the government nevertheless felt it necessary to press the point that the three-judge court had improperly issued the injunction in the *McClung* case.

Justice Stewart interrupted to point out that if the government had welcomed a decision on the merits in the case, it could have counterclaimed as it had in the *Heart of Atlanta Motel* case rather than seeking the dismissal of the case on the jurisdictional issue. Stewart's comment was a signal that the solicitor general was about to face hard going on his jurisdictional objection. Justice Harlan added that "they could have sued you for a declaratory judgment before a single judge," and therefore the Court could treat the *McClung* case as an appeal from a declaratory judgment and proceed to consider the merits.

Solicitor General Cox responded that in this instance "literally, there is absolutely no occasion for these appellees to have taken us to court" because there was no injury or threatened injury to them or their business. "There must be some showing that the complainant had some need for relief," he argued, even in a suit for a declaratory judgment.

Cox, however, encountered a flurry of questions on the jurisdictional point he was raising from Justices Goldberg, Black, Brennan, and White, with most of the justices asking why the Court could not treat the case as an appeal from a declaratory judgment and thus proceed to decide the merits. And Justice Harlan pointed out to the solicitor general that the "injunction no longer exists" because it was stayed by Justice Black.

Cox nevertheless persisted in pressing the jurisdictional issue. "We just don't feel able to waive this point," he told the Court. "I'm not suggesting that the court was without jurisdiction," he added, but that its exercise of equitable jurisdiction under the circumstances was improper. That was what "really concerns me," he said, and if the Court would express its disapproval of the action of the lower court, then he would not object to a ruling on the merits.

The questions on the point from members of the Court continued, however, and the normally unruffled Cox responded with some apparent irritation at the constant interruptions from the bench. "I think if I could have just a minute," he complained, "I do think that I could answer a great many of these questions."

If the solicitor general sometimes appeared to be lecturing the Court during argument, the tables were now turned, and Justice Harlan proceeded to deliver a lecture to Cox. Since he had said that the resolution of the validity of the Civil Rights Act was of the "utmost public importance," Harlan asked, why should not the Court treat the *McClung* case as an appeal from a declaratory judgment and reach the issues in the case on the merits? While the issues of the 1964 act's validity and scope were unresolved, Harlan said, perhaps a declaratory judgment suit was appropriate on behalf of parties like the McClungs who might be subject to the act. Such suits, however, might be inappropriate once the validity of the act was established, when a proliferation of such suits would impede the government's enforcement of the act.

Still unwilling to abandon his jurisdictional objection, Cox replied to Harlan that in the *McClung* case there was no showing of any real injury or threatened injury to the McClungs justifying the issuance of the injunction by the lower court. The act was not enforced by penalties, civil or criminal, he pointed out, and the only method of enforcement was the preventive remedy of an injunction. "What we have here is simply no occasion for picking a quarrel with us," the solicitor general argued.

His jurisdictional objection, Cox continued, was also predicated on the fact that it was important that the government have the ability to pick and choose what cases to litigate in order to further the administration of justice. "We aren't directed to litigate every case, we can't afford to litigate every case, as big as the government is," he pointed out, "and it's important that the ones we do litigate be those which we think are most suited for litigation in the sense that they will do most to promote universal compliance with the statute." The federal courts must avoid the abuse of their jurisdiction like that which had occurred during the 1930s, Cox added, when the lower federal courts by prematurely and unnecessarily ruling on constitutional issues had delayed the enforcement of important federal programs, sometimes for years. Having made his point, however, the solicitor general conceded that when "the case is here, I should agree that the situation has very radically changed," but "I do ask this Court to disapprove" the issuance of the injunction by the lower court.

Probably to his relief, as well as that of the Court, Cox then addressed the merits in the *McClung* case. "On the merits," he said, "the only question is the constitutionality of section 201" of the 1964 act, which applied the prohibition of racial discrimination to restaurants that served food a substantial portion of which had moved in interstate commerce. "The legal principles we rely on here," he said, were the same as those relied on by the government in the *Heart of Atlanta Motel* case. Discrimination in restaurants like the McClungs' affected commerce because the practice resulted in demonstrations protesting it, he argued, and the demonstrations in turn not only reduced the volume of interstate products purchased by the restaurants that were the targets of the demonstrations but also adversely affected businesses generally in the areas where they occurred, with a resultant diminution of purchases of interstate goods by businesses generally.

The Court was aware of the effects on commerce produced by demonstrations against racial discrimination in places of public accommodation, Solicitor General Cox pointed out, since in at least two of the *Sit-in* cases, the restaurants affected had been forced to close at least for a time, thus completely cutting off their purchase of interstate goods. The experience in North Carolina with sit-in demonstrations, Cox cited as an example, substantially disrupted business in that state, with attendant substantial effects on commerce. The government also cited in its brief, he said, statistics demonstrating that spending by blacks was considerably reduced in areas where discrimination was practiced in contrast to areas where it was not. The appellees argued that Congress had no evidence that discrimination in a restaurant like the McClungs' that served interstate food actually affected interstate commerce, the solicitor general noted, but there was no necessity for an activity being regulated by Congress to affect commerce in every instance. "We are dealing with practical things here, with tendencies," he said.

"I suppose," Justice Stewart observed, "that this restaurant could get out from under this statute" by simply being careful to serve only food that was locally produced and that had not moved in commerce. Cox agreed, and pointed out that the fact that the McClungs' restaurant had served food from out of state indicated what would happen in the future, "and it is the threatening disruption of that future movement" of goods in commerce that was important.

The appellees also argued that Congress had not made findings of fact in the 1964 act that discrimination in restaurants serving interstate food affected interstate commerce. But, again citing the *Carolene Products* case,[25] Cox argued that such findings were unnecessary and that the Court could infer such facts in the absence of findings by Congress. The "fatal error" here, he said, was that the appellees argued that Congress had relied on a vulnerable theory of commerce that was invalid.

"To sustain your effect on commerce argument in this case, as distinguished from the first case," Justice Harlan asked, "do you . . . rely simply on the fact that the findings or evidence in the legislative record show an effect on commerce in relation to the purchase or use of interstate food, or do you go further than that and rely on the effect on commerce [generally]?"

He relied on both, Cox replied, because Congress in weighing the "effect of this particular link" considered both kinds of effects on commerce, and "I don't like to stand on either one without the other where I've got both."

In *United States v. Sullivan*,[26] the Court had sustained a regulation under the Commerce Clause that applied to drugs a retail druggist had received from interstate commerce, the solicitor general pointed out, although that case was not cited in the government's brief and "I'm not pressing this on the Court." He continued:

It does seem to me that there is a difference between saying that a man shall not beat his wife and making that a federal crime because he . . . smokes cigarettes that come from North Carolina, and saying that one shall not use food that he has gotten in interstate commerce, in order to perpetuate a practice that the Congress regards as damaging.

Justice Brennan then asked, "You are not making any different argument as to what I characterize as general backdrop kind of business interruption in this case than you did in the *Heart of Atlanta* [case]?"

"Actually, exactly the same, and I rely on it to the same extent," Cox replied.

"Do you think that it could be made a federal offense for a man to strike his wife with a baseball bat imported from another state?" Justice Stewart asked.

The solicitor general responded that the holding in the *Sullivan* case would go a long way toward sustaining such legislation, but he immediately disavowed any intention of asking the Court to adopt such an extreme interpretation of the Commerce Clause. It "seems to me that this statute can be upheld under the Commerce Clause under what I have said [are] existing principles or [without] any truly novel application [of those principles]," Cox argued. "This is just the kind of case where it is wise to keep within the established principles and familiar rules that really haven't been questioned for years and go back as I say to Chief Justice Marshall."

The appellees also contended that there had been no specific showing that discrimination in the McClungs' restaurant affected interstate commerce, the solicitor general pointed out. But, citing *United States v. Darby*,[27] he argued that Congress had frequently in the past made for itself determinations of what affected commerce, and when such determinations were made by Congress the only question for the Court was whether the means chosen by Congress to alleviate those effects on commerce were reasonably adapted to further a legitimate end. The parallel to the Fair Labor Standards Act [FLSA] of 1938, which had been sustained in the *Darby* case, and the Civil Rights Act of 1964 was complete, Cox argued, since in the FLSA Congress had determined that the payment of substandard wages by employers adversely affected interstate commerce and then had left it to the courts in each case to determine whether a particular employer produced products for interstate trade and was thus subject to the FLSA. In the 1964 act, Cox contended, Congress had similarly determined that racial discrimination in restaurants like the McClungs' affected commerce and left it to the court to determine in each instance if a particular restaurant served interstate food and was thereby subject to the act. The 1964 act, he argued, was also analogous to the National Labor Relations Act in that regard.

Cox argued in conclusion, obviously with the facts in *Wickard v. Filburn* in mind:

This particular establishment is tied to its trickle of goods that will be coming in in the future, a trickle Congress could find might be enlarged, if the effect of artificially narrowing the market were removed, and a trickle which might be dammed up and the movement of the flow of goods [stopped] if a dispute occurred as a result of this [racial discrimination].[28]

He finished, "I . . . rely on the general conditions . . . to make the obvious point that this trickle is representative of thousands, hundreds of thousands, of similar trickles, and that together they are a great stream, a national economic problem" affecting interstate commerce.

Chief Justice Warren then called upon Robert McDavid Smith to argue the *McClung* case on behalf of the appellees. October 5, 1964, was a doubly important day for Robert Smith, since not only was he arguing an important case before the U.S. Supreme Court but it was also his forty-fourth birthday. At the outset, Smith announced that since the Court had already heard hours of argument in the *Heart of Atlanta Motel* case as well as the *McClung* case, he would direct his argument to what he believed to be the central issues in the case:

> We do not have any disagreement with the solicitor general as to Congress having a very broad power to regulate local activities wholly within a state where they have a close and substantial relationship to interstate commerce. Nor do we contend that Congress may not under the Commerce Clause deal with the question of racial discrimination and segregation, including certainly some restaurants.

Smith continued:

> What we do contend is that this act . . . has brought within its scope of coverage restaurants over which Congress does not have any demonstrated or demonstrable authority under the Commerce Clause, and it must therefore be held unconstitutional, certainly as applied to these appellees whose factual situation in and of itself shows a typical restaurant that it cannot constitutionally apply to.

Responding to questions from Justice Goldberg as to whether the 1964 act could validly apply to any restaurants, Smith conceded that "we would not question that Congress would have the power to regulate certain restaurants that are related directly to the instrumentalities of commerce." But the McClungs' restaurant was not such an establishment, he insisted. "Certainly on this record, there's no way on earth to conclude that any interstate traveler has ever been served in this restaurant, and the court below on substantial evidence found that there is no offer to serve" interstate travelers by Ollie's Barbecue.

Smith continued his argument:

> Nor is it our purpose, may it please the Court, to try to urge upon this Court any restrictions upon the Commerce Clause or any retrenchments of positions that have been maintained in other cases. What we say is that the decided cases and the statutory precedents that these proponents of this act relied upon are not precedents, and there are no authorities on which to find that this is constitutional.

He also disavowed any intention of arguing that the 1964 act violated the Ninth or Tenth Amendment, although he noted that it was a truism that if Congress exceeded its power under the Commerce Clause a violation of the Tenth Amendment would result. And "certainly we have rights under the Fifth Amendment," Smith added, "but we are constrained to concede that those rights are subject to a considerable amount of influence at least under the Commerce Clause. We think the case must be decided under the Commerce Clause."

Unlike Moreton Rolleston's broadside attack on the validity of the Civil Rights Act in the *Heart of Atlanta Motel* case, Robert Smith's argument, even more than his brief, was a narrow attack on the validity of the act as applied to the McClungs' restaurant and those similarly situated. And in contrast to Rolleston's impassioned and at times histrionic demeanor during oral argument, Smith's argument was restrained and conversational in tone.

"Are you arguing this question just in terms of your own restaurant?" Justice White asked. "Are you saying that this act couldn't validly be applied to any other restaurant?"

"We take the position, Mr. Justice White," Smith replied, "that this act, as it is drawn with respect to the food test, applies to restaurants to which it may not validly be applied, and therefore on that test is unconstitutional—"

"And yours is one of them?" White persisted.

"And ours is one of them that happens to illustrate it," Smith agreed. What about other restaurants, White continued, perhaps a restaurant that purchased more food in interstate commerce than the McClungs' establishment? "No, sir, I don't think the act could be used on this basis to apply to any restaurant [simply because it purchased and served interstate food]," Smith said.

"And . . . you are saying even if, even if, Congress could reach a restaurant based solely on its purchases in interstate commerce, even if that were true, nevertheless Congress cannot necessarily conclude that discrimination in that restaurant affects commerce?" White asked.

"We're making the point," Smith responded, but perhaps in a somewhat different way. "We say first that Congress had to somehow determine that a policy of racial exclusion or selection in a restaurant would have an effect on interstate commerce—they had to find that."

Did Congress have to express such a conclusion in findings of fact in the statute? Justice Brennan asked.

Congress did not have to make findings of fact in the act, but its failure to do so in this statute was "highly significant," Smith said.

"Congress has declared in the act that any restaurant that makes certain kinds of purchases, its operations do affect commerce, it declared that, but you object to that as applied to all restaurants, or to any restaurants?" Justice White continued his questioning.

Smith replied that Congress had said that in the 1964 act but had not found it to be a fact.

"One thing they haven't said in the act is that in . . . this kind of establishment discrimination would affect commerce," White observed.

"They have not said that," Smith agreed.

When the president requested that Congress enact a broad public accommodations statute, Smith contended, Congress "cast about to find some constitutional basis for it, and we think the legislative history if nothing else shows a considerable amount of doubt as to the proper constitutional basis." Many eminent authorities had variously suggested the Thirteenth and Fourteenth Amendments as constitutional bases of the act, rather than the Commerce Clause, he pointed out. "We think what they did," he argued, was to rely on the Court's decision in *Wickard v. Filburn,* which although correctly decided by the Court was nonetheless "an oddity," and also on the cases sustaining the National Labor Relations Act (NLRA) of 1935.

In response to questions from Justice Brennan, Smith contended that under the 1964 act, it must be found that a restaurant engaging in racial discrimination and serving a substantial amount of food that had moved in interstate commerce in fact affected interstate commerce, and that in each case a court or an administrative agency had to make such a determination. But in a restaurant serving interstate food, he insisted, the movement of the food in interstate commerce had ended and therefore the operations of the restaurant would not affect interstate commerce.

"What about the labor board cases, the wages and hours cases?" Justice Black asked.

In the labor board cases, Smith replied, the NLRA was applied to employers who used interstate products or produced goods intended for interstate commerce, and thus a labor dispute in such an employer's business would presumably interrupt the future movement of products in commerce. "I am saying, if it please your honor," he continued, "you could have a restaurant under this statute that might never again make use of any food that crossed state lines and therefore might not affect interstate commerce at all."

"But don't you think that such a restaurant, insofar as the provisions of the statute are concerned, could go in and get an injunction lifted?" Justice Stewart asked. "The restaurant," Stewart continued, "could simply go in and say that we do not . . . now serve food in the restaurant a substantial portion of which has moved in commerce, and the injunction would be lifted insofar as this provision of the statute is concerned."

Responding to continuing questions from Justice Black regarding how he could distinguish the cases arising under the NLRA from the *McClung* case, Smith confessed that he was "afraid I am inept at making my position clear to the Court. I'm not talking in terms now of what Congress's power might have been. . . . Let us assume . . . that they had enough before them just to say that all racial exclusion in restaurants in the whole United States has some kind of cumulative effect on commerce and therefore we will proscribe all of it."

"As far as I am concerned, that'd raise quite a different question," Justice Black interjected.

"Well, let's say that they had done that," Smith continued.

> They didn't do that . . . instead they have purported to apply . . . [the act] to only the restaurants whose operations affect commerce. Now those words have to mean something. And what Congress has said is that in every case, one meaning that has to be attributed to them is that a substantial portion of the food they serve once moved in commerce.

The 1964 act thus applied to any restaurant that had served interstate food, he argued, even if the restaurant never again served interstate food, whereas in the labor board cases, in every case an actual disruption of the use of interstate products by a labor dispute had to be found.

Under questioning by Justice White, Smith conceded that Congress could legitimately regulate restaurants that served interstate travelers. "But, may it please the Court," he continued, "I do not believe there is anything in this legislative record that has anything at all to do with the movement of goods across state lines and the impact on that movement because of discrimination. I can't find anything in the legislative record." He added, "We are confident that none exists, because certainly the solicitor general would have called our attention to it." There was "ample evidence" before Congress when it enacted the Civil Rights Act that racial discrimination might impede interstate travel, Smith conceded, "but we suggest that the same is not true of the food test, and it's not merely a matter of what Congress did undertake to do, it's also that they did not have any basis on which to do that which the solicitor general claims they did." What the Congress had actually done, he argued, was to equate the Civil Rights Act to the National Labor Relations Act as a method of regulating local activities that affected commerce, but the equation was in fact insufficient constitutionally.

Justice Black, however, persisted in questioning Smith regarding whether Congress could have rationally reached the judgment that discrimination in restaurants serving food that had moved in interstate commerce adversely affected commerce and could thus be subjected to regulation under the Commerce Clause.

Smith responded:

> Your honor, may we make it entirely clear we're not in any sense urging that Congress does not have great power or that the gentlemen in Congress that favored this legislation were not conscientious, sincere, and very intelligent Americans. We just feel that this act was not enacted in the usual manner at all; we don't believe that most of the members of Congress had any occasion to really study the impact of the Commerce Clause cases.

Justice Black nevertheless persisted in his questions and inquired whether Smith was arguing that Congress had to include a finding of fact in the 1964 act that discrimination by restaurants serving interstate food affected interstate commerce.

Smith answered:

> Certainly we don't contend you have to have legislative findings in all legislation, however, if you do not . . . in some way, may it please the Court, we think there must be some way to demonstrate that the local activity that on its face is not within the Congress's power under the Commerce Clause comes within that power. We don't think that this Court can presume that Congress is always right.

Justice Black was still not satisfied, and inquired of Smith how he could distinguish decisions of the Court that had sustained exercises of power by Congress under the Commerce Clause that were virtually equivalent to the police power of the states, such as *United States v. Sullivan* and *Wickard v. Filburn.* Those cases, Smith responded, both sustained the regulation under the Commerce Clause of local activities that demonstrably had to be regulated in order for Congress to effectively regulate interstate commerce itself. In the *McClung* case, in contrast, he said, the "question is since . . . [the Civil Rights Act] chooses to use the terms 'affect commerce,' has it been limited to those activities that can be reasonably said to affect commerce, and we think not."

Justice Douglas then questioned Smith regarding whether the purchases of interstate food by the McClungs' restaurant were substantial. "We concede," Smith replied, "that $70,000 out of this restaurant's expenditures is substantial."

Apparently somewhat surprised at this concession, Justice Brennan asked, "You concede, you concede that the statute covers you by its terms?"

"We and the government," Smith agreed, "concede that the statute covers us and that we are in violation."

"You say . . . that the purchases of this restaurant that is involved in this case from outside the state are substantial?" Justice White inquired.

"I've never had occasion to take a position, but we've never questioned it," Smith said. "I don't think there is any question that they are substantial."

"Your point is, I gather," White continued, "that Congress's power cannot be rested upon just mere purchases from outside the state?"

"We think that Congress's power cannot be rested on a connection with interstate commerce that is related solely and exclusively to past movements in commerce, yes, sir," Smith answered.

"But this was a regular pattern of purchases in interstate commerce," Justice Douglas interjected, yet Smith was arguing that the operations of the McClungs' restaurant did not affect commerce and were not validly within the statute. "Maybe this is premature," Douglas suggested, and if the case had been tried under the regular enforcement procedures under the act, Smith could have proved the restaurant was not within the statute's provisions.

Smith, however, immediately disavowed any argument that might result in the *McClung* case being dismissed as having been prematurely brought. "We've showed we come under this statute," he said. "Please don't let me leave the Court in any doubt about our position. We're under the statute, we're not complying with it, it does cover us."

"You're under the words of the statute, as you and the government both agree," Justice Stewart said, "but you say that's not enough constitutionally?"

"We do contend that we have to have a hearing and an opportunity to show we [do not] affect commerce," Smith replied.

"And the statute doesn't give you an opportunity," Stewart added.

"Yes, sir," Smith said, "thank you for that question."

"It's not a matter of hearings," Justice Harlan interrupted, "it is a matter of an . . . irrational definition for Congress to have made in the statute."

"Yes, sir, in the light of common experience," Smith agreed. Findings of fact were not necessary in a statute "in and of themselves," but "where the matter that Congress was dealing with does not have a rational relationship to the regulation in common experience then certainly something must be shown to show that there is a connection" between the subject being regulated and interstate commerce. "Now, what we are saying," he continued, "is that . . . unless the legislative history shows a relationship, you then have to fall back on common experience, and in common experience, there is no relationship here between the matter regulated and an effect on interstate commerce."

"There is no rational connection between discrimination and purchases or between purchases and discrimination?" Justice White asked. "I didn't know that you denied that if purchases were substantially decreased that that was not a burden on commerce."

"Well, under the statute, I don't understand that there is any place to determine that purchases are decreased" because of racial discrimination, Smith answered. "That's the very point I'm trying to make, under this statute, whether it would affect your purchases in volume, increase them or decrease them, it doesn't make any difference, you'd still be covered. And I don't think that there's anything on which Congress could have based that determination and certainly I don't think it's common experience" that racial discrimination in a restaurant necessarily would affect the volume of its purchases in interstate commerce.

Justice Harlan then again intervened and commented that he might well agree with Smith if the Civil Rights Act's validity were predicated solely on the theory that racial discrimination in the McClungs' restaurant affected commerce by affecting the volume of food that it purchased in commerce. "What do you do with the second point of the government's argument," he inquired, "that this statute does cover, and there . . . is evidence to support it, any kind of restraint on commerce, maybe this restaurant would never have purchased a nickel's worth of food again in commerce, but the fact that it is discriminating prevents people from coming to . . . [Birmingham][29] and buying in department stores, etc., which as I understand it, is the second branch of their argument."

"I thought they had expressed no willingness to stand on it here," Smith replied.

The government had "not abandoned it," Harlan pointed out.

At this point, it was apparent that Smith did not fully understand Harlan's question. Was the argument Harlan was inquiring about that Congress had concluded that discrimination generally in all restaurants all over the country affected commerce, and on that basis proscribed it, he asked, "is that the argument?"

"No, that isn't quite the argument," Harlan said.

> I understood the . . . government's argument was that Congress stopped short of that, and they said we will deal with a restaurant that has purchased goods . . . that have moved in commerce, but when it comes to the effect on commerce, we're not limited in showing an effect on commerce to the question as to whether that restaurant or restaurants generally are going to purchase food in commerce, but they can rely on the general evidence, as I got it, that trade generally, interstate trade generally in . . . [Birmingham] is affected by . . . discrimination in that category of restaurants. That's the way I understood their argument.

When Smith again appeared to be puzzled by Harlan's question, saying, "I did not understand them to press that argument," Justice Brennan intervened and attempted to bail Smith out of his predicament. "Maybe we'd better wait and have that cleared up by the solicitor general," he commented.

"I think it's quite important," Harlan persisted, "that that argument be either fleshed [out] or taken out of the case. Because I think your argument on the premise you're arguing is a very persuasive argument, frankly."

Smith then denied that Congress had intended to apply the act as broadly as Justice Harlan had suggested, and he insisted that there was no basis upon which Congress could have concluded that demonstrations protesting segregation interrupted interstate commerce. Whatever effect on commerce the demonstrations of 1963 had produced, he argued, the Court should not rely on the effects on commerce caused by demonstrations because there was no evidence regarding what had caused the demonstrations.

"Well, there was certainly throughout the hearings [on the Civil Rights Act in Congress] . . . and throughout the solicitor general's argument here, there's a clear suggestion that there was an effort to remove . . . the cause of the demonstrations and . . . the basic cause back then was discrimination in restaurants," Justice Stewart observed. "There was an attempt to remove the cause."

Smith responded that he was referring to discrimination in restaurants particularly.

"The demonstrations were about restaurants," Stewart insisted.

"We had about a hundred cases, I guess, sit-ins," Justice Clark added.

"Most were variety and department store restaurants," Smith responded.

"We had all kinds, Mr. Smith," Justice Brennan said, joining in the exchange, "which suggests something, in the whole picture may we take some judicial notice from the hundred-odd cases we have had here, what this is all about in restaurants?" Smith replied that he assumed that the Court was free to take judicial notice, in its discretion, of conditions that were a matter of general knowledge.

Justice Harlan refused to be deflected from his point regarding the impact on commerce generally of demonstrations against discrimination in restaurants. The statute was limited in its application to restaurants that served food that had moved in interstate commerce, and once that was established, there was no further factual issue, Harlan said. He continued:

> I thought you said, if I get you correctly, I thought your argument was twofold, namely that Congress has put in a self-liquidating, self-defining term of affecting commerce, that the definition it's chosen is an irrational one because one's purchase of food doesn't mean that you are

now purchasing or serving food that has moved in commerce, and since the Congress did not provide for a hearing on that question, this is an invalid exercise, there is no effect on commerce shown.

Smith agreed that Harlan had accurately summarized his position, and he pointed out that the McClungs' restaurant was far distant from interstate highways, the train and bus stations, or the airport, and that "it's completely off by itself," and thus its operations did not affect commerce.

Smith then briefly addressed the issue of whether the lower court had properly issued an injunction in the *McClung* case, and he argued that the lower court had acted properly.

There was never any question that the appellees were covered by the act . . . and it has never been contended that they were not covered by the act. So they were in violation of a statute that had immediate application to them. Two days earlier, the Department of Justice had filed a suit in the same court against fifteen restaurants in one case, lumping them all together, and asking for a joint trial as to all of them.

While the solicitor general had suggested that the McClungs would have not had any additional expense in defending themselves against the application of the act to them when and if that occurred, Smith suggested that defending themselves in a joint trial including many other restaurants would have in fact been more expensive and difficult, and the remedy afforded by the lower court was the more convenient alternative.

"May it please the Court," Smith said,

we would like to close our presentation of this case . . . by simply reminding the Court that we are dealing here not with any effort to restrict Congress's power to regulate interstate commerce or local matters that truly affect it, but if the federal system is to be maintained, then Congress cannot have under the commerce power as broad discretion as states have under the police power. And we don't believe that historical precedents show that they have.

And he added, "Now, we do not urge any restriction of any . . . line of authority that exists today, but it's just plain, I'm sure to every justice of this Court, that this does represent an area for which there is no immediate authority and for which there is no really close analogy."

Although it was obvious that Smith intended to conclude his argument at this point, Justice Black refused to allow the argument to conclude without additional comments, just as he had prevented Moreton Rolleston from concluding his argument. Black told Smith:

> It seems to me . . . that [well-established precedent] has settled your basic point against you, which is that the mere ending of commerce, coming to rest, or whatever you want to call it, doesn't take away congressional power to regulate in that field in order to prevent burdens on commerce. At least twenty-five to fifty cases [have held that].

In every such case, Smith replied, the holding of the Court had to do with the regulation of transportation of goods in commerce. Justice Black, however, cited cases in which that was not the fact, and again pointed out that Smith's "point was foreclosed by past cases."

Justice Harlan then inquired of Smith whether his client was willing for the case to be treated as an appeal from a declaratory judgment. "You're properly here?" he asked.

"Yes," Smith replied, and with that his argument ended.

"Mr. Chief Justice, it's late," Solicitor General Cox said, beginning his rebuttal argument and indicating that he would briefly address only two points that Justice Harlan had raised. He would acquiesce in the Court's treatment of the *McClung* case as an appeal from a declaratory judgment, he assured the Court. Regarding the effects of demonstrations against segregation in places of public accommodation, Cox continued,

> our view with respect to that . . . is that it would be quite possible for us to argue, and we do argue . . . , that as racial discrimination in places of public accommodation generally causes disturbances and demonstrations that interfere with the course of retail business generally and so lessen the flow of goods into the state . . . that that is sufficient to justify prohibiting discrimination in all such places under the Commerce Clause.

That was not the whole of his argument, he noted, but he thought he did not have to "go that far in this case." Restaurants serving food that moved in commerce were an additional link to interstate commerce, he added, again citing *Wickard v. Filburn,* and "Congress took the cumulative effect into view" in concluding that discrimination in all such restaurants burdened or affected interstate commerce.

The 1964 act, the solicitor general maintained, did not apply to every restaurant that had ever received food in commerce, but only to those serving such food as a continuing practice or pattern of business related to commerce.

"I might just say one final and general word here," Cox concluded. "A good deal has been said that if Congress can do this, then it can do that, and if Congress can do that, it can go further and thus may swallow up the distinction between the nation and the states." No such drastic result would occur, the solicitor general assured the Court, if it sustained the constitutionality of the Civil Rights Act of 1964.

And with that, the arguments in the public accommodations cases came to an end. The fate of the public accommodations provisions of the Civil Rights Act of 1964 was now in the lap of the Court.

6

THE PUBLIC ACCOMMODATIONS CASES
INSIDE THE COURT

Following the conclusion of the oral arguments in the *Heart of Atlanta Motel* and *McClung* cases, the justices of the Supreme Court met in Conference to decide the cases on the merits. Chief Justice Warren had notified the brethren on September 25 that they would "convene for our first Conference for the 1964 Term immediately after the conclusion of the session on Monday, October 5, and will meet thereafter at 10:00 A.M. every day until the Conference Lists [of cases pending review] are completed."[1] Conferences of the Court by tradition include only the justices themselves, and no law clerks or other aides are present. If additional materials are needed by the justices during their discussion in Conference, or messages to the justices are received, it is the custom of the Court that the junior associate justice is the Conference's doorkeeper, and it is he or she who must obtain the materials needed by the justices or receive messages at the door and deliver them to the appropriate justice. When he was the junior associate justice, Justice Tom Clark thus once remarked, he "was the highest paid doorkeeper in the world."[2] In 1964, the junior associate justice and therefore the doorkeeper of the Conference was Justice Arthur Goldberg, who had been appointed by President Kennedy in 1962.[3]

In the Court, the Conference of the justices serves two important functions. First, the justices discuss those cases pending before it for review that have been included on the Discuss List. The Discuss List is initiated by the chief justice and includes those cases pending review that the chief justice believes raise issues of sufficient importance to at least merit discussion by the justices in Conference. Each of the other justices may also add cases to the Discuss List, but those cases not on the Discuss List are automatically denied review by the Court, since the failure of a case to be included on the Discuss List indicates that none of the justices believes that the case raises issues of sufficient importance to even be discussed in Conference. After the discussion of the cases on the Discuss List in Conference, if at least four justices (the rule of four) vote to grant a case a review on the merits, the case is granted review by the Court. A case included on the Discuss List that does not receive the votes of at least four justices favoring review of the case on the merits is denied review by the Court.[4]

The second function of the Conference of the justices is the decision on the merits of those cases in which oral arguments have occurred, a posture that the *Heart of Atlanta Motel* and *McClung* cases were in on October 5, 1964. By tradition, the discussions in Conference are initiated by the chief justice, followed by remarks of each of the members of the Court in order of seniority, with the most junior associate justice speaking last. Conference discussions are not debates, but rather statements by each of the justices regarding each case, usually without interruptions or comments by other members of the Court. Formal votes on the decision of argued cases on the merits are not taken in the Conference. Rather, each of the justices during his or her discussion of the case at hand announces how he or she believes the case should be decided by either reversing or affirming the decision of the court below.[5]

According to custom, the discussion of how the *Heart of Atlanta Motel* and *McClung* cases should be decided on the merits was opened by Chief Justice Warren in the Conference on the afternoon of October 5. Warren wasted no time in making clear his position that the public accommodations provisions of the 1964 act were constitutional as an exercise of the power of Congress under the Commerce Clause and as applied to the Heart of Atlanta Motel and to Ollie's Barbecue in Birmingham. The jurisdiction of the Court in the *Heart of Atlanta Motel* case was clear, and despite the government's objection to the granting of the injunction in the *McClung* case, the chief justice argued that both cases should be decided on the merits.

Regarding the merits, Warren continued, both sides in each of the cases conceded that the Heart of Atlanta Motel and Ollie's Barbecue were covered by the public accommodations provisions, and therefore the question of the constitutionality of those provisions was squarely presented. The Court, Warren urged, ignoring the advice he had received from one of his clerks, should not reach the Fourteenth Amendment question of whether Congress could have based the public accommodations provisions on its section five power to enforce the provisions of the amendment.

Warren was aware, of course, that the Court ordinarily avoided unnecessary rulings on constitutional issues. If the Commerce Clause was an adequate constitutional basis for the enactment of the public accommodations provisions of the 1964 act, then the issue of whether Congress could have relied on section five of the Fourteenth Amendment as the constitutional basis of those provisions was irrelevant. The chief justice was also acutely aware that the issue of whether the convictions of sit-in demonstrators violated the Fourteenth Amendment standing alone had splintered the Court in the *Sit-in* cases. And while the question of whether Congress could prohibit racial discrimination in facilities of public accommodation under section five of the Fourteenth Amendment presented a different issue from that presented in the *Sit-in* cases, Warren was undoubtedly wary of the Fourteenth Amendment issue in the *Heart of Atlanta Motel* and *McClung* cases, with its potential of perhaps similarly splintering the Court.

Congress had made no findings regarding the effects of racial discrimination in facilities of public accommodation on interstate commerce in the 1964 act, Warren conceded. But such findings were unnecessary, he said, as far as a decision of the Court sustaining the act under the Commerce Clause was concerned. He indicated that he would not, however, as the government had argued, rely on the effects of demonstrations against racial discrimination on commerce as a basis for sustaining the act. The Commerce Clause was an adequate constitutional basis upon which the act could be sustained by the Court, he said. The precedents sustaining the act under the Commerce Clause were all in a line, Warren concluded, and he would therefore affirm in Number 515 [the *Heart of Atlanta Motel* case] and reverse in Number 543 [the *McClung* case].[6]

Following Chief Justice Warren's discussion of the cases, Justice Hugo Black, as the senior associate justice, was the next to speak, according to the custom of the Court. Black began his discussion by concurring in Chief Justice Warren's view that the Commerce Clause was clearly a sufficient basis on which the Court could sustain the constitutionality of the public accommodations provisions of the act. He would have preferred, he added, to have rested the decisions of the Court on the Fourteenth Amendment, but it seemed to him clear that Congress had relied primarily on the Commerce Clause as the constitutional basis of the public accommodations provisions. Otherwise, Black said, he would have supported the overruling of the *Civil Rights Cases* of 1883, which had denied to Congress the power to prohibit racial discrimination in facilities of public accommodation under section five of the Fourteenth Amendment. Black expressed misgivings regarding the issuance of the injunction prohibiting the enforcement of the public accommodations provisions by the three-judge district court in the *McClung* case, since there had been no showing that the government was threatening to enforce the 1964 act against Ollie's Barbecue or otherwise had engaged in harassment of the McClungs. But since the enforcement of the three-judge court's injunction had been stayed by the Court, the *McClung* case was in the posture of a suit for a declaratory judgment regarding the validity of the public accommodations provisions, and as such, was reviewable by the Court.

On the merits of the *McClung* case, Black continued, the facts demonstrated that food used by Ollie's Barbecue had moved in interstate commerce, and the 1964 act provided that restaurants serving or selling a "substantial" amount of food or products that had moved in commerce sufficiently affected commerce to be covered by the act. If the act had not used the term "substantial," he said, he would be bothered, but in his view the act fell well within the Court's precedents sustaining congressional regulation of activities that affected interstate commerce. He would consequently affirm the decision of the three-judge court in Number 515 [the *Heart of Atlanta Motel* case] and reverse in Number 543 [the *McClung* case]. The Commerce Clause, as supplemented by the Necessary and Proper Clause, supported the power of Congress to pass the Civil Rights Act, Black concluded, as indicated by decisions of the Court as early as some written by Charles Evans Hughes. Here Black seems to have had particularly in mind the opinion of Hughes for the Court in the *Shreveport Case* of 1914, in which the Court sustained federal regulation of purely intrastate rail rates in Texas that though reasonable in themselves nevertheless resulted in discrimination against interstate commerce.[7]

Justice William O. Douglas, as the senior associate justice after Black, addressed the Conference next, and his remarks were quite brief. He would sustain the constitutionality of the public accommodations provisions, he said, but unlike the chief justice and Justice Black, would rest the decision on the Fourteenth Amendment, and he referred his colleagues to his concurring opinion in *Edwards v. California,* decided by the Court in 1941.[8]

In the *Edwards* case, Justice Douglas, joined by Justices Black and Murphy, concurred in the judgment of the Court invalidating California's "anti-Okie" law, but disavowed any reliance on the Commerce Clause as the basis for invalidating the California statute as the majority of the Court had done. He was "of the opinion that the right of persons to move freely from State to State occupies a more protected position in our constitutional system," Douglas said, "than does the movement of cattle, fruit, steel and coal across state lines." "The right to move freely from State to State is an incident of *national* citizenship," Douglas continued, "protected by the privileges and immunities clause of the Fourteenth Amendment against state interference."[9]

Douglas's rather cryptic reference to his concurrence in the *Edwards* case was thus an indication during the Conference of the Court that while he would sustain the public accommodations provisions of the 1964 act, he would rest his decision not on the Commerce Clause but on the Fourteenth Amendment. Congressional power to guarantee freedom from racial discrimination and to protect basic human rights, Douglas obviously felt, should rest upon the principles of equality embodied in the Fourteenth Amendment rather than being based on the commerce power under which Congress customarily regulated or protected much more mundane and less exalted subjects.

Speaking next, Justice Tom Clark disagreed with Douglas's reliance on the Fourteenth Amendment as the basis for sustaining the public accommodations provisions, but instead stated his view that the provisions were sustainable under the Commerce Clause. He would therefore affirm the decision of the three-judge court in the *Heart of Atlanta Motel* case, he said, and reverse the decision below in the *McClung* case. He also doubted that the issuance of the injunction by the three-judge court in the *McClung* case had been proper, but the Court had in the past sustained congressional power to regulate when goods or products had moved in interstate commerce, as had the food served by Ollie's Barbecue. Commerce was also affected by the racial discrimination practiced by the Heart of Atlanta Motel, Clark concluded, since the record indicated 75 percent of the motel's patronage involved interstate travelers.

Following Clark, Justice John Marshall Harlan II, whose grandfather had been the lone dissenter in the *Civil Rights Cases* of 1883, stated his agreement with what had been said regarding the propriety of the district court's issuance of the injunction in the *McClung* case, and also agreed that the decision of the district court in that case should be treated by the Court as an appeal from a declaratory judgment. On the merits, Harlan continued, he was inclined to agree with Justice Douglas that both cases raised issues more related to the Fourteenth Amendment than the Commerce Clause. The real purpose of the public accommodations provisions of the 1964 act, he pointed out, was after all the protection of civil rights rather than interstate commerce. He would, however, stand by the *Civil Rights Cases* of 1883 and hold the public accommodations provisions unconstitutional if they had been based solely on section five of the Fourteenth Amendment. In the 1964 act, he noted, Congress had defined state action as the Court had defined that doctrine in the *Civil Rights Cases,* thus indicating no intention of inviting a revision of the Court's decisions in those cases.

Despite these considerations, Harlan said on the other hand, the public accommodations provisions could be sustained under the Commerce Clause, and in the *Heart of Atlanta Motel* case, he had no problem sustaining the provisions under the commerce power. Congress was not required to include findings in the 1964 act indicating how racial discrimination in facilities of public accommodation affected commerce, he agreed, but there must be in the legislative record of the act material demonstrating the relation of the activity being regulated to interstate commerce, since otherwise the courts would not be able to know if an activity in fact affected commerce. In the *Heart of Atlanta Motel* case, he said, the legislative record compiled during the consideration of the 1964 act by Congress relative to the substantial effects on commerce produced by racial discrimination in motels and hotels sustained the application of the act to the Heart of Atlanta Motel. He nevertheless reserved judgment, Harlan noted, on the question of whether the act could be validly applied to discrimination by hotels and motels against noninterstate travelers.

During the oral argument of the *McClung* case, Justice Harlan had of course expressed serious doubt regarding the application of the Civil Rights Act to Ollie's Barbecue based on the fact that the restaurant served food that had moved in interstate commerce. And he had indicated agreement with Robert McDavid Smith's argument that there was an insufficient link between the racial discrimination practiced by the McClungs and the food they purchased that had moved in commerce.

Regarding the *McClung* case, Harlan therefore stated in the Conference that he was not yet prepared to vote because he was uncertain regarding what effects on interstate commerce the government was relying on to justify the application of the act to Ollie's Barbecue. Was the effect on commerce justifying the application of the act in the *McClung* case the effect of racial discrimination in the restaurant on sales of food in commerce, he asked, or was it more broadly the effect of racial discrimination on interstate commerce generally? If the effect on commerce being relied on was the effect on food sales, then he had serious doubts regarding the validity of the act's applicability to Ollie's Barbecue, since he could not discern any substantial effect on interstate food sales resulting from the racial discrimination practiced by that restaurant. If, on the other hand, the act's applicability to Ollie's Barbecue was based on the broader impact of segregation on commerce generally, then he believed the act was valid as applied. Harlan concluded by indicating that in light of these doubts regarding the *McClung* case, he would only tentatively agree to a reversal in that case.

Justice William Brennan opened his discussion of the cases by announcing that he would affirm the decision below in the *Heart of Atlanta Motel* case and reverse the decision in the *McClung* case. With regard to the *McClung* case, he agreed that the U.S. district courts ought to be cautioned against entertaining suits for injunctions under the circumstances of that case. Brennan agreed with Harlan that Congress in the 1964 act had defined state action as the Court had defined it in the *Civil Rights Cases* of 1883, and consequently he agreed that the cases should be decided on the basis of the Commerce Clause. He also agreed that the failure of Congress to include findings in the 1964 act pointing out the effect on commerce of discrimination in facilities of public accommodation was irrelevant, and that the Court could rely on the adequacy of the legislative record on that question. Unlike Justice Harlan, Brennan entertained no doubt regarding the validity of the act as applied in the *McClung* case, since food served by the restaurant had moved in commerce and the Court's prior cases sustained congressional regulation based on the movement of goods or articles in interstate commerce.

Justice Potter Stewart was very brief in his remarks. Relying on the Commerce Clause, he said, he would affirm the decision in the *Heart of Atlanta Motel* case and reverse in the *McClung* case.

Justice Byron White also spoke briefly, noting his agreement with Justice Stewart. Apparently responding to Justice Harlan's concerns in the *McClung* case, White added that although Congress had relied on the effect of racial discrimination in restaurants on interstate food sales to trigger the act's application, that fact did not preclude the Court from finding other grounds under the Commerce Clause on which to sustain the validity of the act's application to Ollie's Barbecue.

Finally, as the junior associate justice, Arthur Goldberg announced his views to the Conference. He shared some of Justice Douglas's difficulties in sustaining the act resting solely on the Commerce Clause, he said, since the act was after all a civil rights act and Congress had relied on both the Commerce Clause and the Fourteenth Amendment when enacting the public accommodations provisions. Consequently, Goldberg said, he was prepared to sustain the validity of the act on either the Commerce Clause or the Fourteenth Amendment or both. If the Court relied on the Commerce Clause, he continued, it would subsequently be getting a lot of messy cases testing the validity of the act's applicability to a variety of businesses. Nonetheless, he said, he would favor an opinion sustaining the act under the Commerce Clause if it was written broadly. Congress had exercised its full commerce power regarding the applicability of the public accommodations provisions to hotels and motels but had limited the applicability of those provisions regarding restaurants, since under the full power of Congress under the Commerce Clause, all restaurants could have been regulated and not just those serving food that had moved in commerce or that catered to interstate travelers. With regard to the *McClung* case, Goldberg pointed out, apparently in response to Harlan's concerns, the movement of food was not the only valid basis for congressional regulation under the Commerce Clause, but rather the effect of racial discrimination on business generally was a relevant basis on which the act could also be sustained.

At the conclusion of Justice Goldberg's remarks, it was thus clear that the Court was unanimous in agreeing to sustain the constitutionality of the application of the public accommodations provisions of the Civil Rights Act of 1964 to the Heart of Atlanta Motel, and that at least eight members of the Court also favored sustaining the act's validity as applied to Ollie's Barbecue in Birmingham. Only Justice Harlan appeared to entertain doubts regarding whether the decision of the three-judge court should be reversed in the *McClung* case. It was also clear that Chief Justice Warren and Justices Black, Clark, Harlan, Brennan, Stewart, and White would support basing the Court's decisions in the *Heart of Atlanta Motel* and *McClung* cases on the

Commerce Clause rather than on congressional power under section five of the Fourteenth Amendment. Only Justice Douglas, and more tentatively, Justice Goldberg, had expressed the view that the Court should sustain the public accommodations provisions under the Fourteenth Amendment. Following the Conference of the justices, it therefore appeared most likely that the public accommodations provisions would be constitutionally sustained in an opinion of the Court based on the Commerce Clause and joined by seven or perhaps eight of the members of the Court. Justice Douglas, and perhaps Justice Goldberg, might file opinions concurring in the result but basing their opinions on the Fourteenth Amendment.

Had the majority of the justices indicated a disposition to sustain the public accommodations provisions under the Fourteenth Amendment, it was also apparent from the Conference discussion that such a decision would not be unanimous, since Justice Harlan had clearly indicated in the Conference that he continued to adhere to the ruling in the *Civil Rights Cases* of 1883 that Congress lacked power to prohibit discrimination in facilities of public accommodation under section five of the Fourteenth Amendment. Unanimity of the Court in the *Heart of Atlanta Motel* and *McClung* cases was therefore only achievable with an opinion of the Court relying on the Commerce Clause and not the Fourteenth Amendment.

It was also clear from the Conference discussion of the justices that the challenges to the validity of the public accommodations provisions under the Fifth, Tenth, and Thirteenth Amendments were regarded as essentially frivolous by the Court, since not one justice appears to have addressed those issues during the Conference on the *Heart of Atlanta Motel* and *McClung* cases. Finally, while there were misgivings among several members of the Court regarding the issuance of the injunction by the three-judge court in the *McClung* case, there appeared to be no inclination by any member of the Court to avoid the issues raised in the *McClung* case on the merits by disposing of that case on jurisdictional grounds.

By the tradition of the Court, apparently dating from Chief Justice John Marshall's time, if the chief justice is in the majority in the decision of a case, the chief justice may select who among the majority justices will write the majority opinion of the Court. If the chief justice is not in the majority, then the senior associate justice in the majority assigns the writing of the majority opinion. Since Chief Justice Warren was in the majority in the *Heart of Atlanta Motel* and *McClung* cases, Warren could therefore choose the author of the majority opinion. The chief justice assigns to himself the writing of opinions in many cases of great significance, yet there is also apparently an expectation among the justices that the chief justice will share the writing of majority opinions in important cases with the other justices.[10]

In exercising the responsibility of opinion assignment, the chief justice must consider a variety of factors. First, the chief justice must consider the fair distribution of the work of the Court among the justices, weighing in addition the varying abilities of the members of the Court to produce acceptable opinions in a timely fashion. In assigning a majority opinion, the chief justice must also consider who among the justices in the majority is most likely to produce an opinion acceptable to the other members of the majority. A justice with extreme views or ones that deviate substantially from the consensus of views of the other members of the Court is thus a less attractive candidate for the assignment of a majority opinion, since such a justice is less likely to write an opinion that the other members of the majority may comfortably join.[11]

An additional factor was undoubtedly operative as Chief Justice Warren pondered the assignment of the majority opinions in the *Heart of Atlanta Motel* and *McClung* cases, and that was the sensitivity of the issue of desegregating facilities of public accommodation in the South. An issue similarly sensitive to the South had been confronted by the Court in 1944, when it held the white primary unconstitutional under the Fifteenth Amendment. Through the white primary, blacks had been deprived of meaningful participation in the political process in the South by being excluded from voting in Democratic primary elections.[12] Chief Justice Harlan Fiske Stone initially assigned the writing of the majority opinion in the white primary case to Justice Felix Frankfurter. After consulting with other members of the Court and discussing the matter with Frankfurter himself, Justice Robert H. Jackson wrote to Chief Justice Stone pointing out that the assignment of the opinion in the white primary case to Frankfurter would "grate on Southern sensibilities." Frankfurter, Jackson pointed out to the chief justice, "unites in a rare degree factors which unhappily excite prejudice. In the first place, he is a Jew. In the second place, he is from New England, the seat of the abolition movement. In the third place, he has not been thought of as a person particularly sympathetic with the Democratic party in the past." The contemplation of these factors, Jackson acknowledged, was utterly distasteful, but in light of the sensitivity of the invalidation of the white primary in the South, an opinion by a member of the Court less offensive to the South might make the decision of the Court more palatable there. Chief Justice Stone apparently realized the validity of Jackson's views and subsequently reassigned the white primary opinion to Justice Stanley Reed, a Protestant, native-born Kentuckian, and longtime Democrat.[13]

In light of the resentment the Court's decisions upholding the constitutionality of the public accommodations provisions of the 1964 act was likely to arouse in the South, it is not unlikely that Chief Justice Warren in selecting the author of the opinions in the *Heart of Atlanta Motel* and *McClung* cases sought to select a member of the Court who also would be less likely to "grate on Southern sensibilities." With that consideration in mind, Warren perhaps eliminated himself as a possible author of the opinions, since he was both a Republican and most prominently identified as the author of the Court's unanimous opinion in the *School Desegregation Cases,* a ruling that had stirred deep resentment and resistance in the South.[14]

Similar considerations eliminated most of the other members of the Court who had supported upholding the public accommodations provisions in the Conference. Justice Harlan was a New Yorker and a Republican, while Justice Stewart was an Ohioan and a Republican, and Justice White, while a Democrat, was from Colorado. Justice Brennan was also a Democrat, but from New Jersey, and Justice Goldberg was not only a Jew but originally from Chicago, Illinois, while Justice Douglas was a Democrat from Washington and had additionally indicated that he would sustain the public accommodations provisions under the Fourteenth Amendment, a position not shared by most of his colleagues. Justices Hugo Black and Tom Clark appeared to be the most likely candidates for the opinion assignment, since both were southerners, Black from Alabama and Clark from Texas, and both were Democrats. Black, however, had become a pariah in the South because of his staunch commitment to civil rights, including school desegregation.[15] Justice Clark thus seemed to be the logical choice to write the opinions in the *Heart of Atlanta Motel* and *McClung* cases, since as a Texan of moderately conservative judicial views, he could write opinions that might cause the least resentment in the South. In any case, whatever factors weighed most heavily in his choice, it was to Justice Tom Clark that Chief Justice Warren assigned the writing of the majority opinions in the public accommodations cases.

The views expressed by the members of the Court in Conference are sometimes only tentative, since it is not uncommon for the minds and votes of the justices to change during the opinion-writing stage of the Court's decisional process. "I myself have changed my opinion after reading the opinions of the members of the Court," Justice Robert H. Jackson once remarked. "And I am as stubborn as most. But I sometimes wind up not voting the way I voted in conference because the reasons of the majority didn't satisfy me." And similarly, Justice Brennan once observed, "I converted more than one proposed majority [opinion] into a dissent before the final decision was announced. I have also, however, had the more satisfying experience of rewriting a dissent as a majority opinion for the Court."[16]

The task of the justice assigned the writing of a majority opinion, such as Justice Clark in the public accommodations cases, is to produce an opinion that reflects a consensus of the views of the other members of the majority and to avoid if possible adopting language that may induce members of the majority to write concurring opinions or dissenting opinions that will dilute the stature and impact of the majority opinion. Pride of authorship by the writer of a majority opinion of the Court therefore becomes an early casualty in the opinion-writing process, since the author of a majority opinion must be willing to modify or even delete language originally included in the opinion, the inclusion of which is objected to by other members of the majority. A successful opinion consequently becomes essentially a compromise of the views of the justices composing the majority of the Court.[17]

Having been assigned the task of writing the opinions of the majority in the *Heart of Atlanta Motel* and *McClung* cases, Justice Clark and his clerks began drafting the opinions. Clark, however, was soon put on notice that at least one member of the Court would not be joining the opinions of the majority. As his remarks in Conference had indicated, Justice Douglas persisted in his belief that the Court's decisions should rest on the Fourteenth Amendment rather than the Commerce Clause, and early on he advised his colleagues that he would be concurring separately in the majority opinions on that basis.

In considering his decision to concur in the judgment of the Court on Fourteenth Amendment grounds, Justice Douglas had assigned one of his clerks to research the question of the extent to which Congress had relied on the Fourteenth Amendment as the constitutional basis of the public accommodations provisions of the 1964 act, as well as any precedents of the Court in which it had relied on a constitutional provision other than that relied on by Congress as the basis for sustaining acts of Congress. On the first point, Douglas's clerk reported that

> a reasonably persuasive case can be made that Congress intended to rely on its powers under the Fourteenth Amendment as well as its powers under the Commerce Clause when it enacted . . . [the public accommodations provisions] of the Civil Rights Act; that is to say, I believe that it can be argued that Congress intended to rest in part on the Fourteenth Amendment to sustain even those parts of . . . [the public accommodations provisions] which are phrased almost entirely in Commerce language.[18]

On the question of whether there were previous cases in which the Court had relied on a constitutional source of congressional power to sustain an act of Congress, although Congress itself had relied on a different source of power when enacting legislation, Douglas's clerk was less successful:

My search for U.S. Supreme Court cases saying that the constitutional label (or lack of a label) which Congress puts on an exercise of power makes no difference when this Court is passing on the constitutionality of the exercise—my search was largely fruitless. I found only two passages touching on this question (and these largely by accident since none of the search methods with which I am familiar is very helpful on this problem).[19]

Undaunted, on October 12 Douglas circulated a memorandum to his colleagues informing them that he would concur separately in the judgment of the Court sustaining the public accommodations provisions. "I think we should rest on the legislative power contained in Sec. 5 of the Fourteenth Amendment which states, 'The Congress shall have power to enforce, by appropriate legislation, the provisions of this article,'" Douglas said. In determining the reach of an exertion of congressional power, he continued, it was customary to read various granted powers together. "The 'means' used in the present Act are in my view 'appropriate' and 'plainly adapted' to the end of enforcing Fourteenth Amendment rights as well as protecting commerce." State action within the meaning of the Fourteenth Amendment, Douglas concluded, was being used to enforce discrimination in facilities of public accommodation "by the state judiciary under the trespass laws," and he cited the Court's decision in *Shelley v. Kraemer* on this point.[20]

As Justice Clark proceeded to draft the opinions in the public accommodations cases, the Court's attention was also briefly diverted in late October by the filing with the Court of a motion by Moreton Rolleston to expedite the decision in the *Heart of Atlanta Motel* case.[21] "A presidential election is imminent," Rolleston argued in his motion. "One of the candidates has endorsed the Civil Rights Act of 1964 and the other voted against it in the U.S. Senate. The people of this country are entitled to know the answer to the questions raised by this law suit so they can intelligently evaluate the candidates."[22]

Chief Justice Warren drew Justice Black's attention to the motion to expedite the decision in the *Heart of Atlanta Motel* case on October 29. "While this motion is addressed to the Court," Warren said, "it would not come up until the Conference a week from tomorrow. As Circuit Justice, I thought you should see it immediately." Although the Civil Rights Act of 1964 was a central national concern in the 1964 national elections, it was soft-pedaled as an issue by both presidential candidates. But the Republican nominee, Senator Barry Goldwater of Arizona, had voted against the act in the Senate and thus came to be identified in the public mind as the anti-black candidate in the race for the presidency, and early decisions of the Court sustaining the 1964 act's validity would doubtless have had some impact on the elections.[23]

Justice Black, however, informed Chief Justice Warren that he opposed announcing the decisions of the Court in the public accommodations cases prior to the elections. And Black soon had an ally on that point in Justice Clark, who wrote Warren on October 30 that as "you know, I am opposed to handing down either the judgment or opinion prior to the election and therefore concur in the views of Brother Black." The motion to expedite the public accommodations decisions was accordingly denied by the Court on November 9.[24]

With that momentary diversion eliminated, Justice Clark circulated his first draft of the *Heart of Atlanta Motel* opinion to the members of the Court on November 20, followed five days later by the circulation of his first draft of the opinion in the *McClung* case. When the draft opinion in the *Heart of Atlanta Motel* case was circulated, however, the Court and Clark learned that there would be yet another concurring opinion in the public accommodations cases. On November 20, Justice Black circulated a draft concurring opinion in which both public accommodations cases were discussed together, but unlike Douglas, Black relied primarily on the Commerce Clause as the basis for sustaining the constitutionality of the 1964 act.[25] Clark was thus aware that his task was to produce majority opinions that the remaining seven members of the Court could join, and the process of negotiating such an opinion among Clark and the majority justices now began in earnest, a process that would require four circulations by Clark of the draft opinion in the *Heart of Atlanta Motel* case and three circulations in the *McClung* case.

On November 21, the first draft of the *Heart of Atlanta Motel* opinion drew a mostly positive response from Justice White. In a memo to Clark, White said, "Please join me in your opinion. I have only one or two very minor suggestions. I would prefer not to rely on *Hall v. DeCuir*," which Clark had cited in his opinion. In *Hall v. DeCuir*, decided in 1878, the Court had invalidated a Reconstruction-era Louisiana statute prohibiting racial discrimination by operators of public transportation facilities within the state. The Court held that the application of the statute to a steamboat operating in interstate commerce on the Mississippi River was an unconstitutional state regulation of an aspect of interstate commerce exclusively reserved to Congress for regulation under the Commerce Clause. Clark's point was of course that the necessary implication of the decision in *Hall v. DeCuir* was that Congress could regulate public accommodations under the Commerce Clause, but in response to White's objection, *Hall v. DeCuir* was mentioned only in a quotation from another case in the final draft of the *Heart of Atlanta Motel* opinion.[26]

Justice Stewart responded to Clark's first draft of the *Heart of Atlanta Motel* opinion on November 24. "I am in substantial agreement with your thorough and well-reasoned opinion in this case," Stewart informed Clark.

"There is, however, one small portion which gives me pause." Clark seemed to suggest in the opinion, Stewart noted, that the Court was required in passing on the constitutional validity of congressional legislation to confine itself to relying on the constitutional basis on which Congress had itself relied in enacting the legislation. But in his view, Stewart said, the Court could rely on any provision of the Constitution if it sustained congressional action, whether relied on by Congress or not. "In order to give specificity to my thoughts, I enclose a draft suggesting the kind of language I have in mind to eliminate the implication which causes me concern," Stewart said, but added a rather direct threat of filing a concurring opinion on the point if Clark refused to modify the opinion. "If you find such change in emphasis unacceptable," he concluded, "I can, of course, write a short separate concurrence, but I'd much prefer to join your excellent opinion for the Court."[27]

Clark immediately incorporated Stewart's views in a draft opinion in the *Heart of Atlanta Motel* case that was recirculated on November 27, and on Stewart's memo Clark wrote, "All incorporated." On the same day as the recirculation, Stewart was successfully brought into the fold. "I am glad to join the fine opinion you have written for the Court in this case," Stewart informed Clark.[28] Chief Justice Warren also approved Clark's second draft of the *Heart of Atlanta Motel* opinion on December 2. As to the second draft, Warren wrote, "*I agree* and of course the tail (No. 543) [the *McClung* case] goes with the hide," indicating that the same reasoning that sustained the application of the public accommodations provisions to the Heart of Atlanta Motel would sustain their application in the *McClung* case. "*Bueno,*" Warren added.[29]

Justice White's acquiescence in Clark's work, however, was somewhat more difficult to obtain. In a November 30 memo to Clark addressing both the *Heart of Atlanta Motel* and the *McClung* opinions, White said, "I like the *McClung* opinion better," although he was still troubled by one paragraph in that opinion. "With regard to the *Heart of Atlanta* opinion," he added, "the material at the top of page 10 gives me some pause. Perhaps we can chat about this, too."[30] The material troubling White was a discussion of the *Civil Rights Cases* of 1883 by Clark, in which he attempted to demonstrate that the Court in those cases had not rejected the idea that a public accommodations act could be based on the Commerce Clause. In the 1883 cases, however, the Court had said, "Of course, no one will contend that the power to pass . . . [the Civil Rights Act of 1875] was contained in the Constitution before the adoption of the last three amendments [the Thirteenth, Fourteenth, and Fifteenth Amendments]."[31]

Since the Commerce Clause had been a source of congressional power since 1789, well before the adoption of the Civil War amendments, this passage could be construed to deny that Congress possessed the power to pass a public accommodations act under the Commerce Clause, a point that had been raised by Moreton Rolleston on behalf of the Heart of Atlanta Motel. In his draft opinion in the *Heart of Atlanta Motel* case, however, Clark denied that this was the meaning to be attributed to this language in the 1883 cases. This "expressed what was universally acknowledged prior to these [Civil War] Amendments—that the Constitution recognized slavery prior to the adoption and that problem was left to the states," Clark argued. "Hence Congress had no power, even under the Commerce Clause, to enact a public accommodation statute requiring equal treatment for slaves."[32]

Apparently in response to Justice White's reservations regarding this paragraph, it was dropped by Justice Clark from the final version of the *Heart of Atlanta Motel* opinion. Instead, Clark in the final version said:

> Though the Court observed that "no one will contend that the power to pass . . . [the Civil Rights Act of 1875] was contained in the Constitution before the adoption of the last three amendments [Thirteenth, Fourteenth, and Fifteenth]," the Court went on specifically to note that the Act was not "conceived" in terms of the commerce power and expressly pointed out: "Of course, these remarks [as to the lack of congressional power] do not apply to those cases in which Congress is clothed with direct and plenary powers of legislation over the whole subject, accompanied with an express or implied denial of such power to the States, as in the regulation of commerce with foreign nations, among the several States, and with the Indian tribes. . . . In these cases Congress has power to pass laws for regulating the subjects specified in every detail, and the conduct and transactions of individuals in respect thereof."

When this language was included along with other more minor changes in Clark's December 4 circulation of the *Heart of Atlanta Motel* opinion, White responded positively on December 7. "Dear Tom," White wrote, "I am with you on your December 4 circulation."[33]

On the Warren Court, Justice William Brennan was recognized as the member of the Court most adept at marshaling a consensus among the members of the Court in the resolution of cases, and he appears to have assumed that role in the public accommodations cases by advising Clark regarding how to avoid pitfalls that might divide the majority justices.[34] Just such a pitfall was identified by Brennan in Clark's first circulation of the draft of the *Heart of Atlanta Motel* opinion. In that draft Clark had written:

> Nor is there any merit in the contention that Title II [the public accommodations provisions] is invalid because it requires motels to fur-

nish lodging to Negroes traveling solely on intrastate journeys. To permit covered establishments to require proof of interstate status would perpetuate the very burden that the Act seeks to eliminate.

Clark continued:

Congress therefore had ample basis for extending coverage to include intrastate travelers. It is well settled that Congress may "choose [any] means reasonably adapted to the attainment of the permitted end, . . . and necessary to effectuate its regulation of interstate commerce. . . ." It has acted well within that power in requiring that motels furnish accommodations to "transients."[35]

Justice Brennan apparently believed that this language might prove troublesome with regard to building a consensus among the majority justices, and he expressed his concerns to Clark on November 25. "Dear Tom," Brennan wrote,

I fully agree that travelers on intrastate journeys are covered in the case of any motel which also caters to interstate transients. It is in that context that I understand you discuss the problem. But what of the case of the motel which deals exclusively with intrastate customers? Should that question be expressly laid to one side or should we go all out and say that this must be such a rare motel that it is swept within the congressional power to deal generally with local activities having a substantial and harmful effect upon commerce? Your present treatment lends itself to the latter reading and I am fully content with it. I had supposed that someone else, particularly John [Harlan], might be concerned about it. If no one else is concerned perhaps we ought to let sleeping dogs lie.[36]

As Brennan and Clark were undoubtedly aware from the expressions of views in the Conference regarding the public accommodations cases, the member of the Court whose agreement with the majority opinions in the cases might be the most difficult to obtain was Justice Harlan. Although in Conference he had expressed no doubt regarding the validity of the 1964 act's applicability to the Heart of Atlanta Motel, Harlan had expressed serious doubt regarding the Commerce Clause rationale for the act's applicability to Ollie's Barbecue and thus had only tentatively voted to reverse in the *McClung* case. Harlan was also the most conservative member of the Court on many issues, and he had an abiding belief in the principle of federalism in the constitutional order and the importance of preserving the powers of the states from federal encroachment.[37] The very broad interpretation of the reach of the commerce power embodied in Clark's first draft, Brennan thus perceived, might have the effect of driving Harlan from the majority fold. Harlan's participation as a member of the majority, on the other hand, was quite important, since he was greatly respected for his well-considered and well-reasoned opinions and the care that he devoted to the work of the Court. His participation as a member of the majority in the public accommodations cases was also probably of considerable symbolic importance, since he was the grandson of the sole dissenter in the *Civil Rights Cases* of 1883, John Marshall Harlan I.

While Justice Brennan anticipated opposition from Justice Harlan to any language in the majority opinion sustaining the application of the public accommodations provisions to intrastate travelers, one of Harlan's clerks expressed no such reservations in a memo to Harlan discussing the constitutional issues in the public accommodations cases. "If motels and hotels may be regulated if they offer lodging to interstate travelers, it would also seem permissible for Congress to regulate them if they also serve intrastate travelers whenever it would be burdensome to separate the two," the clerk advised Harlan.

> It is probably clear that no white person would be asked whether or not he was moving in interstate commerce, but Negroes might be subjected to the test of proving their interstate status if the Act were so limited. Ever since the *Shreveport Rate Case* . . . , the Court has upheld congressional regulation of intrastate commerce when it involved a reasonable choice of means to aid interstate commerce. . . . I think Congress could have determined that Negroes should not be put to the proof of showing that they are traveling interstate before they must be offered lodging, and that in order to protect interstate travelers, Congress can legitimately cover all transients.[38]

Justice Harlan's clerk also expressed no reservations regarding the application of the Civil Rights Act to Ollie's Barbecue in Birmingham, although Harlan himself of course expressed serious misgivings on that point both during the oral argument and in the Conference. The clerk advised Harlan:

> The Civil Rights Act of 1964, in title II, carefully defines each public accommodation covered by the Act in terms of its effect upon interstate commerce. Given the legislative fact-finding upon which this act was probably based, I think that those portions of title II which rely on the Commerce Clause are constitutional.[39]

As Justice Brennan had correctly perceived, however, Justice Harlan had serious concerns regarding not only the validity of the application of the public accommodations provisions to Ollie's Barbecue but also the broad scope of the commerce power supported by the government in the public accommodations cases. Those concerns led Harlan at one point to draft a separate opinion in the cases, in which he concurred in the majority opinion's conclusion that the act was valid as applied to the Heart of Atlanta Motel but dissented from the judgment of the Court upholding the application of the act to Ollie's Barbecue. In this draft opinion, Harlan clearly expressed his views regarding the proper scope of the commerce power as well as his initial belief that the Civil Rights Act was unconstitutional as applied to restaurants serving interstate food.

Harlan said in his draft opinion:

The Civil Rights Act of 1964 was passed in furtherance of a noble ideal; the intent of the bill is to remove a blot on the national conscience of which the nation has become acutely aware since the pioneering decision of this Court in *Brown v. Board of Education*. But worthy as is the object of this Act, I cannot commend its method of passage. The legislative history clearly reveals that its framers, once having settled upon its general objective, rummaged in the closet of constitutional powers to find a constitutional peg on which to hang it. The Civil Rights amendments to the Constitution apparently would not support legislation directed at private citizens acting in a private capacity. Therefore, faith was placed primarily on the commerce clause which served in the 30s as the basis of the far-reaching economic legislation of the New Deal. It is argued that Congress holds plenary powers over all phases of American life which affect commerce, and that these broad powers clearly encompass the Civil Rights Act of 1964. I intend to take a lawyer-like look at the scope of this power, to inquire as to its limits and to determine, free of any preconceived bias that this legislation is morally good or bad, whether the commerce clause encompasses the power to enact the sections of the Civil Rights Act of 1964 involved in the cases before the Court.[40]

"Two obvious, but to me startling and unsettling, observations may be made at the outset," Harlan continued.

First, if the commerce power is what some now suppose it to be, the people of the United States went to a great deal of unnecessary trouble in passing an amendment to prohibit states from discriminating. By a simple majority vote of Congress not only could discriminatory state action have been foreclosed, but, as this Act bears witness, a substantial measure of discriminatory private action could have been foreclosed as well. Second, in this modern world, it must be conceded that nearly every phase of daily life has an effect on commerce. An interpretation of the commerce clause permitting Congress to regulate all activities which affect commerce would leave Congress free to regulate virtually anything. To those upset by such a possibility the sole comfort offered, short of the safeguards of the Bill of Rights, is the hope that a majority of the people's representatives in Congress will choose never to abuse such an extraordinary power.[41]

In language reminiscent of Moreton Rolleston's argument in the *Heart of Atlanta Motel* case, Harlan said:

Our federal system was originally created by the delegation of certain powers to the national government and the reservation of all other powers to the states and to the people. If we are to accept a proposition that Congress may, if it chooses, regulate all things which have any effect on commerce, then it should be clearly recognized that the federal structure, as originally conceived, is a dead letter—that a new order has been introduced in which the states hold their regulatory powers at the sufferance of the national government. I, for one, am not anxious to accept an interpretation of the commerce clause which leads to such conclusions, and will not do so unless cases decided by this Court compel me.[42]

There had been continual conflict on the Court among those justices who feared that a limitless commerce power could be used to undermine state sovereignty, Harlan said, and those who desired to uphold congressional power under the Commerce Clause in the case at hand and to leave worries regarding possible limits of the commerce power to those occasions when abuses arose. One line of the Court's commerce decisions sustained congressional power to regulate or prohibit the movement in interstate commerce of certain evil or harmful subjects, such as prostitutes, lottery tickets, products manufactured by child labor, and the like, he acknowledged, while another line of cases sustained congressional legislation regulating activities that substantially affected interstate commerce. And it was under the latter line of cases that the Civil Rights Act of 1964, it was argued, could be constitutionally sustained.[43]

At one time, Harlan pointed out, the Court had

framed limitations on the commerce power in conceptual terms—burdens on the "flow" of commerce were "direct" or "indirect"—but

NLRB v. Jones [and] Laughlin Corp. turned away from any such conceptual approaches and looked directly to the substantiality of the effect on commerce of the activity regulated. *Wickard v. Filburn* pointed out that substantiality "is a matter of degree."[44]

Because *Wickard v. Filburn* "is regarded as one of the most far-reaching of the commerce cases," Harlan said, "I think it profitable to observe how truly substantial were the effects on commerce on which it was based." While Filburn grew wheat on his farm for home consumption as food, feed, and seed, Harlan pointed out that the total production of wheat for home consumption nationally constituted approximately 20 percent of the average wheat production. Effective congressional regulation of the interstate price of wheat could thus not be effective without regulation of the production of wheat for home consumption, since farmers might sell such wheat in interstate commerce if induced to do so by rising prices, with the resultant effect of reducing the price of wheat in commerce. The *Wickard* case, Harlan argued, therefore "demonstrated a high degree of substantiality, a degree which, if required of all congressional action under the commerce clause, would provide an effective substitute for the conceptual limitations discarded by *Jones [and] Laughlin.*"[45]

In addition to the limitation imposed on the power of Congress under the Commerce Clause by the requirement that activities being regulated must substantially affect interstate commerce, Harlan noted, were the limitations on governmental power included in the Bill of Rights:

> This, then, is the approach which I derive from existing cases—that Congress may regulate activities which affect commerce if the effect is substantial and if the need for economic regulation is not outweighed by the degree of infringement it entails upon the rights guaranteed citizens by the Bill of Rights.[46]

The Civil Rights Act of 1964, he continued, contained no legislative findings of fact demonstrating how racial discrimination in facilities of public accommodation substantially affected interstate commerce beyond "conclusory declarations" that such effects existed. This circumstance, he said, "makes the Court's role difficult," but he refused to accept the proposition that the Court

> should look to any theory which might have supported the legislation on any factual basis which Congress could, within the bounds of rationality, have found to be true. Adoption of such an abject approach

by the Court would render the "degree of substantiality" limitation on the commerce power largely illusory, for merely by passing legislation regulating activities asserted to affect commerce Congress would greatly foreclose Court inquiry.

For the courts to surrender their power to determine independently the validity of the facts and theories upon which Congress based its exercise of the commerce power, Harlan argued, would result in an essentially limitless power under the Commerce Clause. To the argument that the integrity of Congress would prevent abuses of such a power, Harlan answered that

> as our Constitution was designed, this was not meant to be the only check on the use of power. Our system of government was meant to be more sophisticated than simple majority rule. The duty rests upon the Court to determine if the facts exist necessary to bring the commerce power to bear. It would be an abdication of the judicial function to do otherwise.

In determining whether activities regulated by Congress substantially affected commerce, he argued, detailed legislative findings incorporated in an act "based on solid evidence" should be given "great weight"; findings embodied in committee reports but not in the act itself should be given less weight; and evidence produced at congressional hearings and floor debates should be given yet less weight by the courts.[47]

Harlan then proceeded to examine the evidence in the legislative record regarding the Civil Rights Act indicating that racial discrimination by motels and hotels in fact substantially affected interstate commerce, and he concluded that discrimination by hotels and motels did substantially affect commerce by discouraging and burdening interstate travel by blacks. He reserved judgment, however, on the question of whether the act could validly be applied to intrastate travelers. With regard to the validity of the act's application to Ollie's Barbecue, on the other hand, he concluded that discrimination by restaurants serving food a substantial amount of which had moved in interstate commerce had not been shown by the legislative record to substantially affect commerce. The act as applied in the *McClung* case, he therefore concluded, was constitutionally invalid.[48]

The legislative record of the Civil Rights Act contained no evidence "dealing particularly with restaurants serving only intrastate patrons but buying substantial amounts of food through interstate channels, *e.g.,* Ollie's Barbecue," Harlan pointed out.

The theory which most clearly fits this section of the statute is that segregation in restaurants serving interstate food may lead to civil rights protests, picketing and sit-ins, which in turn might have the effect of reducing the restaurants' patronage with a consequent reduction in the restaurants' demand for food which has moved in interstate commerce. But there was no evidence beyond conjecture to show that reduction in demand for interstate food had actually taken place. Nor was the fact dealt with that the people who do not eat at picketed restaurants must eat somewhere else. A real demand reduction would be brought about only if racial discrimination caused people to eat less, not eat elsewhere.

It was also significant that Ollie's Barbecue purchased its food from a local wholesaler rather than directly in interstate commerce, Harlan argued, since if the McClungs lost business because of civil rights protests, "it is likely that some other restaurants or grocery stores having accounts with the wholesaler will pick up the business."[49]

Harlan acknowledged that Congress had considered evidence that racial disputes and disorders that were largely caused by racial discrimination in facilities of public accommodation, including restaurants, adversely affected interstate commerce, and he conceded that it could not "be doubted that these disturbances have had an effect on commerce." But he rejected the contention that Congress could validly prohibit racial discrimination by restaurants serving interstate food as a means of eliminating the causes of racial disputes and their adverse effects on commerce. He argued:

> First, the statute does not fit the theory. Its logic calls for statutory coverage of all restaurants; there is no indication whatsoever that restaurants serving insubstantial amounts of interstate food do not contribute as much to civil rights disturbances as restaurants serving substantial amounts of interstate food. Second, if this theory is accepted, there are no limits short of the Bill of Rights to the forms of discrimination within congressional reach.

General federal legislation would be permissible, he warned, on any subject "which a psychoanalysis of the Negro disturbances reveals to be a contributing cause."[50]

Harlan concluded:

> Without specific evidence that racial discrimination has given rise to a substantial disruption of the lines of interstate food distribution or to a substantial decrease in the overall demand for interstate food, the fact

that a restaurant serves food which has moved in interstate commerce is not sufficient to empower Congress to ban discrimination on its premises under the asserted theory. The application of the Act to Ollie's Barbecue solely on the basis that a substantial part of the food sold by it at one time moved in commerce is unconstitutional, and the decision of the court below must be affirmed.[51]

As Harlan's draft opinion indicated, Justice Brennan was correct in his judgment that Harlan would not accept Justice Clark's initial language in the *Heart of Atlanta Motel* opinion that the public accommodations provisions were valid as applied to intrastate travelers. And it was also clear that a dissent by Justice Harlan in the *McClung* case could be avoided only (if at all) by language in Justice Clark's opinion for the majority in that case demonstrating that racial discrimination in restaurants serving interstate food had substantial effects on interstate commerce beyond the possible reduction of food purchases in commerce. Justice Clark's principal task consequently became one of producing majority opinions in both of the public accommodations cases that would satisfy Justice Harlan on these points and keep him in the majority fold.

Justice Brennan's perception that Clark's discussion of the applicability of the public accommodations provisions to intrastate travelers might be troublesome for Justice Harlan proved to be prescient, since on December 1 Harlan responded to Clark's draft of the *Heart of Atlanta Motel* opinion and raised the same issue. "I have indicated on the enclosed copy of your opinion a few suggestions," Harlan informed Clark, "only three of which seem to require special comment." He suggested a minor change in the discussion of the Court's jurisdiction and the deletion of a paragraph that "seemed to me a bit tangential in the context of this case." But his most significant objection was to Clark's discussion of the applicability of the public accommodations provisions to intrastate travelers:

I don't see why we have to get into the "transients" problem in the context of this case where there is no dispute that this motel did serve interstate travelers, and I would leave for another day the question of whether the Act can constitutionally be applied to motels serving only *intrastate* travelers. With these and other changes indicated on the enclosed copy, I am ready to join your opinion.[52]

Instead of Clark's discussion of the power of Congress to regulate intrastate travelers under the Commerce Clause, Harlan suggested that Clark add a footnote to the opinion on that point. The footnote, he said, could read, "Nor need we decide whether the Act is constitutional as applied to a motel which serves only intrastate transients, since it was stipulated in this case that appellant served interstate travelers, and the Act contains a broad severability clause." Clark responded by not only deleting the disputed passages on intrastate travelers in his December 4 draft circulation but also adding the footnote as suggested by Harlan. Even the footnote, however, was eliminated from the final opinion in the *Heart of Atlanta Motel* case.[53]

Justice Clark circulated the first draft of the opinion in the *McClung* case on November 25, and although the application of the public accommodations provisions to Ollie's Barbecue raised a much more problematic question under the Commerce Clause than that raised in the *Heart of Atlanta Motel* case, the *McClung* opinion produced fewer suggestions for changes from the majority justices than did the opinion in the motel case. The most substantial changes in the *McClung* opinion were suggested by Justice Brennan and, not surprisingly, Justice Harlan. In the first draft of the *McClung* opinion, Clark cited *McDermott v. Wisconsin*[54] and *United States v. Sullivan*[55] in discussing the scope of congressional power under the Commerce Clause. In the *McDermott* case, the Court invalidated a Wisconsin statute requiring the labeling of food items offered for retail sale on the ground that the statute conflicted with the labeling requirements of the federal food and drug act, and in doing so, sustained under the Commerce Clause the application of the federal food and drug act's labeling requirements to goods offered for retail sale after the interstate movement of the goods had clearly ceased. And in the *Sullivan* case, the Court similarly sustained under the Commerce Clause the labeling requirements of the federal food and drug act to the retail sale of pills that had moved in interstate commerce.

In citing the *McDermott* and *Sullivan* cases, Justice Clark was of course attempting to demonstrate the broad reach of the commerce power, but his reliance on those cases drew an objection from Justice Brennan on November 25. "I think *McClung* is a really fine job and I am happy to join it," Brennan wrote Clark, but added that he had "only some minor suggestions."

> I think reliance on *Sullivan* and *McDermott* presents the danger of expanding federal power without a visible stopping place, and I do think the problem of regulating the goods themselves as a reason for barring products from interstate commerce is quite different from the problem we are dealing with here. Your opinion without that material fully supports the exercise of federal power in this case.[56]

In response to Brennan's objection, Clark removed any reference to the *McDermott* and *Sullivan* cases in the *McClung* opinion.

In addition to Justice Clark as the author of the majority opinion, Justice

Brennan was also apparently concerned that the *McClung* opinion should rely on substantial effects on interstate commerce resulting from discrimination in restaurants other than food purchases in commerce. And indeed he assigned one of his clerks to lobby Harlan's clerks regarding the effects on commerce of racial discrimination in restaurants. "I have spoken to Justice Harlan's clerks concerning his doubt about evidence in the record of economic effects of discrimination in restaurants serving interstate food," the clerk reported to Brennan. Three kinds of effects were possible, he suggested: (1) the distortion of purchasing patterns caused by the limited access blacks had to restaurants; (2) the impact of sit-ins and demonstrations against segregated restaurants, thus affecting the amount of interstate food they purchased; and (3) the economic effects of such demonstrations on other businesses, also reducing their purchases of interstate products.[57]

For his part, Justice Clark also sought to remove Harlan's doubts regarding the effect on commerce produced by racial discrimination in restaurants. In his November 25 draft of the *McClung* opinion, citing *Wickard v. Filburn*,[58] Clark thus argued that while racial discrimination in a small restaurant like Ollie's Barbecue in Birmingham might result in a quite limited reduction in the amount of food purchased by the restaurant in interstate commerce, racial discrimination in all similarly situated restaurants nationally would result in reductions in food purchases in commerce that were "far from trivial." Clark continued:

> This principle takes on added significance in view of the further testimony [before congressional committees considering the act of 1964] that racial discrimination by one restaurant in a city encouraged the practice throughout the area because of the other proprietors' fear of the competitive advantage gained by the segregated restaurant in increased white trade. Thus if Congress had limited coverage of the Act to those large restaurants which clearly cater to interstate patrons there would have existed a very real danger of injury to interstate commerce resulting from this competitive disadvantage.[59]

Clark's language on this point produced a divided reaction on the part of Justice Harlan's clerks as they advised him on the *McClung* opinion. In a memo to Harlan on Clark's November 25 draft of the opinion, one of Harlan's clerks pointed out that his fellow clerk "takes issue with the language . . . relating to competition on the ground that it may be a dangerous precedent for extending congressional power to any business in competition with a business which could be reached under the Commerce Clause." As to his own viewpoint, the clerk said, "I am not troubled by it, since I don't think that this would extend congressional power any further, and I believe the argument has force in the context of this case."[60]

The language regarding competition in the *McClung* opinion, however, also disturbed Justice Harlan, and in a memo to Clark on November 27, he urged its deletion from the *McClung* opinion. "The paragraph on p. 7, which I have marked for deletion, may have repercussions for the future which I am sure that you do not intend," Harlan informed Clark. From this language, he pointed out, "it might be taken that the commerce power extends to organizations and individuals in competition with those over whom such power exists, even though the former would not otherwise be subject to congressional power." "I would prefer to see the paragraph eliminated," Harlan said, "and do not think its omission could weaken the argument made at this juncture."[61]

In his November 25 draft of the *McClung* opinion, Clark had also discussed the overall effects on interstate commerce of racial discrimination in restaurants as justifying congressional application of the public accommodations provisions to restaurants, leaving aside any effects such discrimination might have by reducing interstate food purchases. On this point, however, Justice Harlan had a further suggestion for the inclusion of additional language in the opinion. "The absence of evidence directly connecting discriminatory restaurant service with the flow of interstate food," he suggested as additional language, "a factor on which the appellees place much reliance, is not, given the evidence as to the effect of such practices on other aspects of commerce, a crucial matter." With the adoption of the changes he had suggested, Harlan added, "I shall be happy to join your opinion and I think you have done a very good job."[62]

In his November 27 recirculation of the *McClung* opinion, Clark adopted all of the changes that had been suggested by both Harlan and Brennan and included word for word the additional language Harlan had suggested, despite its awkwardness.[63] In response to the November 27 circulation, Justice Stewart wrote Clark that "I am glad to join the fine opinion you have written for the Court in this case." And after another, and final, recirculation of the *McClung* opinion on December 4, Justice White also approved Clark's effort. "I am with you on your circulation of December 4," White informed Clark on December 7.[64]

Even after the adoption of the changes in the November 27 draft of the *McClung* opinion that he had suggested, however, Justice Harlan remained unsatisfied. On November 30, he therefore wrote Clark that after "careful deliberation, I have decided that I can join your recirculation of November 27," but he insisted on yet more changes. Regarding the discussion of the effects on interstate commerce of racial discrimination in restaurants, Harlan said, he would add, "and finally there was plentiful evidence of the fact that discrimination created profound and continuing unrest with the resultant reduction in sales by business in general." In response, Clark added in the final draft of the *McClung* opinion, "In addition, there were many references to discriminatory situations causing wide unrest and having a depressant effect on general business conditions in the respective communities."[65] Harlan also suggested that language be added indicating the fact that racial discrimination discouraged the location of new businesses in areas where the practice was widespread and that the language be rephrased to discuss the point that findings by Congress on the effects of racial discrimination on commerce were unnecessary, changes that were also incorporated by Clark in the December 4 draft of the *McClung* opinion. Finally, with these changes in the opinion, Harlan was satisfied.[66]

By early December, therefore, it appeared that Clark had successfully drafted opinions in the *Heart of Atlanta Motel* and *McClung* cases that were joined by seven members of the Court, with Justices Black and Douglas concurring separately. Justice Goldberg, however, continued to hesitate to join Clark's opinions because of their reliance exclusively on the Commerce Clause as the constitutional basis of the public accommodations provisions and their failure consequently to discuss the Fourteenth Amendment as an alternative basis for the act. Indeed, one of Justice Douglas's clerks reported to the justice in late November that apparently

> it is Justice Goldberg's intention to urge Justice Clark to include in his opinion for the Court a statement to the effect that the 14th Amendment supports even the commerce-language sections of the Act, together with some elaboration on the point. If the Court will buy that, then Justice Goldberg will not concur separately. But I think he will end up writing himself, or joining you if you incorporate something to meet his point. (All this is gleaned from one of his law clerks, as you no doubt guessed.)[67]

At one point, Goldberg in fact circulated but then withdrew a brief concurring opinion, in which he stated his agreement with Clark's opinions but noted his view that the public accommodations provisions could also have been enacted by Congress under section five of the Fourteenth Amendment, and that "the primary purpose of the Civil Rights Act of 1964 is the vindication of human dignity and not mere economics." But since the public accommodations provisions were plainly valid under the Commerce Clause, Goldberg added, "it is unnecessary to consider whether . . . [they are] additionally supportable by Congress' exertion of power under sec. 5 of the Fourteenth Amendment." On his copy of this draft concurrence by Goldberg, Justice Clark wrote, "He withdrew this."[68]

On December 7, Goldberg wrote Clark that if "the suggestions I have made to you are agreeable, I gladly join in your excellent opinions in the above cases."[69] Goldberg's "suggestions" undoubtedly regarded a discussion of the Fourteenth Amendment as an alternative constitutional basis for the 1964 act, but any inclusion of such a discussion would have driven Justice Harlan from the majority fold, since he had indicated in the Conference that he continued to support the holding in the *Civil Rights Cases* of 1883 denying that Congress could validly enact a public accommodations statute under section five of the Fourteenth Amendment.

Justice Goldberg's bargaining power with Justice Clark was consequently weak, since acceptance of his Fourteenth Amendment views would probably trigger a partial dissent from Justice Harlan. On the other hand, Goldberg had previously indicated in Conference his support for the validity of the public accommodations provisions under the Commerce Clause as well as the Fourteenth Amendment, and a refusal by Clark to accept Goldberg's Fourteenth Amendment views would at most trigger a concurring opinion by Goldberg expressing those views. The potential cost of including Goldberg's views in the opinions of the Court was thus relatively high, while the cost of refusing to accept them was relatively low.

On the same day as his memo to Clark, Goldberg consequently wrote Justice Douglas, enclosing a draft of a possible concurring opinion. "I am more and more reluctant to let Hugo's [Justice Black's] separate opinion stand alone in these cases. What do you think about the attached?" Finally, on December 11, Goldberg circulated his concurring opinion in the public accommodations cases, and Justice Clark thus learned that his opinions would now speak for six rather than seven members of the Court.[70]

With Clark's opinions for the majority in the *Heart of Atlanta Motel* and *McClung* cases now receiving the approval of six members of the Court, and the concurring opinions of Justices Black, Douglas, and Goldberg finalized, the Court's decisions in the cases were ready to be announced. On December 14, 1964, the public at large thus learned the fate of the public accommodations provisions of the Civil Rights Act of 1964.

7

THE SUPREME COURT'S DECISIONS
AND THEIR AFTERMATH

The decisions of the Supreme Court in the *Heart of Atlanta Motel* and *Mc-Clung* cases were publicly announced on December 14, 1964. As the internal deliberations of the Court had indicated, the result was a total victory for Solicitor General Archibald Cox and the government as the public accommodations provisions of the Civil Rights Act of 1964 were unanimously sustained by the Court. Justice Tom Clark announced the majority opinions in the two cases, while Justices Goldberg, Douglas, and Black concurred in the decisions of the majority.[1]

After reciting the proceedings before the three-judge court in Atlanta, the factual background of the case and the contentions of the parties, along with the legislative history and description of the provisions of the Civil Rights Act, Justice Clark noted that while the public accommodations provisions at issue in the *Heart of Atlanta Motel* case were partially based on section five of the Fourteenth Amendment, they were primarily based on the Commerce Clause. Clark said:

> Our study of the legislative record, made in the light of prior cases, has brought us to the conclusion that Congress possessed ample power in this regard, and we have therefore not considered the other grounds relied upon. This is not to say that the remaining authority upon which it acted was not adequate, a question upon which we do not pass, but merely that since the commerce power is sufficient for our decision here we have considered it alone.[2]

Clark then addressed the relevance of the *Civil Rights Cases* of 1883 and the Court's ruling that the Civil Rights Act of 1875 was invalid under the Fourteenth Amendment, decisions that had been so heavily relied on by Moreton Rolleston in his attack on the public accommodations provisions of the 1964 act. Clark pointed out that the Civil Rights Act of 1875 had been based on section five of the Fourteenth Amendment and that consequently the Court considered the *Civil Rights Cases* "inapposite, and without precedential value in determining the constitutionality of the present Act," since the 1964 act was based on the Commerce Clause and not the Fourteenth Amendment. Even if the 1875 act had been based on the Commerce

Clause, Clark indicated, a ruling that the 1875 act was invalid under the Commerce Clause would not be dispositive of the validity of the 1964 act. The fact "that certain kinds of businesses may not in 1875 have been sufficiently involved in interstate commerce to warrant bringing them within the ambit of the commerce power is not necessarily dispositive of the same question today," he said.

> Our populace had not reached its present mobility, nor were facilities, goods and services circulating as readily in interstate commerce as they are today. Although the principles which we apply today are those first formulated by Chief Justice John Marshall in Gibbons v. Ogden . . . , the conditions of transportation and commerce have changed dramatically, and we must apply those principles to the present state of commerce. The sheer increase in volume of interstate traffic alone would give discriminatory practices which inhibit travel a far greater impact upon the Nation's commerce than such practices had on the economy of another day.[3]

Although in the *Civil Rights Cases* of 1883, the Court had stated that no one would have contended that Congress possessed the power to enact the Civil Rights Act of 1875 prior to the Civil War Amendments, Clark admitted, other language of the Court in those cases indicated that it had not considered the validity of the 1875 act under the Commerce Clause. "Since the commerce power was not relied on by the Government and was without support in the record [in the *Civil Rights Cases* of 1883], it is understandable that the Court narrowed its inquiry and excluded the Commerce Clause as a possible source of power," he continued.

> In any event, it is clear that such a limitation renders the opinion devoid of authority for the proposition that the Commerce Clause gives no power to Congress to regulate discriminatory practices now found substantially to affect interstate commerce. We, therefore, conclude that the Civil Rights Cases have no relevance to the basis of decision here where the Act explicitly relies upon the commerce power, and where the record is filled with testimony of obstructions and restraints resulting from the discriminations found to be existing.[4]

Justice Clark then reviewed the evidence in the legislative record of the 1964 act, which indicated that discrimination in facilities of public accommodation, particularly hotels and motels, had the effect of discouraging interstate travel by blacks because of the difficulties they encountered in finding accommodations willing to serve them. After citing numerous examples of testimony before Congress on this point, Clark declined to "burden this opinion with further details since the voluminous testimony presents overwhelming evidence that discrimination by hotels and motels impedes interstate travel."[5]

"The power of Congress to deal with these obstructions depends on the meaning of the Commerce Clause," Clark then pointed out. "Its meaning was first enunciated 140 years ago by the great Chief Justice John Marshall in Gibbons v. Ogden." He then quoted extensively from Marshall's opinion in *Gibbons v. Ogden,* in which Marshall had defined not only interstate commerce but also the power of Congress to regulate commerce in the broadest of terms. In light of Marshall's interpretation of the Commerce Clause, Clark said, "the determinative test of the exercise of power by the Congress under the Commerce Clause is simply whether the activity sought to be regulated is 'commerce which concerns more States than one' and has a real and substantial relation to the national interest."[6]

Justice Clark pointed out that, contrary to Moreton Rolleston's contention, the Court had held as early as 1849 that the movement of persons among the states was interstate commerce, and that holding had been reaffirmed on numerous subsequent occasions, including rulings sustaining under the Commerce Clause congressional prohibitions of racial discrimination in facilities of interstate commerce. Congress had also utilized its power under the Commerce Clause, Clark noted, to enact a host of legislation regulating such various subjects as gambling, criminal enterprises, deceptive trade practices, fraudulent securities transactions, misbranding of drugs, wages and hours, the protection of the right of workers to form labor unions, crop control, and many others. "That Congress was legislating against moral wrongs in many of these areas rendered its enactments no less valid," Clark added.

> In framing Title II of this [Civil Rights] Act Congress was also dealing with what it considered a moral problem. But that fact does not detract from the overwhelming evidence of the disruptive effect that racial discrimination has had on commercial intercourse. It was this burden which empowered Congress to enact appropriate legislation, and, given this basis for the exercise of its power, Congress was not restricted by the fact that the particular obstruction to interstate commerce with which it was dealing was also deemed a moral and social wrong.[7]

To Moreton Rolleston's argument that the operations of the Heart of Atlanta Motel were local in character, Justice Clark answered, citing such precedents as the *Jones and Laughlin* case and *United States v. Darby,* that the power of Congress under the Commerce Clause and Necessary and Proper

Clause included the power to regulate not only interstate commerce itself but also local activities that substantially affected interstate commerce. He continued:

> Thus the power of Congress to promote interstate commerce also includes the power to regulate the local incidents thereof, including local activities in both the States of origin and destination, which might have a substantial and harmful effect upon that commerce. One need only examine the evidence which we have discussed above to see that Congress may—as it has—prohibit racial discrimination by motels serving travelers, however "local" their operations may appear.[8]

Having sustained the public accommodations provisions as applied to the Heart of Atlanta Motel as a valid exercise of the Commerce Clause, Justice Clark proceeded to give short shrift to Moreton Rolleston's contentions that the provisions deprived the Heart of Atlanta Motel of liberty and property without due process of law in violation of the Fifth Amendment and imposed involuntary servitude on the owners of the motel in violation of the Thirteenth Amendment. The only question under the Due Process Clause of the Fifth Amendment, he said, was whether Congress had a rational basis for concluding that racial discrimination in motels and hotels affected interstate commerce and whether the means chosen by Congress to alleviate the problem were reasonable and appropriate. "If they are," he continued, "appellant has no 'right' to select its guests as it sees fit, free from governmental regulation." Thirty-two states had adopted public accommodations policies similar to the provisions of Title II of the Civil Rights Act, Clark pointed out, and in no case, state or federal, had such policies been held to deprive those to whom they were applicable of either liberty or property without due process of law, a circumstance that supported a like conclusion regarding Title II. Also, he noted, even if the effect of the application of the public accommodations provisions to the Heart of Atlanta Motel might cause it economic loss, which was "doubtful in the long run," Clark said, the Court had repeatedly held that the mere fact that a governmental regulation imposed economic costs on those regulated did not render the regulation invalid.[9]

"We find no merit in the remainder of appellant's contentions," Clark said, "including that of 'involuntary servitude.'" The public accommodations policies adopted by thirty-two states had merely codified the traditional common law requirement that operators of public accommodations must serve all orderly persons on an equal basis, he pointed out, and it was "difficult to believe that the [Thirteenth] Amendment was intended to abrogate this principle." In any case, the Court could not say that requiring nondiscriminatory service by facilities of public accommodation, Clark continued, was "in any way 'akin to African slavery.'"[10]

> We, therefore, conclude that the action of the Congress in the adoption of the Act as applied here to a motel which concededly serves interstate travelers is within the power granted it by the Commerce Clause of the Constitution, as interpreted by this Court for 140 years. It may be argued that Congress could have pursued other methods to eliminate the obstructions it found in interstate commerce caused by racial discrimination. But this is a matter of policy that rests entirely with the Congress not with the courts. How obstructions in commerce may be removed—what means are to be employed—is within the sound and exclusive discretion of the Congress. It is subject only to one caveat— that the means chosen must be reasonably adapted to the end permitted by the Constitution. We cannot say that its choice here was not so adapted. The Constitution requires no more.[11]

After upholding the validity of the application of the public accommodations provisions of the Civil Rights Act to the Heart of Atlanta Motel, Justice Clark then announced the opinion in *Katzenbach v. McClung,* sustaining the act as it applied to Ollie's Barbecue in Birmingham. Clark first addressed Solicitor General Cox's objection to the exercise of jurisdiction by the three-judge court in the *McClung* case because the McClungs had not alleged sufficient irreparable injury to justify the exercise of federal judicial power in the circumstances of their case. Since the Civil Rights Act provided for a statutory proceeding in which the respective rights and duties of those subject to the act could be determined, Clark acknowledged, "courts should, therefore, ordinarily refrain from exercising their jurisdiction in such cases." The *McClung* case was, however, in a "unique position," he continued.

> The interference with governmental action has occurred and the constitutional question is before us in the companion case of Heart of Atlanta Motel as well as in this case. It is important that a decision on the constitutionality of the Act as applied in these cases be announced as quickly as possible. For these reasons, we have concluded, with the above caveat, that the denial of discretionary declaratory relief is not required here.[12]

Having disposed of the jurisdictional issue and acceded to Solicitor Cox's request that the lower courts be admonished not to exercise jurisdiction in such cases, Justice Clark then recited the facts in the *McClung* case and the fact that the Civil Rights Act applied to Ollie's Barbecue because it served

$69,683 worth of meat that had moved in interstate commerce. The discrimination practiced by Ollie's Barbecue was unsupported by any action of the State of Alabama, he noted, and there was no claim that interstate travelers frequented the restaurant. "The sole question, therefore," Clark said, "narrows down to whether Title II, as applied to a restaurant annually receiving about $70,000 worth of food which has moved in commerce, is a valid exercise of the power of Congress."[13]

To answer that question, Justice Clark reviewed the evidence and testimony that had been presented to Congress on the impact of discrimination in restaurants on interstate commerce during its consideration of the Civil Rights Act, and found that the legislative record "is replete with testimony of the burdens placed on interstate commerce by racial discrimination in restaurants." Evidence before Congress, he pointed out, included statistics demonstrating that spending by blacks in restaurants and other public accommodations, even when income differences were discounted, was reduced in areas where racial discrimination was practiced as compared to areas where it was not. "This diminutive spending springing from a refusal to serve Negroes and their total loss as customers has, regardless of the absence of direct evidence, a close connection to interstate commerce," Clark said. "The fewer customers a restaurant enjoys the less food it sells and consequently the less it buys." Racial discrimination in restaurants, he noted, also had the effect of restricting the market for products from interstate commerce, evidence before Congress had indicated, and it also tended to produce unrest and disturbances that adversely affected general business conditions in communities in which such disturbances occurred.[14]

There was also evidence before Congress, Justice Clark noted, that racial discrimination in restaurants

> had a direct and highly restrictive effect upon interstate travel by Negroes. This resulted, it was said, because discriminatory practices prevent Negroes from buying prepared food served on the premises while on a trip, except in isolated and unkempt restaurants and under most unsatisfactory and often unpleasant conditions. This obviously discourages travel and obstructs interstate commerce for one can hardly travel without eating.

Finally, Clark noted, Congress had before it testimony that racial discrimination tended to deter professional and other skilled persons from moving into areas where it was commonly practiced and caused industry to be reluctant to locate in such areas. The resultant negative economic effect also adversely impacted on interstate commerce.[15]

Justice Clark summed up the evidence before Congress:

We believe that this testimony afforded ample basis for the conclusion that established restaurants in such areas sold less interstate goods because of the discrimination, that interstate travel was obstructed directly by it, that business in general suffered and that many new businesses refrained from establishing there as a result of it. Hence the District Court was in error in concluding that there was no connection between discrimination and the movement of interstate commerce. The court's conclusion that such a connection is outside "common experience" flies in the face of stubborn fact.[16]

"It goes without saying that, viewed in isolation, the volume of food purchased by Ollie's Barbecue from sources supplied from out of state was insignificant when compared with the total foodstuffs moving in commerce," Justice Clark conceded. But, citing *Wickard v. Filburn,* he pointed out that it was not just the economic effect of Ollie's Barbecue on interstate commerce that the Court had to consider, but rather the economic effect on commerce produced by all other similarly situated restaurants. Clark continued:

We noted in Heart of Atlanta Motel that a number of witnesses attested to the fact that racial discrimination was not merely a state or regional problem but was one of national scope. Against this background, we must conclude that while the focus of the legislation was on the individual restaurant's relation to interstate commerce, Congress appropriately considered the importance of that connection with the knowledge that the discrimination was but "representative of many others throughout the country, the total incidence of which if left unchecked may well become far-reaching in its harm to commerce."[17]

Even though the operations of Ollie's Barbecue were essentially local in nature, the Court had affirmed on numerous occasions, Justice Clark noted, the power of Congress to regulate under the Commerce Clause not only interstate commerce itself but local activities that either burdened or substantially affected commerce. "The activities that are beyond the reach of Congress are 'those which are completely within a particular State, which do not affect other States, and with which it is not necessary to interfere, for the purpose of exercising some of the general powers of the government,'" Clark added. "This rule is as good today as it was when Chief Justice Marshall laid it down almost a century and a half ago" in *Gibbons v. Ogden.*[18]

Justice Clark then addressed Robert McDavid Smith's argument, which had been sustained by the lower court, that Congress had enacted a conclusive presumption that the operations of any restaurant serving food that had moved in commerce necessarily affected interstate commerce, and had failed to provide for a mechanism allowing for the determination on a case-by-case basis of whether the presumption was correct in fact. Clark pointed out that Congress had itself in the past made the determination that a particular practice or activity affected interstate commerce, as in the Fair Labor Standards Act of 1938, and such determinations had been sustained by the Court. In the Civil Rights Act, he said, Congress had likewise determined for itself that racial discrimination in restaurants serving food that had moved in commerce imposed burdens on interstate commerce. "Of course, the mere fact that Congress has said when particular activity shall be deemed to affect commerce does not preclude further examination by this Court," Clark conceded.

> But where we find that the legislators, in light of the facts and testimony before them, have a rational basis for finding a chosen regulatory scheme necessary to the protection of commerce, our investigation is at an end. The only remaining question—one answered in the affirmative by the court below—is whether the particular restaurant either serves or offers to serve interstate travelers or serves food a substantial portion of which has moved in interstate commerce.[19]

The absence of specific findings of fact regarding the relationship between discrimination in restaurants serving interstate food and interstate commerce, Clark added, was not fatal to the validity of the Civil Rights Act. The evidence presented to Congress during its consideration of the act led the Court to "conclude that it had a rational basis for finding that racial discrimination in restaurants had a direct and adverse effect on the flow of interstate commerce." Congress had prohibited discrimination only in those restaurants having a close tie to interstate commerce, Clark pointed out.

> We think in so doing that Congress acted well within its power to protect and foster commerce in extending the coverage of Title II only to those restaurants offering to serve interstate travelers or serving food, a substantial portion of which has moved in interstate commerce. The absence of direct evidence connecting discriminatory restaurant service with the flow of interstate food, a factor on which the appellees place much reliance, is not, given the evidence as to the effect of such practices on other aspects of commerce, a crucial matter.[20]

Justice Clark concluded:

The power of Congress in this field is broad and sweeping; when it keeps within its sphere and violates no express constitutional limitations it has been the rule of this Court, going back almost to the founding days of the Republic, not to interfere. The Civil Rights Act of 1964, as here applied, we find to be plainly appropriate in the resolution of what Congress found to be a national commercial problem of the first magnitude. We find it in no violation of any express limitations of the Constitution and we therefore declare it valid.[21]

In his concurring opinion, Justice Black agreed that the Civil Rights Act was constitutionally valid under the Commerce and Necessary and Proper Clauses. Citing *Gibbons v. Ogden* and the *Shreveport Case,* Black emphasized that the power conferred upon Congress by the Commerce and Necessary and Proper Clauses included the power to regulate local activities that adversely affected or burdened interstate commerce. The racial discrimination practiced by the Heart of Atlanta Motel and Ollie's Barbecue, he said, could therefore be legitimately prohibited by Congress. Chief Justice John Marshall in his classic exposition of the meaning of the Necessary and Proper Clause in *McCulloch v. Maryland,* Black pointed out, had said: "Let the end be legitimate, let it be within the scope of the constitution, and all means which are appropriate, which are plainly adapted to that end, which are not prohibited, but consist with the letter and spirit of the constitution, are constitutional."

"By this standard Congress acted within its power here," Black said.

In view of the Commerce Clause it is not possible to deny that the aim of protecting interstate commerce from undue burdens is a legitimate end. In view of the Thirteenth, Fourteenth and Fifteenth Amendments, it is not possible to deny that the aim of protecting Negroes from discrimination is also a legitimate end. The means adopted to achieve these ends are also appropriate, plainly adapted to achieve them and not prohibited by the Constitution but consistent with both its letter and spirit.[22]

The Civil Rights Cases, Black added, were not inconsistent with the Court's affirmation of the validity of the Civil Rights Act of 1964, since in those cases the Court had left undecided whether the Civil Rights Act of 1875 could have been validly based on the Commerce Clause. Nor was his dissenting opinion in the Maryland sit-in case, *Bell v. Maryland,* which had been joined by Justices Harlan and White, inconsistent with the result in the *Heart of Atlanta Motel* and *McClung* cases, he maintained. In his *Bell v.*

Maryland dissent, he had only argued that the Fourteenth Amendment, standing alone, did not prohibit racial discrimination by owners of facilities of public accommodation. "The opinion did not discuss," he pointed out, "the power of Congress under the Commerce and Necessary and Proper Clauses or under section 5 of the Fourteenth Amendment to pass a law forbidding such discrimination."[23]

As his remarks in the Conference of the justices had indicated, Justice Douglas concurred in the judgment of the Court, but based his concurrence on his view that the Civil Rights Act was a valid exercise of the power conferred on Congress by section five of the Fourteenth Amendment to enforce its provisions by appropriate legislation. And he reiterated the view he had expressed in the *Sit-in* cases that racial discrimination in facilities of public accommodation was prohibited by the Fourteenth Amendment and that state enforcement of trespass laws against persons seeking nondiscriminatory service in such facilities was state action violative of the Fourteenth Amendment.[24]

Douglas argued:

A decision based on the Fourteenth Amendment would have a more settling effect, making unnecessary litigation over whether a particular restaurant or inn is within the commerce definitions of the Act or whether a particular customer is an interstate traveler. Under my construction, the Act would apply to all customers in all the enumerated places of public accommodation. And that construction would put an end to all obstructionist strategies and finally close one door on a bitter chapter in American history.[25]

While Justice Clark was announcing from the bench of the Court the majority opinions in the *Heart of Atlanta Motel* and *McClung* cases, Justice Douglas passed a note to Justice Goldberg in which he said "that the more I heard of the majority opinion, the happier I was we had written separately." Goldberg in turn passed a note to Douglas which said: "Bill: I agree most emphatically. It sounds like hamburgers are more important than human rights. Arthur."[26]

As this exchange indicated, Justice Goldberg also concurred in the judgment of the Court in a brief opinion. He agreed with the majority that the Civil Rights Act was well within the power of Congress under the Commerce Clause, he said. "The primary purpose of the Civil Rights Act of 1964, however, as the Court recognizes, is the vindication of human dignity and not mere economics," he said. And he reiterated the position he had taken in his concurring opinion in *Bell v. Maryland* that the Fourteenth Amendment guaranteed to all Americans the right to equal access to public accommodations. In his view, Goldberg therefore concluded, "Congress clearly had authority under both sec. 5 of the Fourteenth Amendment and the Commerce Clause to enact the Civil Rights Act of 1964."[27]

In addition to announcing the decisions in the public accommodations cases on December 14, the Court also announced its decisions in two sit-in cases that were pending before it, *Hamm v. Rock Hill* and *Lupper v. Arkansas*.[28] Over the strong dissents of Justices Black, Harlan, Stewart, and White, Justice Clark held for the majority that the Civil Rights Act abated state trespass prosecutions of sit-in demonstrators for seeking non-discriminatory service in public accommodations covered by the Civil Rights Act. Thus ended the long line of sit-in cases that had occupied the Court since the early 1960s.

In response to the Court's decisions in the *Heart of Atlanta Motel* and *McClung* cases, Justice Clark received what must have been a heartening letter from Jack Todd of Cleveland, Ohio:

Dear Justice Clark, Thanks to you good men for your wonderful decision. God Bless your hearts. And thanks again. You kind gentlemen has given twenty million or more people the greatest Xmas possible. Never did i think i would live to see this day. But i have and i thank God and also you good people. Now we Negroes know we can get justice in this our native mother land. Merry Christmas and a happy new year to all you gentlemen.[29]

Solicitor General Archibald Cox had predicted that sustaining the Civil Rights Act under the Commerce Clause would be for the Supreme Court "as easy as falling off a log." And that had indeed proven to be the case in the *Heart of Atlanta Motel* case, if not in the *McClung* case. Although Moreton Rolleston believed Cox to be "a typical Harvard Law School man who thinks they're better than everyone else in the world," Rolleston now learned that the solicitor general had bested him in the clash of argument before the Court.[30]

Rolleston received the news of the Supreme Court's unanimous decision sustaining the constitutionality of the public accommodations provisions of the Civil Rights Act by telephone in Atlanta. And given the largely ideological arguments he had advanced against the act, his reaction was predictable. Rolleston announced to the press:

We have charged that the fundamental question before the tribunal was whether Congress has the right to take from a private business concern the owner's choice of running the firm as he wishes and choosing his customers. The decision nullifies the rights and principles which the Constitution was designed to perpetuate. This decision opens the frightful door to unlimited power of a centralized government in Washington, in which the individual citizen and his personal liberty are of no importance. It makes possible a socialistic state and eventual dictatorship. This a sad day for the cause of individual freedom.[31]

The Heart of Atlanta Motel had of course been operating on a desegregated basis since the injunction by the three-judge court had taken effect on August 11, and Rolleston now recognized that the injunction would not be lifted. "This is the end of the line," he admitted. "I've gone as far as I can." In a more philosophical vein, however, Rolleston conceded that with "my grandchildren, there won't be any problems at all. They won't even know there was any."[32]

In the 1970s, Moreton Rolleston purchased his partner's shares in the Heart of Atlanta Motel and thus became the motel's sole proprietor. The motel, however, was razed in 1973, and the property upon which it had stood is now occupied by the Atlanta Hilton and Towers. Now in his eighties, Moreton Rolleston himself continues (in 2000) to be active in his law practice in Atlanta.[33]

In reaction to the Supreme Court's decisions, the *Atlanta Constitution* editorially declared that the "cause of orderly government can only be served now by acceptance of the law. Further defiance means anarchy and disorder. Those who respect law and order surely will place this respect above lesser feelings concerning the civil rights statute." The president of the Atlanta Hotel Association reflected similar sentiments and pledged that the "hotels will obey the law." And Calvin Bradshaw, the president of the Atlanta Restaurant Association, also conceded that the Civil Rights Act "now is the law of the land. As responsible law-abiding citizens, our duty to obey the law is clear. I urge that all our members comply. I am confident that our patrons, customers and friends will understand this position and we shall look forward to continued service to our fellow citizens."[34]

Atlanta black attorney Donald Hallowell, one of the leaders in the fight to desegregate Lester Maddox's Pickrick restaurant, said that the Supreme Court's decisions were

> most important and extremely gratifying. It is another step toward effecting human dignity for all Americans. Some have said, and I agree, that the great story relative to the public accommodations section has been the substantial compliance with rather than defiance of it. Now that the Supreme Court has spoken, I sincerely trust that all public officials will actively advocate and businessmen will practice full compliance.

Lester Maddox's attorney Sidney Schell, however, pledged continued resistance to the Civil Rights Act. If Maddox were held in contempt of court, he predicted, "we're going on up to the Supreme Court regardless of today's ruling. We'll fight with 'em to the finish."[35]

Lester Maddox's Pickrick restaurant had been closed on August 18 after the federal injunction had been issued ordering the desegregation of the establishment, but on September 26 the restaurant reopened as the Lester Maddox Cafeteria. The Pickrick restaurant, a corporation, had leased the premises to Maddox as an individual in a transparent attempt by Maddox and his counsel to evade the federal injunction. The Lester Maddox Cafeteria continued to operate on a segregated basis, although Maddox claimed he was only refusing to serve "integrationists" because of their political beliefs rather than their race, as well as also refusing to serve interstate travelers. Signs were thus posted at the cafeteria notifying potential customers that integrationists and interstate travelers would not be served. In practice, however, blacks were automatically presumed to be integrationists and refused service, while whites were assumed to be neither integrationists nor interstate travelers and were served.[36]

Because of Lester Maddox's rather sophomoric attempts to evade the mandate of the federal injunction ordering him to end racial discrimination in his establishment, the government requested that U.S. District Judge Frank Hooper hold Maddox in contempt of court for violating the injunction. Judge Hooper held a hearing on the contempt charge beginning on February 1, 1965; during it Maddox's attorneys argued that the injunction ordering Maddox to desegregate was applicable only to the Pickrick restaurant, which had closed, and not to the Lester Maddox Cafeteria. Also, they contended, Maddox was not discriminating against persons because of their race in operating his cafeteria but rather was discriminating on the basis of political beliefs, depending on whether individuals were integrationists or not.[37]

Defending Maddox at the contempt hearing, Sidney Schell admitted that his client's "conduct might not be ideal," but portrayed Maddox as a misguided individual who was unable to adjust to modern conditions. Maddox had grown up when an owner could operate his business as he saw fit, Schell contended. "It may be that the law has changed, but full understanding of that principle comes slowly to a man over 50." His client had lost $40,000 defending his principles, Schell maintained, and he had been "confused by what the Congress of the United States had done and what the law is," and his actions had been based on his own interpretation of the law and bad advice from others.[38]

NAACP attorney William Alexander, however, argued that the lease of the former Pickrick restaurant premises to Lester Maddox and the Lester Maddox Cafeteria was a transparent subterfuge designed to evade the federal injunction to desegregate. "The Pickrick and Lester G. Maddox are for all practical purposes one and the same," Alexander argued, "and the Pickrick and the Lester Maddox Cafeteria are one and the same."

"I don't think there's any question about that," Judge Hooper agreed. "The mere fact that he does business under a trade name doesn't change the entity at all."

Lester Maddox must be held responsible for his acts, Alexander contended,

> whether on the advice of others or not. A survey of restaurants in Atlanta, Georgia, and the South would show almost universal compliance [with the Civil Rights Act]. If hundreds of restaurants throughout the South and throughout the country can abide by it, how can he come into court and claim he had trouble understanding it? The act is not ambiguous, the order is not ambiguous, and he's had counsel to interpret for him.[39]

In response to Maddox's claim that he was only refusing to serve integrationists and thus was not discriminating on the basis of race, Civil Rights Division attorney St. John Barrett responded that "apart from what I think is the patent ridiculousness of such assertions in view of what Mr. Maddox has said in the courtroom and publicly from the time the order was entered," if Maddox's position was sustained by the court the result would "punish or penalize people for exercising their privileges under the [Civil Rights] Act." There was "no alternative" other than to find Maddox in contempt of court, Barrett said. "The only question is what sanctions [are needed] to compel obedience." And Barrett recommended that the court fine Maddox one thousand dollars per day, with the fine to be cumulative.[40]

Lester Maddox had become a national symbol of resistance to the Civil Rights Act, and the Civil Rights Division obviously put a high priority on compelling his compliance with the act without, however, at the same time making him a martyr in the segregationist cause. St. John Barrett had conferred with Charles Goodson, the U.S. attorney in Atlanta, regarding what the appropriate sanction for contempt the government should recommend to the court, and Barrett reported to John Doar of the Civil Rights Division his thoughts on the strategy he believed should be pursued to bring Maddox into compliance with the act. "We both are of the view that a fine, rather than imprisonment, should be imposed," Barrett reported to Doar.

> The fine could escalate as the contempt continues. For instance, the fine could be $25 for the first day, $50 for the second, $75 for the third, etc. We would seek to have it made clear in the order that failure of Negroes to seek service on any particular days would not interrupt the escalation

of the fine. Thus, if on the third day after the order Negroes sought and were refused service the fine would be $25 plus $50, plus $75.

The collection of the fine would not occur until blacks were actually refused service, Barrett informed Doar. "We can anticipate an almost immediate test [of compliance with the act] as soon as an order is entered. After such test, however, it might be some time before Negroes again sought service."[41]

On February 5, Judge Hooper found Lester Maddox to be in contempt of court for his failure to comply with the injunction requiring him to operate his restaurant on a nondiscriminatory basis. While Hooper imposed a fine of two hundred dollars per day rather than the one thousand dollars per day recommended by the government, he did accept the government's recommendation that the fine should be cumulative. If, for example, Maddox refused service to blacks thirty days following February 5, he would owe a six thousand dollar fine. To sustain Maddox's defense that he was not engaged in racial discrimination but only refusing to serve integrationists because of their political beliefs "would create an anomaly hitherto unheard of," Judge Hooper remarked in imposing the sanctions for contempt. Hooper added:

Should the continued refusal of defendant Maddox to comply with the law and the orders of the court cause him in the future to lose the fruits of his endeavors under our free enterprise system, it would be a matter of deep regret to all, but the responsibility for his losses would rest upon his shoulders.[42]

After being held in contempt, Lester Maddox conferred with his accountant and his attorneys, Sidney Schell and William McRae. "You've done everything you could do, Lester," they advised him. "You have to comply now, or everything you've got will go down the drain." After arguing the matter for three hours, Maddox finally agreed that he would have to desegregate his restaurant. He called a press conference and announced his decision publicly. But when a black man, Jack Googer, appeared at the restaurant door on February 8 at 1:15 P.M., Maddox changed his mind and permanently closed the establishment. "This business is available to the first person with a reasonable offer," he announced. And he posted a sign on the restaurant door saying, "Closed. Out of business resulting from act passed by the U.S. Congress, signed by Pres. Johnson and inspired and supported by deadly and bloody communists." The restaurant was subsequently leased to some of Maddox's former employees, but when the business was unsuccessful, the property was sold to Georgia Tech University and became part of its campus. In the fall of 1965, Lester Maddox opened a furniture store in Atlanta, and the following year he was elected governor of Georgia.[43]

In Alabama, Governor George Wallace denounced the Supreme Court's decisions in the public accommodations cases as a "staggering blow to the free enterprise system and the rights of private property owners." "Despite this setback," he added, "there should be continuing resistance to such attacks on the system that has made this nation great and strong." In Birmingham, the *Birmingham News* criticized the decisions in much the same vein, while conceding that the unanimity of the Court indicated that the other sections of the Civil Rights Act would be upheld as well. The Court, the *News* said, "has joined Congress in protecting some rights at the expense of rights of others. A grave danger may lie in the uses of this opinion as further precedent in cases involving governmental power to act against private enterprise practices." And columnist James J. Kilpatrick warned, "It is right for us to look at Ollie's in Birmingham, how it serves a local trade; but we ought better to look at the high court, how it shapes a federated republic into a single consolidated mass."[44]

When the news of the Supreme Court's decisions in the public accommodations cases reached Birmingham, Robert McDavid Smith was not surprised, since he had concluded following the oral argument in the *McClung* case that the case was lost. He believed, however, that Justices Harlan and Stewart would vote in his favor, based upon their questions and comments during the argument. Smith's strategy had been to target Justice Black in his argument with the hope of convincing him that Ollie's Barbecue insufficiently affected interstate commerce to be regulated by Congress under the Commerce Clause. But when Justice Black had commented that Smith's argument was "foreclosed by past cases," Smith knew that he had lost the *McClung* case. Ollie McClung Sr. had been present incognito during the oral argument before the Court, and Smith had informed McClung as they left the Court following the argument that they had no chance of winning.[45]

"I'm shocked over the decision," Ollie McClung Sr. nevertheless said to the press following the announcement of the Supreme Court's ruling. "We will have to confer with our attorneys. It seems to me that the ownership and use of private property is basic to the American way of life. I'm sad that the U.S. Supreme Court didn't see it our way." Asked if Ollie's Barbecue would now serve blacks on the premises, McClung replied, "We have made no decision as to what we'll do or whether we'll change our operation. We will work on it with our attorneys."[46]

Ollie McClung had demonstrated by his conduct that he was no Lester Maddox, however, and consequently his defiance of the Civil Rights Act seemed unlikely. That proved to be the case when, after conferring with

Robert McDavid Smith, the McClungs announced on December 15 that Ollie's Barbecue would desegregate. "As law-abiding Americans we feel we must bow to this edict of the Supreme Court," they announced to the press.

> We are deeply concerned that so many of our nation's leaders have accepted this edict, which gives the federal government control over the life and behavior of every American. This could prove to be the most important and disastrous decision handed down by this court. We plan no further legal action, but shall continue to pray that somehow the freedom of our citizens will one day be restored.

And they added, "We will accept customers at our restaurant without regard to race or color."[47]

The McClungs also expressed concern that their challenge of the Civil Rights Act had been widely misunderstood, and they denied that their actions had been motivated by racial animosity. Many people "are misinformed as to the nature of our [court] action and the consequences of this decision," they said. "The issue seems to be clouded by the racial overtones."

> The racial issue just happened to be the issue over which this controversy of federal control of private property and dictation of private business operations arose. Our reaction would have been the same if the federal government had intruded upon our right to manage any aspect of our business, for example, what products to use, dress of customers, etc.[48]

On Wednesday, December 16, five blacks entered Ollie's Barbecue and requested service. They were served without incident, and the desegregation of the McClungs' restaurant thus occurred peacefully and quietly. There was not "a single incident," one of the blacks said later. "Everything was lovely. Lovely."[49]

Commenting on the McClungs' decision to desegregate, the *Birmingham News* said that it was "rather strange still to think of the name of the proprietor of Ollie's Barbecue, long a Birmingham landmark, becoming identified with one of the major U.S. Supreme Court rulings of our times—yet it happened." Ollie McClung and Moreton Rolleston "had every right" to challenge the Civil Rights Act, the *News* said, and they "did so correctly, as citizens." The *News* continued:

> Now Birmingham's Ollie McClung has said of course that he will meet the court's verdict without further delay. Throughout the case, and now

in its aftermath, he has conducted himself properly, in dignity, and in accordance with law. Not only did Ollie McClung seek to serve his own proprietary ends; in making his case doubtless he has contributed to an earlier settlement of this particular matter, no matter how much many persons still disapprove. As Mr. McClung now adjusts to the reality, he provides a further lesson to many citizens—of grace in fulfilling his citizen's duty after full recourse through channels of law. We commend him.

And accompanying the editorial was a picture of Ollie McClung Sr., captioned, "McClung . . . example."[50]

Ollie's Barbecue did not suffer any adverse financial consequences because of the desegregation of its premises. Ollie McClung Sr. died on August 4, 1989, at the age of seventy-three. Ollie's Barbecue has relocated since 1964 and now operates near an interstate highway in Birmingham, where the establishment continues to thrive financially under the management of Ollie McClung Jr.[51]

The editorial responses of the press to the Supreme Court's decisions in the *Heart of Atlanta Motel* and *McClung* cases were generally favorable, with many newspapers expressing the view that the decisions were what had been anticipated. Outside the South, an unusual dissenting view was expressed by columnist David Lawrence. "On this date," he said, "what many historians will describe as a federal dictatorship was established in the United States." The more common view was reported by Anthony Lewis of the *New York Times*. "The decision was no surprise to experts in constitutional law," he reported. "From the time President Kennedy first proposed the public accommodations section in June, 1963, Justice Department lawyers and outside scholars generally forecast it would be sustained under the commerce clause." The decisions were nevertheless important both politically and legally, Lewis said. They "cleared the way for full-scale enforcement of the act. Justice Department lawyers and conciliators in the new Community Relations Service have been waiting until the constitutionality of the section was settled." Politically, he added, the decisions were "a definitive answer to those in the South and elsewhere who have made an issue of the new law's constitutionality. Most prominent among those is Senator Barry Goldwater, who voted against the law, saying it was unconstitutional."[52]

The editorial response of the *New York Times* was also reflective of press response nationally. The *Times* praised the decisions as "a profoundly important victory for the cause of justice in our society." The *Times* said:

The defenders of segregation and racially biased discrimination had relied upon a sweeping view of property rights to defend the morally reprehensible treatment of Negroes. In a forcefully worded unanimous opinion, the Court has swept aside this antiquated and presumptuous assertion of the sanctity of private property. From this time forward the right to operate a business for private gain no longer carries with it the implied prerogative of humiliating and embarrassing otherwise well-intentioned private citizens because of their color. Interstate commerce need no longer bear the destructive burden of those gratuitous humiliations and irrational restraints.[53]

Civil rights leaders were of course delighted with the public accommodations decisions as well as the Court's ruling that prosecutions of sit-in demonstrators were abated by the Civil Rights Act. Jack Greenberg, general counsel of the NAACP Legal Defense and Education Fund, estimated that as many as three thousand cases involving demonstrators would now be dismissed. The 120 NAACP cooperating attorneys in the South, he said, would participate in a "massive mop-up operation to secure the release of all these defendants." Since the sit-in demonstrations had begun in 1960, the Legal Defense and Education Fund had represented thirteen thousand individuals arrested in demonstrations in the South.[54]

Student Non-Violent Coordinating Committee (SNCC) chairman John Lewis declared that the Court's decisions were "the most heartening thing since SNCC was founded." NAACP executive secretary Roy Wilkins had received word of the Court's decisions in a telegram from the counsel of the NAACP's Washington bureau just after noon on December 14. "Supreme Court unanimously upholds civil rights act in hotel and restaurant cases," the telegram said. "Holds act abates prosecution in Rock Hill and Little Rock Sit-in cases." Reacting to this news, Wilkins announced to the press that the Court's decisions "should promptly end discrimination in public accommodations everywhere in the country." The rulings, he added, should "reinforce public confidence in the orderly processes of law" and "enhance the image and prestige of our country throughout the world." And Martin Luther King Jr., just returned from Oslo, where he had received the 1964 Nobel Peace Prize, said that the decisions should make all Americans "proud of the Supreme Court in its constant vigilance to assure equal protection of the law."[55]

In Washington, a relieved President Johnson, who had feared massive and perhaps violent resistance to the Civil Rights Act in the South, had seen his fears proved unfounded by the widespread and peaceful compliance with the public accommodations provisions by southern businesses. The Supreme Court's decisions, he said, assured "reasonable and responsible acceptance of the law," and he pointed out,

The Civil Rights Act of 1964 was proposed by two Presidents. It was overwhelmingly approved by Congress and now the constitutionality of the public accommodations section has been upheld by a unanimous vote of the Supreme Court. The nation has spoken with a single voice on the question of equal rights and equal opportunity.

The president continued:

I have been heartened by the spirit with which the people of the South have accepted this act even though many of them were opposed to its passage. There already has been encouraging and widespread compliance with the act during the five months it has been law. Now that the Supreme Court has also ruled, I think we all join in the hope and the resolution that this kind of reasonable and responsible acceptance of the law will continue and increase.[56]

The Supreme Court's decisions in the public accommodations cases were certainly a victory for President Johnson, who had resurrected the Civil Rights Act after President Kennedy's assassination and steadfastly insisted on its enactment by Congress. And the decisions were also a victory for Attorney General Kennedy, Senators Humphrey and Dirksen, and Congressman McCulloch and the overwhelming majority of Congress that had ensured the act's successful passage by Congress.

The Supreme Court's decisions were also a substantial victory for Burke Marshall and the Civil Rights Division of the Department of Justice. The public accommodations provisions of the Civil Rights Act of 1964, Burke Marshall said, had been "an overwhelming success." Rather than the massive resistance to the act many, including the Johnson administration, had feared, Marshall pointed out, the public accommodations provisions had instead met with "massive compliance." The public accommodations provisions "had worked," he added. "There is not a major city in the United States where there is not substantial compliance with this provision of the law. Many business organizations and many public officials—including Senators from the southern states who vehemently opposed the bill—have called for compliance and acceptance, and it has come."[57]

On December 18, just four days following the Supreme Court's decisions, Burke Marshall's resignation as head of the Civil Rights Division was announced. In his letter of resignation to President Johnson, Marshall noted that now that

the Civil Rights Act of 1964 has become law, and the nation has overwhelmingly endorsed your leadership and ratified the decision of the

Congress, I believe that the policy direction of the Department of Justice, and of my Division, is clear beyond question. Compliance with the law has been general. The task of eliminating discrimination in voting, education, and those places of public accommodation that are engaged in a pattern of resistance to the law is now a straightforward matter of litigation, requiring primarily administrative skills, hard work and good lawyers.

In his response, President Johnson noted that during the past four years,

the Nation has at long last come to grips with the domestic problem that has been the most difficult and complicated during our entire existence. You have played an extraordinary role in this significant area of human progress, and I know that your principal reward and that of your family must be the satisfaction of knowing that, as a Nation, we are well on the way to an enduring and meaningful resolution of this most vexatious problem.

"In 33 years service with the Federal govt," Johnson added in a handwritten postscript, "I have never known any person who rendered a better quality of public service."[58]

But the Supreme Court's decisions in a legal and constitutional sense were even more a victory and vindication for Solicitor General Archibald Cox. Justice Clark's opinions for the majority in the *Heart of Atlanta Motel* and *McClung* cases had essentially tracked the Commerce Clause arguments that Solicitor General Cox had presented to the Court. Cox had also steadfastly resisted taking the position in the *Sit-in* cases that the Fourteenth Amendment itself required the desegregation of facilities of public accommodation because he had feared such a decision by the Supreme Court would be widely resisted and perhaps result in irreparable damage to the Court's legitimacy.

Cox said later, regarding his position in the *Sit-in* cases:

The one clear point, in my view, was that a clear-cut decision either way was wrong and should be avoided if possible—at least as long as there was hope that Congress might outlaw racial discrimination and segregation in places of public accommodation. The ability of the judicial branch to withstand the strains of adjudicating society's most fundamental and divisive public issues is not unlimited. In order to strike effective blows upon critical occasions the Court must be willing, for the most part, to conform its decisions to the binding force of law.[59]

"Granting that the practice of segregation in places of public accommodation was evil, how much of the burden of innovation could the Supreme Court successfully carry?" Cox asked.

> Could a decision sustaining a claim that the Fourteenth Amendment itself required the desegregation of lunch counters and restaurants without the need for legislative action, have ever commanded the degree of voluntary acceptance to make the prohibition effective? The response to the school desegregation decisions suggested a negative answer. Would it not be better to leave the question to Congress, which was beginning to bestir itself?

Cox continued:

> In retrospect, it seems clear that the public-accommodations sections of the Civil Rights Act of 1964, after the Supreme Court decision upholding their constitutionality, commanded far wider and deeper acceptance in all parts of the country, because of the participation of all three branches of the government, than would have been accorded a Supreme Court ruling sustaining the claim that private establishments were required to desegregate by reason of the Fourteenth Amendment.

The events during 1964 following the passage of the Civil Rights Act and the decisions of the Court upholding the public accommodations provisions indicated that Archibald Cox had undoubtedly been correct.[60]

In retrospect, Moreton Rolleston's haste to become the first to challenge the public accommodations provisions of the Civil Rights Act of 1964 furnished the government a test case that could not have been more ideal had the government itself selected the *Heart of Atlanta Motel* case to test the validity of the 1964 act. As a motel of 216 rooms located in downtown Atlanta and conveniently accessible to two interstate highways and two state highways and serving guests 75 percent of whom were interstate travelers, the Heart of Atlanta Motel was ideally suited to test the Commerce Clause basis of the public accommodations provisions.

Consequently, as most contemporary press comment had indicated, the Supreme Court's decision in the *Heart of Atlanta Motel* case was entirely predictable. The precedent most nearly analogous to the *Heart of Atlanta Motel* decision was the Court's decision in the *Jones and Laughlin* case in 1937.[61] If discrimination by employers against union members in manufacturing and production enterprises could be validly prohibited by Congress under the Commerce Clause to prevent the adverse effects of labor disputes on commerce, then racial discrimination in motels and hotels with its obvious detrimental effects on interstate travel by blacks seemed logically to follow.

Katzenbach v. McClung was of course also a test case initiated and financed by the Birmingham Restaurant Association.[62] Unlike the *Heart of Atlanta Motel* case, the *McClung* case was factually far from ideal as a test case from the government's standpoint. The case involving the application of the public accommodations provisions to Lester Maddox's Pickrick restaurant in Atlanta was clearly a factually stronger test of the restaurant provisions than Ollie's Barbecue in Birmingham. The location of the Pickrick on the business route of an interstate highway, its advertising on highway signs, and its use of large volumes of food that had moved in interstate commerce made the linkages between the operations of the Pickrick and interstate commerce factually much stronger than the operations of Ollie's Barbecue. And it was the *Pickrick* case that would have undoubtedly tested the validity of the restaurant provisions of the 1964 act in the Supreme Court had not Lester Maddox and his counsel failed to appeal the decision of the lower court. The *McClung* case consequently became the case testing the restaurant provisions largely by default.

Because of the factually weaker linkage between the operations of Ollie's Barbecue and interstate commerce, the Supreme Court's decision in the *McClung* case appeared at the outset to be more problematic than the decision in the *Heart of Atlanta Motel* case. The *McClung* decision is sometimes portrayed as being predicated primarily on the fact that Ollie's Barbecue purchased about $70,000 worth of meat that had moved in interstate commerce.[63] While the application of public accommodations provisions to Ollie's Barbecue was triggered by the use by the McClungs of food that had moved in interstate commerce and the *McClung* decision was based in part on the cumulative impact discrimination in restaurants serving interstate food would have on the interstate food market, on the *Wickard v. Filburn* analogy, the decision did not rest on that factor alone. Justice Harlan would not have joined an opinion in the *McClung* case resting upon the impact of restaurant discrimination on interstate food sales alone, and in order to keep Harlan in the majority fold, the *McClung* decision rested more on the other effects on commerce produced by racial discrimination in restaurants. The detrimental impact of restaurant discrimination on interstate travel by blacks and the economic burdens on restaurants and business in general produced by the practice of segregation and by protests and demonstrations against segregation in restaurants thus formed more important bases of the *McClung* decision than the impact of restaurant discrimination on the interstate food market. "The absence of direct evidence connecting discriminatory restaurant service with the flow of interstate food," the *McClung* opinion thus said at the suggestion of Justice Harlan, "a factor on which the appellees place much reliance, is not, given the evidence as to the effect of such practices on other aspects of commerce, a crucial matter." The decision in the *McClung* case may well be, as has been said, "the Supreme Court's most expansive reading of the constitutional grant of power to Congress to regulate interstate commerce," but the decision rested more on other adverse effects on commerce produced by restaurant segregation than the effects of that practice on the interstate food market.[64]

Despite President Johnson's fear of massive and possibly violent resistance to the public accommodations provisions, and Justice Goldberg's prediction that the Court might face many "messy" cases testing the applicability of the Civil Rights Act to different businesses, the widespread compliance with the public accommodations provisions both before and after the *Heart of Atlanta Motel* and *McClung* decisions resulted in surprisingly little follow-up litigation in the Supreme Court.[65] Only one further, significant decision on the applicability of the public accommodations provisions was rendered by the Court after 1964, and that was *Daniel v. Paul,* decided in 1969.[66]

In *Daniel v. Paul,* the Court upheld the application of the public accommodations provisions to the Lake Nixon Club, located some twelve miles from Little Rock, Arkansas. The club was a 232-acre recreational area providing swimming, boating, sunbathing, picnicking, miniature golf, and dancing facilities, along with a snack bar serving hot dogs, hamburgers, soft drinks, and milk. The club was not on an interstate highway and could be reached only by country roads. Because the Lake Nixon Club advertised in a local monthly magazine that was distributed to guests at Little Rock hotels and motels and a nearby Air Force base, and the club advertised on two Little Rock radio stations, the Court held that it offered to serve and likely did serve interstate travelers within the meaning of the Civil Rights Act. The Court additionally held that a substantial portion of the food and beverages served at the club's snack bar had moved in interstate commerce, and that the club's jukebox, the records played on it, and the club's paddleboats had also moved in commerce. Consequently, the operations of the club affected interstate commerce within the meaning of the public accommodations provisions, the Court held, and racial discrimination by its owners was prohibited by the 1964 act.[67]

In the years following the decisions in the 1964 public accommodations cases, the Supreme Court has introduced a degree of uncertainty regarding what had hitherto been considered settled constitutional principles governing the modern scope of congressional power under the Commerce Clause.

In a mini-revival of the doctrine of dual federalism, a narrowly divided Court in 1976 held that Congress could not validly regulate the wages of state and local governmental employees under the Fair Labor Standards Act without invading the powers retained by the states under the Tenth Amendment.[68] In 1985, however, a similarly divided Court overruled the 1976 decision and upheld congressional regulation of the wages of state and local governmental employees under the Commerce Clause.[69]

The mini-revival of dual federalism nonetheless continued in the 1990s with decisions of the Court that Congress under the Commerce Clause could not require the states to adopt legislation or compel state officers to enforce a federal policy. In *New York v. United States* in 1992, the Court thus invalidated provisions of the Low-Level Radioactive Waste Policy Amendments Act requiring the states to enact legislation taking title to low-level radioactive wastes generated within their jurisdictions;[70] and in *Printz v. United States,* decided in 1997, the Court similarly held that Congress could not require the enforcement by local law enforcement officers of the background checks for gun purchases required by the Brady Handgun Violence Prevention Act.[71] In both cases, the Court ruled that Congress had exceeded its power under the Commerce Clause and infringed on the independence reserved to the states under the Tenth Amendment. Although the Court has consequently revived the Tenth Amendment as a limitation on the power of Congress under the Commerce Clause, its limited revival of dual federalism has not extended to a holding that the Tenth Amendment removes from the reach of the commerce power congressional regulation of certain business or economic activities, as the Court had done under the doctrine of dual federalism in its earlier incarnation prior to the 1930s. Rather, the Court has confined its mini-revival of dual federalism to holdings that the Commerce Clause cannot be the vehicle for federal intrusion upon the basic powers and independence of the states.[72]

The Court has, on the other hand, imposed for the first time since the 1930s limits on the extent to which the commerce power may be used to regulate activities that affect interstate commerce. In *United States v. Lopez,* decided in 1995, the Court thus invalidated the Gun-Free School Zones Act of 1990, which prohibited the possession of firearms in school zones. Again the Court was sharply divided, with the majority opinion written by Chief Justice William Rehnquist, joined by Justice Antonin Scalia, with Justices Anthony Kennedy, Sandra O'Connor, and Clarence Thomas concurring, while Justices Stephen Breyer, Ruth Bader Ginsburg, David Souter, and John Paul Stevens dissented.[73]

The Gun-Free School Zones Act, Chief Justice Rehnquist argued, could only be sustained under the line of the Court's commerce cases upholding congressional legislation regulating local or intrastate activities that affected interstate commerce. And reflecting concerns similar to those expressed by Justice Harlan in his unpublished partial concurrence and dissent in the public accommodations cases, Rehnquist concluded that for such activities to be validly subject to congressional regulation under the Commerce Clause the activities must be shown to have "substantial" effects on interstate commerce. The regulation of the possession of firearms in school zones, the chief justice also noted, was not the regulation of the sort of "commercial" activity that had been sustained by the Court in prior cases.

The government contended nevertheless that possession of firearms in school zones increased violent crime, which in turn increased insurance costs and discouraged the location of business in areas where it occurred, both of which adversely affected interstate commerce. Additionally, the government argued, the possession of firearms in school zones produced violent criminal activity, which was disruptive of the educational process, resulting in less well educated citizens, and this too adversely affected interstate commerce. If the Court were to sustain the government's contentions, Rehnquist nonetheless argued, the result would be a virtually limitless commerce power:

> To uphold the Government's contentions here, we would have to pile inference upon inference in a manner that would bid fair to convert congressional authority under the Commerce Clause to a general police power of the sort retained by the States. Admittedly, some of our prior cases have taken long steps down that road, giving great deference to congressional action.

The chief justice continued:

> The broad language in these opinions has suggested the possibility of additional expansion, but we decline here to proceed any further. To do so would require us to conclude that the Constitution's enumeration of powers does not presuppose something not enumerated, . . . and that there never will be a distinction between what is truly national and what is truly local. . . . This we are unwilling to do.[74]

The dissenting justices in the *Lopez* case warned that the Court was deviating from the rational basis test by which it had determined the validity of congressional legislation under the Commerce Clause since 1937 and that the Court had explicitly endorsed in *Katzenbach v. McClung* in 1964. In the *McClung* case, they noted, the Court had held that "where we find that the legislators, in light of the facts and testimony before them, have a rational basis for finding a chosen regulatory scheme necessary to the protection of commerce, our investigation is at an end."[75] Failure to adhere to the rational basis test, the dissenters warned, could lead the Court into the same pitfalls that had produced decisions such as *Hammer v. Dagenhart* and such substantive due process decisions as *Lochner v. New York,* in which the Court had invalidated a maximum-hour law for bakery workers in 1905.[76] "There is today, however," Justice Souter thus warned, "a backward glance at both the old pitfalls, as the Court treats deference under the rationality rule as subject to gradation according to the commercial or non-commercial nature of the immediate subject of the challenged regulation." "The distinction between what is patently commercial and what is not," he added, "looks much like the old distinction between what directly affects commerce and what touches it only indirectly."[77]

In a dissenting opinion joined by all four of the dissenting justices, Justice Breyer also argued that the standard for determining whether a local activity could be regulated under the Commerce Clause should be whether the activity in question had a "significant" effect on commerce, rather than a "substantial" effect, as the chief justice insisted. And Breyer convincingly argued that school violence had such adverse effects on the educational process that it threatened the prospect for a well-educated workforce so essential to the economic well-being of the nation in an economy that was interdependent on not only an interstate basis but also a global one.[78]

Relying in part on the *Lopez* case, the Court also invalidated the Violence Against Women Act (VAWA) of 1997 in *United States v. Morrison* during the spring of 2000. The act was based on the congressional power derived from the Commerce Clause as well as the power of Congress under section five of the Fourteenth Amendment to enforce the provisions of that amendment, and authorized victims of violent crimes motivated by gender to file civil suits for damages in the federal courts against the perpetrators of such crimes. Writing on behalf of the same justices who had composed the majority in the *Lopez* case, Chief Justice Rehnquist reaffirmed the Court's ruling in the *Civil Rights Cases* of 1883 that the congressional power derived from section five of the Fourteenth Amendment did not extend to actions of private individuals but only to state action violative of the provisions of that amendment, despite expressions of contrary views in previous opinions of the Court.[79] Since the VAWA authorized civil suits for damages by victims of gender-based crimes against private individuals who had committed such crimes, the Court held, the act exceeded congressional power under section five of the Fourteenth Amendment.[80]

Unlike the situation with the Gun-Free School Zones Act invalidated in the *Lopez* case, Congress made extensive findings regarding the effects on interstate commerce produced by violence against women in support of the

Violence Against Women Act. Indeed, Justice Souter, joined in dissent by Justices Breyer, Stevens, and Ginsburg, noted that there was a "mountain of data assembled by Congress, here showing the effects of violence against women on interstate commerce."[81] Despite the congressional findings, however, Chief Justice Rehnquist held for the majority that the VAWA was nonetheless beyond the legitimate scope of congressional power under the Commerce Clause. As in the *Lopez* case, Rehnquist said, under the VAWA Congress was attempting to regulate "non-economic violent criminal conduct based solely on that conduct's aggregate effect on interstate commerce." The majority refused to accept reasoning that "seeks to follow the but-for causal chain from the initial occurrence of violent crime (the suppression of which has always been the prime object of the States' police power) to every attenuated effect upon interstate commerce." Such reasoning, the chief justice said,

> would allow Congress to regulate any crime as long as the nationwide, aggregated impact of that crime has substantial effects on employment, production, transit, or consumption. Indeed, if Congress may regulate gender-motivated violence, it would be able to regulate murder or any other type of violence since gender-motivated violence, as a subset of all violent crime, is certain to have lesser economic impacts than the larger class of which it is a part.[82]

The Court's decisions in the *Lopez* and *Morrison* cases do not appear to portend a wholesale uprooting of the principles governing the scope of congressional power under the Commerce Clause that have prevailed since the 1930s and that were reaffirmed in the *Heart of Atlanta Motel* and *McClung* cases in 1964. The cautious concurring opinion by Justice Kennedy, joined by Justice O'Connor, in the *Lopez* case certainly seems to belie that notion, and only Justice Thomas among the majority justices in the *Lopez* and *Morrison* cases seemed to favor a more fundamental overhauling of the Court's Commerce Clause doctrine.[83]

The *Lopez* and *Morrison* decisions, on the other hand, reemphasize the point made by Justice Harlan in his unpublished partial concurrence and dissent in the 1964 public accommodations cases—that there are boundaries beyond which Congress may not go in exercising the commerce power and that a holding that any activity of any kind having any effect on commerce could be reached and regulated under the Commerce Clause would render the commerce power virtually limitless. It thus appears that Commerce Clause jurisprudence in American constitutional law has at least tentatively entered a new era of limits not seen since the 1930s. So long as the Court avoids paralyzing the national commerce power in a manner similar to what occurred prior to 1937, the *Lopez, Morrison,* and like decisions may in the long run be viewed as healthy reminders that we live under a constitutional system that imposes limitations on the exercise of governmental power that may not be exceeded even when the power being exercised derives from the Commerce Clause.

NOTES

A Note on Sources

As the notes reflect, I have relied on a substantial amount of material drawn from archival sources for the documentation herein. This includes material from the Lyndon B. Johnson Library, Austin, Texas; the Earl Warren, William O. Douglas, William J. Brennan, Hugo L. Black, and National Association for the Advancement of Colored People (NAACP) Papers, all of which are located in the Manuscript Division of the Library of Congress; the Tom C. Clark Papers in the Tarleton Law Library, School of Law, University of Texas–Austin; the John Marshall Harlan II Papers in the Seeley Mudd Library, Princeton University; and the File of the Civil Rights Division, Department of Justice, on *Heart of Atlanta Motel v. United States*. References in the notes to material from the Lyndon B. Johnson Library are prefaced by LBJL; Library of Congress material by LC; the Clark Papers by TLL; and the Harlan Papers by SML; and the materials from the file of the Civil Rights Division, Department of Justice, are cited as Civil Rights Division File.

Preface

1. Brief for Appellees, *Heart of Atlanta Motel v. United States,* 379 U.S. 241 (1964), pp. 42–43.
2. *New York Times,* Dec. 16, 1964, p. 48.
3. *Civil Rights Cases,* 109 U.S. 3 (1883).
4. *Heart of Atlanta Motel v. United States,* 379 U.S. 241 (1964); *Katzenbach v. McClung,* 379 U.S. 294 (1964).

Introduction

1. Record, *Heart of Atlanta Motel v. United States,* 379 U.S. 241 (1964), p. 35; Record, *Katzenbach v. McClung,* 379 U.S. 294 (1964), pp. 87–88.
2. *Heart of Atlanta Motel v. United States,* 379 U.S. 241 (1964); *Katzenbach v. McClung,* 379 U.S. 294 (1964).
3. Bernard Schwartz, ed., *Statutory History of the United States: Civil Rights,* Part 1 (New York: Chelsea House, 1970), pp. 657–58, 661.
4. *Civil Rights Cases,* 109 U.S. 3, 26–62 (1883).
5. Ibid., 10–11.
6. Ibid., 18–19.
7. Ibid., 24–25.
8. *Jones v. Alfred H. Mayer Co.,* 392 U.S. 409 (1968).

9. *Brown v. Board of Education,* 347 U.S. 483 (1954).

10. Thomas P. Lewis, "The Sit-in Cases: Great Expectations," in *Supreme Court Review* (Chicago: University of Chicago Press, 1963), pp. 101–51; Monrad G. Paulsen, "The Sit-in Cases of 1964: But Answer Came There None," in *Supreme Court Review* (Chicago: University of Chicago Press, 1964), pp. 137–70.

11. The classic analysis of the restrictive covenant cases is Clement E. Vose, *Caucasians Only* (Berkeley: University of California Press, 1959).

12. On the Office of U.S. Solicitor General, see Rebecca Mae Salokar, *The Solicitor General: The Politics of Law* (Philadelphia: Temple University Press, 1992); and Donald L. Horowitz, *The Jurocracy* (Lexington, Mass.: Lexington Books, 1977), pp. 54–60.

13. Victor S. Navasky, *Kennedy Justice* (New York: Atheneum, 1971), pp. 280–81.

14. Ibid., p. 280.

15. Ibid., p. 289.

16. Ken Gormley, *Archibald Cox: Conscience of the Nation* (Reading, Mass: Addison Wesley, 1997), p. 159.

17. Gormley, *Archibald Cox,* pp. 156–60; Cox subsequently defended his position in the *Sit-in* cases in his *The Warren Court: Constitutional Decision as an Instrument of Reform* (Cambridge: Harvard University Press, 1968), pp. 39–40.

18. See Tinsley E. Yarborough, *Mr. Justice Black and His Critics* (Durham: Duke University Press, 1988); Robert K. Newman, *Hugo Black* (New York: Pantheon Books, 1994); Gerald T. Dunne, *Hugo Black and the Judicial Revolution* (New York: Simon and Schuster, 1977); Virginia Van Der Veer Hamilton, *Hugo Black: The Alabama Years* (Baton Rouge: Louisiana State University Press, 1972); Hugo Black, *A Constitutional Faith* (New York: Knopf, 1969).

19. See William O. Douglas, *Go East, Young Man* (New York: Random House, 1974); *The Court Years* (New York: Vintage Books, 1980); J. F. Simon, *Independent Journey: The Life of William O. Douglas* (New York: Harper and Row, 1980); Howard Ball and Phillip J. Cooper, *Of Power and Right: Hugo Black, William O. Douglas, and America's Constitutional Revolution* (New York: Oxford University Press, 1992).

20. See Henry J. Abraham, *Justices and Presidents: A Political History of Appointments to the Supreme Court,* 3d ed. (New York: Oxford University Press, 1985), pp. 242–45.

21. *Baker v. Carr,* 369 U.S. 186 (1962).

22. See Richard C. Cortner, *The Apportionment Cases* (Knoxville: University of Tennessee Press, 1970).

23. Bernard Schwartz, *Super Chief: Earl Warren and His Supreme Court* (New York: New York University Press, 1983); Ed Cray, *Chief Justice: A Biography of Earl Warren* (New York: Simon and Schuster, 1997); Earl Warren, *The Memoirs of Chief Justice Warren* (New York: Doubleday, 1977); G. Edward White, *Earl Warren: A Public Life* (New York: Oxford University Press, 1982).

24. See Richard C. Cortner, *The Supreme Court and the Second Bill of Rights* (Madison: University of Wisconsin Press, 1981); Tinsley E. Yarborough, *John Marshall Harlan: Great Dissenter of the Warren Court* (New York: Oxford University Press, 1992).

25. See Phillip Cooper and Howard Ball, *The United States Supreme Court: From the Inside Out* (Upper Saddle River, N.J.: Prentice Hall, 1996), pp. 246–57.

26. See Anthony Lewis, *Make No Law* (New York: Random House, 1991); David E. Marion, *The Jurisprudence of Justice William J. Brennan, Jr.: A Political and Constitutional Study* (Lanham, Md.: Rowman and Littlefield, 1997); Abraham, *Justices and Presidents,* pp. 262–65.

27. See *Chimel v. California,* 395 U.S. 752 (1969); *Katz v. United States,* 389 U.S. 347 (1967).

28. Abraham, *Justices and Presidents,* pp. 267–71.

29. Ibid., pp. 273–77; Cortner, *The Apportionment Cases,* p. 144.

30. Abraham, *Justices and Presidents,* pp. 277–80; Arthur J. Goldberg, *Equal Justice: The Supreme Court in the Warren Era* (Evanston, Ill.: Northwestern University Press, 1971).

31. *Bell v. Maryland,* 378 U.S. 226 (1964).

32. Ibid., 227–41.

33. Ibid., 286–318.

34. Ibid., 260.

35. Ibid., 326.

36. For an analysis of the divisions that the *Sit-in* cases produced inside the Court, see Cooper and Ball, *The United States Supreme Court,* pp. 205–8.

1. The Civil Rights Act of 1964

1. Charles and Barbara Whalen, *The Longest Debate: A Legislative History of the 1964 Civil Rights Act* (Washington, D.C.: Seven Locks Press, 1985), pp. xvi–xx; Hugh Davis Graham, *The Civil Rights Era: Origins and Development of National Policy* (New York: Oxford University Press, 1990), pp. 74–75.

2. Bernard Schwartz, ed., *Statutory History of the United States, Civil Rights,* Part 2 (New York: Chelsea House, 1970), pp. 1017–18; Taylor Branch, *Pillar of Fire: America During the King Years, 1963–65* (New York: Simon and Schuster, 1998), p. 108.

3. Graham, *The Civil Rights Era,* pp. 87–90.

4. Ibid., pp. 87–88; Whalen, *The Longest Debate,* pp. 9–13.

5. Michael R. Beschloss, ed., *Taking Charge: The Johnson White House Tapes, 1963–1964* (New York: Simon and Schuster, 1997), p. 354; Robert D. Loevy, ed., *The Civil Rights Act of 1964: The Passage of the Law That Ended Segregation* (Albany: State University of New York Press, 1997), pp. 245–64. For an analysis of the interaction among Lyndon Johnson, Hubert Humphrey, and Richard Russell on the civil rights issue, see Robert Mann, *The Walls of Jericho: Lyndon Johnson, Hubert Humphrey, Richard Russell, and the Struggle for Civil Rights* (New York: Harcourt, Brace, 1996).

6. Schwartz, *Statutory History,* pp. 1377–79. Senator Dirksen claimed that his "idea whose time has come" quote was from the diary of Victor Hugo. No such diary exists. Rather, Dirksen was paraphrasing words from Hugo's *Histoire d'un Crime,* in which he had said, "A stand can be made against invasion by an army; no stand can be made against invasion by an idea." See Mann, *The Walls of Jericho,* p. 422.

7. Whalen, *The Longest Debate,* pp. 199–200.

8. Schwartz, *Statutory History,* pp. 1401–2.

9. Whalen, *The Longest Debate,* pp. 226–28.

10. *Civil Rights Cases,* 109 U.S. 3 (1883).

11. Graham, *The Civil Rights Era,* pp. 80–81.

12. *Gibbons v. Ogden,* 22 U.S. 1, 6 L.Ed. 23, 69–70 (1824).

13. *McCulloch v. Maryland,* 17 U.S. 316, 4 L.Ed. 579, 605 (1819).

14. *Southern Railway Co. v. United States,* 222 U.S. 20 (1911).

15. *Shreveport Case (Houston and East and West Texas Railway Co. v. United States),* 234 U.S. 342 (1914).

16. Ibid., 353.

17. *Swift and Co. v. United States,* 196 U.S. 375 (1905).

18. *Stafford v. Wallace,* 258 U.S. 495 (1922).

19. *Chicago Board of Trade v. Olsen*, 262 U.S. 1 (1923).

20. *Hammer v. Dagenhart*, 247 U.S. 251 (1918).

21. *Carter v. Carter Coal Co.*, 298 U.S. 238 (1936). The application of the direct-indirect effects doctrine to the commerce power of Congress first occurred in *United States v. E. C. Knight and Co. (Sugar Trust Case)*, 156 U.S. 1 (1895); see also *Adair v. United States*, 208 U.S. 161 (1908).

22. *NLRB v. Jones and Laughlin Steel Corp.*, 301 U.S. 1 (1937). See also Richard C. Cortner, *The Wagner Act Cases* (Knoxville: University of Tennessee Press, 1964).

23. *United States v. Darby*, 312 U.S. 100 (1941).

24. Ibid., 118–19.

25. *Wickard v. Filburn*, 317 U.S. 111 (1942).

26. Ibid., 125.

27. Ibid., 129.

28. See Graham, *The Civil Rights Era*, p. 80.

29. Ibid., p. 81.

30. Ibid., pp. 92–93.

31. Ibid. Brief of Professor Paul A. Freund, Hearings, Senate Commerce Committee, 88th Cong., 1st sess., Part 1 (1963), pp. 1183–90.

32. Ibid.

33. Ibid.

34. Graham, *The Civil Rights Era*, pp. 93–95.

35. Beschloss, *Taking Charge*, pp. 420–21.

36. Ibid., p. 450.

37. Victor S. Navasky, *Kennedy Justice* (New York: Atheneum, 1971), pp. 161–63; Arthur M. Schlesinger Jr., *Robert Kennedy and His Times* (Boston: Houghton Mifflin, 1978), pp. 288–89.

38. Navasky, *Kennedy Justice*, p. 162.

39. LBJL, Burke Marshall Oral History, Oct. 28, 1968, pp. 2–3.

40. See the Brief for the Appellants, *Katzenbach v. McClung*, 379 U.S. 294 (1964), p. 12.

41. Brian K. Landsberg, *Enforcing Civil Rights: Race Discrimination and the Department of Justice* (Lawrence: University Press of Kansas, 1997), pp. 96–97.

2. The Genesis of the *Heart of Atlanta Motel* Case

1. *Atlanta Constitution*, June 19, 1964, p. 1; June 22, 1964, p. 18.

2. Ibid., July 3, 1964, p. 1; Michael R. Beschloss, ed., *Taking Charge: The Johnson White House Tapes, 1963–1964* (New York: Simon and Schuster, 1997), pp. 449, 450 n. 5.

3. LBJL, Papers of LBJ, Human Rights, Box 2, Memorandum to the Files, Subject: Meeting with Negro leadership following Signing Ceremony, by Lee C. White, July 6, 1964.

4. *Wall Street Journal*, July 2, 1964, pp. 1, 16.

5. Ibid.

6. Ivan Allen and Paul Hemphill, *Mayor: Notes on the Sixties* (New York: Simon and Schuster, 1971), pp. 82–83.

7. Ibid., p. 103.

8. Ibid., pp. 104–6.

9. David Andrew Harmon, *Beneath the Image of the Civil Rights Movement and Race Relations: Atlanta, Georgia, 1946–1981* (New York: Garland Publishing, 1996), pp. 153–58;

Clarence N. Stone, *Regime Politics: Governing Atlanta, 1946–1988* (Lawrence: University Press of Kansas, 1989), p. 58; Allen, *Mayor,* p. 107.

10. Harmon, *Beneath the Image,* pp. 156–57; Stone, *Regime Politics,* p. 58; *Atlanta Constitution,* Dec. 23, 1963, p. 14; Dec. 25, 1963, p. 14; Dec. 26, 1963, p. 8; Jan. 1, 1964, p. 16A.

11. Harmon, *Beneath the Image,* pp. 156–57.

12. *Atlanta Constitution,* Dec. 16, 1963, p. 1.

13. *Atlanta Constitution,* Dec. 3, 1963, p. 1; Jan. 7, 1964, p. 1; Jan. 11, 1964, p. 1; Jan. 16, 1964, p. 5; Jan. 21, 1964, p. 4.

14. *Atlanta Constitution,* Jan. 11, 1964, p. 1; Jan. 27, 1964, p. 20; Harmon, *Beneath the Image,* p. 161.

15. *Wall Street Journal,* July 2, 1964, pp. 1, 16.

16. *Atlanta Constitution,* June 19, 1964, pp. 1, 15.

17. *Atlanta Constitution,* July 2, 1964, pp. 4, 5.

18. *Atlanta Constitution,* July 3, 1964, pp. 1, 4; July 4, 1964, p. 1.

19. *Atlanta Constitution,* July 3, 1962, p. 3; March 5, 1998, pp. 10C–11C; June 21, 1963, pp. 1, 13; *Atlanta Journal,* July 6, 1964, pp. 1, 6.

20. *Martindale-Hubbell Law Directory* (Summit, N.J.: Martindale-Hubbell, 1964), biographical section, p. 1746.

21. *Atlanta Journal,* July 7, 1964, p. 3; July 11, 1964, pp. 1, 5.

22. Complaint, *Heart of Atlanta Motel v. United States,* July 2, 1964, Civil Action No. 9017, p. 6 (hereafter Complaint).

23. Complaint, pp. 8–9; Amended Complaint, *Heart of Atlanta Motel v. United States,* July 15, 1964, Civil Action No. 9017, pp. 13–15.

24. Complaint, p. 7.

25. FBI interview with name redacted, July 11, 1964, *Heart of Atlanta Motel v. United States,* Civil Rights Division File.

26. *Atlanta Constitution,* July 4, 1964, p. 1; July 7, 1964, pp. 1, 3; *Time* 84 (July 17, 1964): p. 25.

27. Letter, Burke Marshall to Director, Federal Bureau of Investigation, July 8, 1964, *Heart of Atlanta Motel v. United States,* Civil Rights Division File.

28. Ibid.

29. Lester G. Maddox, *Speaking Out: The Autobiography of Lester Garfield Maddox* (Garden City, N.Y.: Doubleday, 1975), p. 57; Taylor Branch, *Pillar of Fire: America in the King Years, 1963–65* (New York: Simon and Schuster, 1998), p. 388; see also *Atlanta Constitution,* July 18, 1964, p. 1.

30. Dan T. Carter, *The Politics of Rage: George Wallace, the Origins of the New Conservatism, and the Transformation of American Politics* (New York: Simon & Schuster, 1995), pp. 216–17.

31. *Atlanta Journal,* July 5, 1964, p. 1; *Christian Science Monitor,* July 14, 1964, p. 3.

32. LC, NAACP Papers, Group III, C27, Branch Files, Atlanta, Ga., Memo to the Executive Committee from Albert R. Sampson, Aug. 14, 1964; *Atlanta Constitution,* July 8, 1964, pp. 1, 6; April 21, 1965, pp. 1, 8.

33. *Atlanta Constitution,* July 10, 1964, pp. 1, 11.

34. Record, *Heart of Atlanta Motel v. United States,* Civil Action No. 9017, pp. 18–20, 28 (hereafter Record); *Atlanta Constitution,* July 14, 1964, p. 3; July 15, 1964, p. 13; July 16, 1964, pp. 1, 12.

35. *Atlanta Constitution,* Sept. 2, 1954, p. 1; *The American Bench* (Minneapolis: Bishop Forster and Associates, 1977), pp. 43–44.

36. *The American Bench,* p. 472; Jack Peltason, *Fifty-Eight Lonely Men* (New York: Harcourt, Brace and World, 1961), pp. 113, 127–31.

37. *Almanac of the Federal Judiciary* (Chicago: Lawletters, 1989), 11th Circuit, p. 23; *Atlanta Journal,* July 25, 1968, p. 11-C.

38. Letter, Burke Marshall to Director, FBI, July 10, 1964, *Heart of Atlanta Motel v. United States,* Civil Rights Division File. In complying with this request for an investigation of the Heart of Atlanta Motel, as well as the investigation of the Pickrick restaurant, the FBI amassed investigative reports totalling 207 pages and large numbers of photographs of the highway billboards of the Heart of Atlanta Motel.

39. Letter, Olin C. Cooper to Attorney General Robert Kennedy, July 17, 1964, *Heart of Atlanta Motel v. United States,* Civil Rights Division File.

40. Record, pp. 33–35.

41. Ibid., pp. 35–41.

42. Ibid., pp. 42–43.

43. *Civil Rights Cases,* 109 U.S. 3 (1883).

44. Record, p. 45.

45. Ibid., p. 46.

46. Ibid., pp. 46–47.

47. Ibid., pp. 47–52.

48. Ibid., pp. 52–54.

49. Ibid., pp. 55–56.

50. *NLRB v. Jones and Laughlin Steel Corp.,* 301 U.S. 1 (1937).

51. Record, pp. 56–58.

52. *Gibbons v. Ogden,* 22 U.S. 1 (1824).

53. *United States v. Darby,* 312 U.S. 100 (1941).

54. *Wickard v. Filburn,* 317 U.S. 111 (1942).

55. Record, pp. 59–60.

56. Ibid., p. 61.

57. Ibid.

58. Ibid., pp. 61–62.

59. Ibid., p. 62.

60. Ibid., p. 63.

61. Ibid., pp. 63–64.

62. *Shreveport Case (Houston and East and West Texas Railway Co. v. United States),* 234 U.S. 342 (1914).

63. Record, p. 64.

64. Ibid., pp. 64–67.

65. Ibid., pp. 67–68.

66. Ibid., pp. 68–71.

67. Ibid., pp. 72–73.

68. Ibid., p. 73.

69. *Atlanta Constitution,* July 17, 1964, pp. 1, 12; July 18, 1964, pp. 1, 5; July 20, 1964, pp. 1, 6.

70. Ibid., July 17, 1964, pp. 1, 12; July 21, 1964, pp. 1, 6; *Time* 84 (July 31, 1964): p. 62.

71. *Atlanta Constitution,* July 23, 1964, p. 1.

72. *McCulloch v. Maryland,* 17 U.S. 317 (1819).

73. Record, pp. 76–77; *Heart of Atlanta Motel v. United States,* 231 F.Supp. 393 (D.C.N.D.Ga., Atlanta Div., 1964), 395.

74. *Marriott Hotels of Atlanta v. Heart of Atlanta Motel,* 232 F.Supp. 270 (D.C.N.D.Ga., Atlanta Div., 1964), 272–74.

75. *Hotel Employees v. Leedom,* 358 U.S. 99 (1958).

76. Record, pp. 77–78; 231 F.Supp. 393, 395.

77. Record, pp. 78–79; 231 F.Supp. 393, 396.

78. *Willis v. Pickrick Restaurant,* 231 F.Supp. 396 (D.C.N.D.Ga., Atlanta Div., 1964), 398–99.

79. 231 F.Supp. 393, 399–400.

80. 231 F.Supp. 393, 401–402.

81. *Atlanta Constitution,* July 23, 1964, pp. 1, 18–19.

82. Letter, Burke Marshall to Director, FBI, July 19, 1964, *Heart of Atlanta Motel v. United States,* Civil Rights Division File.

83. Ibid.

84. *Heart of Atlanta Motel v. United States* and *Pickrick v. Willis,* 13 L.Ed. 2d 12 (1964).

85. Ibid., 13–14.

86. Ibid., 14.

87. LC, Black Papers, Container No. 382, Case File, No. 515, *Heart of Atlanta Motel v. United States,* Letter, Fred J. Hurst to Black, July 16, 1964; Letter, Jean Burgess to Black, Aug. 11, 1964; Postcard, J. Win to Black, n.d.

88. *Atlanta Constitution,* Aug. 11, 1964, pp. 1, 6.

89. Ibid.; *New York Times,* Aug. 11, 1964, p. 24.

90. *Atlanta Constitution,* Aug. 11, 1964, p. 6; *New York Times,* Aug. 13, 1964, pp. 1, 22.

91. *Atlanta Constitution,* Aug. 12, 1964, pp. 1, 8; Aug. 13, 1964, pp. 1, 16.

92. *Atlanta Constitution,* Aug. 14, 1964, pp. 1, 12.

93. Ibid.

94. Telegrams, [names redacted] to Robert Kennedy, Aug. 14, 1964, *Heart of Atlanta Motel v. United States,* Civil Rights Division File.

95. *Atlanta Constitution,* Aug. 21, 1964, pp. 1, 11.

96. Ibid.; see the Motion to Dismiss or Affirm, *Maddox v. Willis,* 382 U.S. 18 (1965), pp. 4–7, Civil Rights Division File.

97. *Atlanta Journal,* July 7, 1964, p. 15; see Notice of Appeal to U.S. Supreme Court, *Willis v. Pickrick,* July 28, 1964; Motion to Dismiss or Affirm, *Maddox v. Willis,* July 1965, p. 5, Civil Rights Division File. Maddox later claimed that the Supreme Court denied his attorneys' appeal of the *Pickrick* case and instead decided the validity of the public accommodations provisions as they applied to restaurants in a case involving Ollie's Barbecue in Birmingham, Alabama. "I felt then—and now—that the merits of my case were far stronger and that at least a glimmer of hope would have remained for justice being done had my case reached the Supreme Court first," Maddox asserted. "Even if justice had not been dispensed, my arguments would have been heard." These assertions are inaccurate. First, the *Pickrick* case was not heard by the Supreme Court because Maddox and his attorneys failed to pursue the appeal in the case. Although Maddox claimed that $17,000 had been contributed by his supporters for his legal defense, the appeal in the *Pickrick* case was probably abandoned because of Maddox's financial difficulties after the closure of the Pickrick. Maddox reported in January 1965 that between August and the end of November of 1964, he had lost $36,000 in income

and incurred $22,500 in legal expenses. Contributions by supporters, he said, covered some of the legal expenses, but he nonetheless had still lost a total of over $45,000. Secondly, the facts in the *Pickrick* case were more favorable to the government than the facts in the case involving Ollie's Barbecue proved to be regarding the application of the Civil Rights Act to restaurants. See Maddox, *Speaking Out,* pp. 60–61, 65; *Atlanta Constitution,* Jan. 2, 1965, p. 5.

3. Public Accommodations and Ollie's Barbecue in Birmingham

1. Hugh David Graham, *The Civil Rights Era: Origin and Development of National Policy, 1960–1972* (New York: Oxford University Press, 1990), pp. 74–76; Glenn T. Eskew, *But for Birmingham: The Local and National Movements in the Civil Rights Struggle* (Chapel Hill: University of North Carolina Press, 1997), p. 312.

2. Eskew, *But for Birmingham,* p. 191; *New York Times,* July 4, 1964, p. 1.

3. *Atlanta Journal,* July 4, 1964, p. 2.

4. *Time* 84 (July 17, 1964): p. 25.

5. Ibid.

6. Ibid.; *Christian Science Monitor,* July 7, 1964, pp. 1, 14; *Wall Street Journal,* July 6, 1964, p. 2.

7. Author's telephone interview with Robert McDavid Smith, June 19, 1998.

8. Ibid.

9. Michael Durham, "Ollie McClung's Big Decision," *Life* 57 (Oct. 9, 1964): p. 31.

10. Ibid.

11. Ibid.; author's telephone interview with Robert McDavid Smith, June 19, 1998.

12. Author's telephone interview with Robert McDavid Smith, June 19, 1998.

13. *Martindale-Hubbell Law Directory* (Summit, N.J.: Martindale-Hubbell, 1964), biographical section, p. 17.

14. Civil Rights Act of 1964, Title II, section 206(a); *Katzenbach v. McClung,* 379 U.S. 294 (1964).

15. *Birmingham News,* July 16, 1964, p. 44; July 30, 1964, pp. 1, 3.

16. Record, *Katzenbach v. McClung,* Civil Action No. 64-4435, pp. 89–90 (hereafter Record).

17. *Birmingham News,* Aug. 1, 1964, p. 2.

18. Record, p. 2.

19. Ibid., pp. 2–3.

20. Ibid., pp. 5–6, 31–32.

21. Ibid., pp. 3–4.

22. Ibid., pp. 4–5.

23. Ibid., pp. 6–7.

24. Ibid., p. 16.

25. Memorandum from Solicitor General Archibald Cox to Harold H. Greene, Chief, Appeals and Research Section, Civil Rights Division, July 30, 1964, noting that a notice of appeal had been filed in the *Pickrick* case, *Heart of Atlanta Motel v. United States,* Civil Rights Division File.

26. *Birmingham News,* Aug. 5, 1964, p. 18; Sept. 1, 1964, p. 2; Sept. 2, 1964, p. 2; Record, p. 11.

27. Jack Peltason, *Fifty-Eight Lonely Men* (New York: Harcourt, Brace and World, 1961), p. 84; *Almanac of the Federal Judiciary*, vol. 1, 11th Circuit (Chicago: Lawletters, 1989), p. 5.

28. Peltason, *Fifty-Eight Lonely Men*, p. 84; *Almanac of the Federal Judiciary*, vol. 1, 11th Circuit, p. 4.

29. *Birmingham News*, May 16, 1981, p. 12B; *Martindale-Hubbell Law Directory*, Alabama vol. (Summit, N.J.: Martindale-Hubbell, 1961), p. 66.

30. Request for Admissions, Aug. 18, 1964; Request for Additional Admissions, Aug. 24, 1964, Record, pp. 13–23.

31. Response to Request for Admissions, Aug. 24, 1964; Objections to Plaintiffs' Request for Additional Admissions, Aug. 31, 1964, Record, pp. 23–24, 25–29.

32. Record, p. 62.

33. Ibid., pp. 62–63.

34. Ibid., pp. 63–64.

35. Ibid.

36. Ibid., pp. 64–65.

37. Ibid., p. 65.

38. Ibid., pp. 70–72.

39. Ibid., pp. 72–75, 78.

40. Ibid., pp. 76–77.

41. Ibid., pp. 78–79.

42. Ibid., pp. 80–81.

43. Ibid.

44. Ibid., pp. 81–82.

45. Ibid., pp. 82–83.

46. Ibid., pp. 84–85.

47. Ibid., pp. 87–88.

48. Ibid., pp. 89–90.

49. Ibid. The three-judge court subsequently heard oral arguments in the *McClung* case, but unfortunately, these arguments were not recorded. See Record, p. 90.

50. *Birmingham News*, Sept. 3, 1964, p. 1; *McClung v. Katzenbach*, 233 F.Supp. 815 (D.C.N.D. Ala., Sept. 17, 1964).

51. 233 F.Supp. 815, 819.

52. Ibid., at 820–21.

53. Ibid., at 815, 821.

54. Ibid., at 822–23.

55. Ibid., at 824–25.

56. Ibid., at 825.

57. Ibid.

58. *Birmingham News*, Sept. 17, 1964, pp. 1, 18; *New York Times*, Dec. 17, 1964, p. 46.

59. *Birmingham News*, Sept. 17, 1964, pp. 1, 18.

60. *Montgomery Advertiser*, Sept. 18, 1964, pp. 1, 4.

61. *Birmingham News*, Oct. 27, 1964, p. 6.

62. Ibid. Robert McDavid Smith and his firm were not informed of the ad nor were they aware of who had sponsored it. Letter, Robert McDavid Smith to the author, Nov. 20, 1998; Glenn T. Eskew states in his *But for Birmingham*, p. 326, n. 52, that the organization of the defense fund under the auspices of the Exchange Security Bank was "a

reflection of the Big Mules [the dominant business interests in Birmingham] defense of segregation, for directors of the bank included industrialist Alfred M. Shook, [U.S. District]
Judge Seybourn Lynne, and attorneys R. H. Lange and former state senator James A. Simpson of the old-guard law firm of Lange, Simpson, Robinson & Somerville." It nevertheless
appears more likely that the McClung legal defense fund was sponsored by the Restaurant
Association.

63. Durham, "Ollie McClung's Big Decision," p. 31.

64. Ibid.

65. *Katzenbach v. McClung*, 13 L.Ed. 15, 16 (1964).

66. LC, Black Papers, Container 383, Case File, *Katzenbach v. McClung*, Letter, John W.
Nolen to Black, Sept. 23, 1964.

67. Ibid., Letter, Horace C. Bell to Black, Sept. 30, 1964.

68. Ibid., Letter, Arthur Newcomb to Black, Dec. 1964.

69. Ibid., Letter, Moreton Rolleston to Ralph Spritzer, Office of Solicitor General, Aug.
12, 1964; Letter, Archibald Cox to Moreton Rolleston, Aug. 12, 1964, Civil Rights Division File.

70. Ibid., Letter, Chief Justice Warren to Archibald Cox, Aug. 25, 1964.

71. Ibid., Letter Archibald Cox to Chief Justice Warren, Aug. 28, 1964.

72. Joint Motion to Expedite Briefing and Oral Argument, *Katzenbach v. McClung*, Sept.
24, 1964, SML, John Marshall Harlan Papers, Box 235, Case Files, No. 543; Letter, Robert
McDavid Smith to the author, Nov. 20, 1998; *Katzenbach v. McClung*, 379 U.S. 802 (1964);
Heart of Atlanta Motel v. United States, 379 U.S. 803 (1964).

4. The *Heart of Atlanta Motel* Case: The Clash of Argument

1. *Civil Rights Cases*, 109 U.S. 3 (1883); Brief of the Appellant, *Heart of Atlanta Motel v.
United States*, 379 U.S. 241 (1964), p. 16 (hereafter Brief for Appellant).

2. *Bell v. Maryland*, 378 U.S. 226 (1964); Brief for Appellant, pp. 17, 30–33.

3. *New York v. Miln*, 36 U.S. 102 (1837); Brief for Appellant, pp. 32, 40–44.

4. Brief for Appellant, pp. 41, 51–55.

5. Brief for Appellees, *Heart of Atlanta Motel v. United States*, 379 U.S. 241 (1964), p. 15
(hereafter Brief for Appellees).

6. *Gibbons v. Ogden*, 22 U.S. 1 (1824); *McCulloch v. Maryland*, 17 U.S. 316 (1819);
NLRB v. Jones and Laughlin Steel Corp., 301 U.S. 1 (1937); *United States v. Darby*, 312 U.S.
100 (1941); *Wickard v. Filburn*, 317 U.S. 111 (1942); Brief for Appellees, pp. 17–22.

7. *Hotel Employees v. Leedom*, 358 U.S. 99 (1958).

8. Brief for Appellees, pp. 23–46.

9. Ibid., pp. 22, 56–62.

10. *Butts v. Merchants & Marine Transportation Co.*, 280 U.S. 126 (1913); Brief for Appellees, p. 16.

11. Brief for Appellees, p. 22.

12. For an excellent analysis of the evolution of the role of *amicus curiae* briefs in the judicial process, see Samuel Krislov, "The *Amicus Curiae* Brief: From Friendship to Advocacy,"
Yale Law Journal 62 (March 1963): p. 694.

13. Brief on Behalf of the State of New York as *Amicus Curiae* in Support of Affirmance, *Heart of Atlanta Motel v. United States,* 379 U.S. 898 (1964), p. 1.

14. Brief *Amicus Curiae* on Behalf of the Commonwealth of Virginia, *Heart of Atlanta Motel v. United States,* 397 U.S. 898 (1964), p. 8.

15. LC, Douglas Papers, Container No. 1347, Memo, JSC to Douglas, Re *Heart of Atlanta* case, Oct. 4, 1964.

16. LC, Warren Papers, Container No. 267, Conference Memos, Bench Memo, *Heart of Atlanta Motel v. United States,* JCG to Warren, Sept. 30, 1964, pp. 20–22.

17. Ibid., pp. 23–24, 26.

18. Ibid., pp. 30–35.

19. Ibid., pp. 35–36.

20. Ibid., p. 43.

21. LC, Brennan Papers, Case Files, Container 130, Memorandum on the Civil Rights Cases, No. 515, *Heart of Atlanta Motel v. United States,* SPP to Brennan, n.d., p. 20.

22. Ibid., pp. 25–27.

23. Ibid., pp. 31–32.

24. Ibid., p. 32.

25. SML, John Marshall Harlan II Papers, Box 235, Case Files, No. 515, *Heart of Atlanta Motel v. United States,* Bench Memo by Michael M. Maney, Sept. 15, 1964.

26. *Shelley v. Kraemer,* 334 U.S. 1 (1948).

27. SML, Harlan Papers, Box 235, Case Files, No. 515, *Heart of Atlanta Motel v. United States,* Civil Rights Act of 1964: Public Accommodations and the Fourteenth Amendment by Charles R. Nesson, Sept. 13, 1964.

28. Ibid.

29. Ibid.

30. This description of the oral argument in *Heart of Atlanta Motel v. United States* is based on the tape recording of the argument that is available from the Audiovisual Division of the National Archives. A transcript of the oral argument is also available in Philip B. Kurland, ed., *Landmark Briefs and Arguments of the Supreme Court of the United States: Constitutional Law,* vol. 60 (Arlington, Va.: University Publications of America, 1975), pp. 541–95.

31. *Civil Rights Cases,* 109 U.S. 3 (1883).

32. *Bell v. Maryland,* 378 U.S. 226 (1964).

33. Ibid., 289.

34. *New York v. Miln,* 36 U.S. 102 (1837).

35. *Hotel Employees v. Leedom,* 358 U.S. 99 (1958).

36. *Wickard v. Filburn,* 317 U.S. 111 (1942).

37. *Gibbons v. Ogden,* 22 U.S. 1 (1824).

38. *Shreveport Case (Houston and East and West Texas Railway Co. v. United States),* 234 U.S. 342 (1914).

39. *United States v. Yellow Cab Co.,* 332 U.S. 218 (1947).

40. *United States v. Sullivan,* 332 U.S. 68 (1948).

41. *United States v. Carolene Products Co.,* 304 U.S. 144 (1938).

42. *McCulloch v. Maryland,* 17 U.S. 316 (1819).

43. *Edwards v. California,* 314 U.S. 160 (1941).

44. *Passenger Cases,* 7 How. 283 (1849).

45. *United States v. Darby,* 312 U.S. 100 (1941).

46. *Bob-Lo Excursion Co. v. Michigan,* 333 U.S. 28 (1948).

47. *Colorado Anti-Discrimination Commission v. Continental Airlines,* 372 U.S. 714 (1963).

48. *Hammer v. Dagenhart,* 247 U.S. 251 (1918).

5. Of Barbecue and Commerce: The Argument in the *McClung* Case

1. Brief for the Appellants, *Katzenbach v. McClung,* 379 U.S. 294 (1964), p. 12 (hereafter Brief for Appellants). An additional supplemental brief was filed by Solicitor General Cox on behalf of the United States in the *McClung* case. This supplemental brief reiterated the government's objection to the assumption of jurisdiction of the three-judge court in the case and urged the Court to express its disapproval of that action by the lower court.

2. Brief for Appellants, pp. 19–20.

3. Ibid., p. 26.

4. Ibid., pp. 38–39.

5. Ibid., pp. 44–45.

6. Ibid., p. 46; *Wickard v. Filburn,* 317 U.S. 111 (1942).

7. Brief for Appellants, p. 58.

8. Brief of Appellees, *Katzenbach v. McClung,* 379 U.S. 294 (1964), pp. 8–11 (hereafter Brief of Appellees). A supplemental brief for the appellees was also filed in the *McClung* case. This supplemental brief emphasized the contention of the appellees that there was no rational relation between discrimination by restaurants serving interstate food and an effect on interstate commerce. The brief thus reiterated points made in the main brief on behalf of the appellees, and it will therefore not be discussed herein.

9. Brief of Appellees, pp. 9, 13–25.

10. Ibid., p. 26.

11. Ibid., pp. 29–31.

12. Ibid., p. 30.

13. *Amicus Curiae* Brief on Behalf of the State of North Carolina, *Katzenbach v. McClung,* 379 U.S. 294 (1964), pp. 5, 7–9.

14. NAACP Legal Defense and Education Fund, as *Amicus Curiae, Katzenbach v. McClung,* 379 U.S. 294 (1964), p. 2.

15. LC, Warren Papers, Container No. 267, Bench Memo, *Katzenbach v. McClung,* 379 U.S. 294 (1964), JCG to Warren, Oct. 3, 1964, p. 3.

16. Ibid., pp. 13–14.

17. Ibid., p. 4.

18. Ibid., pp. 14–15.

19. LC, Brennan Papers, Case Files, Container 130, Memorandum on the Civil Rights Cases, No. 515, *Heart of Atlanta Motel v. U.S.,* SPP to Brennan, n.d., pp. 5–7.

20. Ibid., p. 22.

21. Ibid., pp. 27–30.

22. Ibid., pp. 31–32.

23. Ibid., pp. 32–33.

24. This description of the oral argument in *Katzenbach v. McClung* is based on the tape recording of the argument that is available from the Audiovisual Division of the National Archives.

25. *United States v. Carolene Products Co.,* 304 U.S. 144 (1938).

26. *United States v. Sullivan,* 332 U.S. 68 (1948).

27. *United States v. Darby,* 312 U.S. 100 (1941).

28. *Wickard v. Filburn,* 317 U.S. 111 (1942).

29. Justice Harlan actually said "Atlanta," obviously having the *Heart of Atlanta Motel* case in mind, but it is clear that he meant Birmingham.

6. The Public Accommodations Cases Inside the Court

1. TLL, Clark Papers, Box B124, General Correspondence, Memo, Warren to the Conference, Sept. 25, 1964.

2. David M. O'Brien, *Storm Center: The Supreme Court in American Politics,* 3d ed. (New York: Norton, 1986), p. 239.

3. On the operation of the Conference of the justices, see William H. Rehnquist, *The Supreme Court: How It Was, How It Is* (New York: William Morrow, 1987), pp. 287–95; on Goldberg's appointment to the Court, see Henry J. Abraham, *Presidents and Justices,* 2d ed. (New York: Oxford University Press, 1984), pp. 277–80.

4. See Rehnquist, *The Supreme Court,* p. 289. During the period of the Warren Court, the case selection procedure differed somewhat from that just described. At that time, the chief justice circulated a "dead list" of cases that were considered unworthy of discussion in conference, and each of the justices could remove cases from the dead list for consideration in conference. The discuss list replaced the dead list in the early 1970s. See Phillip Cooper and Howard Ball, *The United States Supreme Court: From the Inside Out* (Upper Saddle River, N.J.: Prentice Hall, 1996), pp. 112–13.

5. Rehnquist, *The Supreme Court,* pp. 289–90. At one time, however, it appears that votes on the merits were taken following the Conference discussion; see Tom C. Clark, "Inside the Court," in Alan F. Westin, ed., *The Supreme Court: Views from the Inside* (New York: Norton, 1961), p. 48.

6. The discussion in the above paragraphs and those that follow of the Conference of the justices in the *Heart of Atlanta Motel* and *McClung* cases is based on the handwritten notes of the Conference discussion taken by Justice William O. Douglas. The notes may be found in LC, William O. Douglas Papers, Container No. 1347, Supreme Court File, 1939–1980, Case No. 543. Since Douglas's notes are rather cryptic, I have elaborated on the points each of the justices was obviously making for purposes of clarity, but I have attempted to carefully avoid attributing to the justices views that were not clearly implied by their remarks.

7. *Shreveport Case (Houston and East and West Texas Railway Co. v. United States),* 234 U.S. 342 (1914); see Black's concurring opinion in the *Heart of Atlanta Motel* and *McClung* cases, 379 U.S. 241, 271–72 (1964).

8. *Edwards v. California,* 314 U.S. 160 (1941).

9. Ibid., 177–81.

10. See Rehnquist, *The Supreme Court,* p. 297.

11. Cooper and Ball, *The United States Supreme Court,* pp. 144–52.

12. *Smith v. Allwright,* 321 U.S. 649 (1944).

13. For an account of this episode, see Alpheus T. Mason, *Harlan Fiske Stone: Pillar of the Law* (New York: Viking, 1956), pp. 514–16.

14. *Brown v. Board of Education,* 347 U.S. 483 (1954).

15. Gerald T. Dunne, *Hugo Black and the Judicial Revolution* (New York: Simon and Schuster, 1977), pp. 324–26.

16. O'Brien, *Storm Center,* p. 315.

17. See Lee Epstein and Jack Knight, *Choices Justices Make* (Washington, D.C.: Congressional Quarterly Press, 1998), especially ch. 3, "Strategic Interaction," pp. 56–107; Rehnquist, *The Supreme Court,* pp. 301–3.

18. LC, Douglas Papers, Container No. 1347, Memo, JSC to Douglas, Re Legislative History of the Civil Rights Act and Its Constitutional Basis, Oct. 9, 1964.

19. Ibid., Memo, JSC to Douglas, Oct. 10, 1964.

20. Ibid., Memorandum, Oct. 12, 1964; *Shelley v. Kraemer,* 334 U.S. 1 (1948).

21. See *Heart of Atlanta Motel v. United States,* 379 U.S. 898 (1964).

22. *Atlanta Journal,* Nov. 9, 1964, p. 1.

23. LC, Warren Papers, Correspondence, 1953–1969, Container 348, Memo, Warren to Black, Oct. 29, 1964; Theodore H. White, *The Making of the President 1964* (New York: Atheneum Publishers, 1965), p. 304.

24. TLL, Clark Papers, Box A179, Memo, Clark to Warren, Oct. 30, 1964; Box A211, Record of Circulations, *Heart of Atlanta Motel v. United States,* 379 U.S. 898 (1964).

25. TLL, Clark Papers, Box A211, Record of Circulations, *Heart of Atlanta Motel v. United States* and *Katzenbach v. McClung.*

26. *Hall v. DeCuir,* 95 U.S. 485 (1878); TLL, Clark Papers, A179, Case No. 515, Memo, White to Clark, Nov. 21, 1964.

27. TLL, Clark Papers, A179, Case No. 515, Memo, Stewart to Clark, Nov. 24, 1964.

28. Ibid., Memo, Stewart to Clark, Nov. 27, 1964.

29. LC, Warren Papers, Container 520, Opinions, Associate Justices, 1953–69.

30. TLL, Clark Papers, Box A179, Case No. 515, Memo, White to Clark, Nov. 30, 1964.

31. *Civil Rights Cases,* 109 U.S. 3, 10 (1883).

32. TLL, Clark Papers, Box A179, Case No. 515, Draft Opinion, *Heart of Atlanta Motel v. United States,* Nov. 27, 1964.

33. See *Heart of Atlanta Motel v. United States,* 379 U.S. 241, 251–52 (1964); TLL, Clark Papers, Box A179, Case No. 515, Memo, White to Clark, Dec. 7, 1964.

34. See Cooper and Ball, *The United States Supreme Court,* pp. 248–59.

35. TLL, Clark Papers, Box A179, Case No. 515, Draft of the Opinion, *Heart of Atlanta Motel v. United States,* Nov. 21, 1964.

36. LC, Brennan Papers, Container 130, Case Files, No. 515, Memo, Brennan to Clark, Nov. 25, 1964; the memo is also in TLL, Clark Papers, Box A179, Case No. 515.

37. Anthony Lewis, *Make No Law: The Sullivan Case and the First Amendment* (New York: Random House, 1991), p. 171.

38. SML, John Marshall Harlan II Papers, Box 235, Case Files, No. 515, *Heart of Atlanta Motel v. United States,* Bench Memo by Michael M. Maney, Sept. 15, 1964.

39. Ibid. Harlan's other clerk, Charles R. Nesson, also expressed no reservations regarding the validity of the act and submitted a memorandum to Harlan suggesting a theory on which the act could be upheld under section five of the Fourteenth Amendment, rather than the Commerce Clause. See ibid., Civil Rights Act of 1964: Public Accommodations and the Fourteenth Amendment, Sept. 13, 1964.

40. Ibid., Draft opinion in Nos. 515 and 543, pp. 1–2 (footnotes omitted).

41. Ibid., pp. 2–3.

42. Ibid., p. 3.

43. Ibid., pp. 5–6.

44. Ibid., p. 6.

45. Ibid., pp. 6–7.

46. Ibid., p. 8.

47. Ibid., pp. 8–11.

48. Ibid., pp. 14–17.

49. Ibid., pp. 18–19.

50. Ibid., pp. 21–23.

51. Ibid., pp. 21, 25.

52. TLL, Clark Papers, Box A179, Case No. 515, Memo, Harlan to Clark, Dec. 1, 1964.

53. Ibid., Draft of the *Heart of Atlanta Motel* opinion, Dec. 4, 1964.

54. *McDermott v. Wisconsin,* 228 U.S. 115 (1913).

55. *United States v. Sullivan,* 332 U.S. 68 (1948).

56. TLL, Clark Papers, Box A179, Case No. 543, Memo, Brennan to Clark, Nov. 25, 1964.

57. LC, Brennan Papers, Container 130, Case No. 543, Memo, SPP to Brennan, n.d.

58. *Wickard v. Filburn,* 317 U.S. 111 (1942).

59. TLL, Clark Papers, Box A179, Case No. 543, Draft Opinion in *Katzenbach v. McClung,* Nov. 25, 1964.

60. SML, Harlan Papers, Box 235, Memo from Mike [Michael M. Maney], Nov. 25, 1964.

61. TLL, Clark Papers, Box A179, Case No. 543, Memo, Harlan to Clark, Nov. 27, 1964.

62. Ibid.

63. See *Katzenbach v. McClung,* 379 U.S. 294, 304–5 (1964).

64. TLL, Clark Papers, Box A179, Case No. 543, Memo, Stewart to Clark, Nov. 27, 1964; Memo, White to Clark, Dec. 7, 1964.

65. See 379 U.S. 294, 300 (1964).

66. TLL, Clark Papers, Box A179, Case No. 543, Memo, Harlan to Clark, Nov. 30, 1964.

67. LC, Douglas Papers, Container No. 1347, Case No. 543, Memo, JSC to Douglas, Nov. 24, 1964.

68. TLL, Clark Papers, Box A179, Case No. 515, Draft Concurring Opinion by Justice Goldberg.

69. Ibid., Case No. 543, Memo, Goldberg to Clark, Dec. 7, 1964.

70. LC, Douglas Papers, Container No. 1347, Case No. 515, Memo, Goldberg to Douglas, Dec. 7, 1964; TLL, Clark Papers, Box A211, Record of Circulations, Case No. 515.

7. The Supreme Court's Decisions and Their Aftermath

1. *Heart of Atlanta Motel v. United States,* 379 U.S. 241 (1964); *Katzenbach v. McClung,* 379 U.S. 294 (1964).

2. *Heart of Atlanta Motel v. United States,* 379 U.S. 241, 242–50.

3. Ibid., 250–51.

4. Ibid., 251–52.

5. Ibid., 252–53.

6. Ibid., 253–55.

7. Ibid., 255–57.

8. Ibid., 258.

9. Ibid., 258–61.

10. Ibid., 261.

11. Ibid., 261–62.

12. *Katzenbach v. McClung,* 379 U.S. 294, 296–98.

13. Ibid., 296–98.

14. Ibid., 299–300.

15. Ibid., 300.

16. Ibid.

17. Ibid., 300–301.

18. Ibid., 302.

19. Ibid., 302–4.

20. Ibid., 304–5.

21. Ibid., 305.

22. Ibid., 270–72, 276.

23. Ibid., 378–79.

24. Ibid., 279–80, 281–86.

25. Ibid., 280.

26. LC, William O. Douglas Papers, Container No. 1347, No. 543, *Katzenbach v. Mc-Clung.* Douglas's recounting of this episode is in his handwriting, while Goldberg's reply was in his handwriting.

27. 379 U.S. 241, 291–93.

28. *Hamm v. Rock Hill; Lupper v. Arkansas,* 379 U.S. 306 (1964).

29. TLL, Clark Papers, Box A179, Case No. 515, *Heart of Atlanta Motel v. United States,* Letter, Jack Todd to Justice Clark, n.d.

30. Ken Gormley, *Archibald Cox: Conscience of the Nation* (Reading, Mass.: Addison Wesley, 1997), pp. 189–90.

31. *Atlanta Journal,* Dec. 14, 1964, p. 14; *Atlanta Constitution,* Dec. 15, 1964, p. 1; *Birmingham News,* Dec. 14, 1964, p. 25.

32. *Chicago Tribune,* Dec. 15, 1964, p. 2; *Time* 84 (Dec. 25, 1964): pp. 13–14.

33. *Atlanta Constitution,* March 5, 1998, pp. 10C–11C.

34. *Atlanta Constitution,* Dec. 15, 1964, p. 4; *Atlanta Journal,* Dec. 14, 1964, p. 14.

35. *Atlanta Journal,* Dec. 14, 1964, pp. 1, 14.

36. *Atlanta Constitution,* Jan. 30, 1965, p. 3; Feb. 1, 1965, p. 3; Feb. 2, 1965, pp. 1, 11.

37. *Atlanta Constitution,* Feb. 2, 1965, pp. 1, 11.

38. *Atlanta Constitution,* Feb. 4, 1965, pp. 1, 15.

39. Ibid.

40. *Atlanta Constitution,* Feb. 3, 1965, p. 1.

41. Letter, St. John Barrett to John Doar, Jan. 21, 1965, Civil Rights Division File.

42. *Atlanta Constitution,* Feb. 6, 1965, pp. 1, 11. Lester Maddox's attorneys appealed the contempt decision directly to the Supreme Court, but Solicitor General Cox filed a motion to dismiss or affirm the appeal on the ground that Judge Hooper's decision was properly reviewable in the first instance by the U.S. Court of Appeals for the Fifth Circuit and not the Supreme Court. On October 11, 1965, the Supreme Court granted the motion to dismiss. See *Maddox v. Willis,* 382 U.S. 18 (1965); Motion to Dismiss or Affirm, *Maddox v. Willis,* Civil Rights Division File.

43. Lester G. Maddox, *Speaking Out: The Autobiography of Lester Garfield Maddox* (Garden City, N.Y.: Doubleday, 1975), pp. 65–70, 92; *Atlanta Constitution,* Feb. 8, 1965, pp. 1, 9.

44. *Mobile Register,* Dec. 15, 1964, p. 1; *Birmingham News,* Dec. 15, 1964, p. 10; Dec. 22, 1964, p. 11.

45. Author's Telephone Interview with Robert McDavid Smith, June 19, 1998.

46. *Birmingham News,* Dec. 14, 1964, p. 1.

47. *Birmingham News,* Dec. 16, 1964, pp. 1, 7.

48. Ibid.

49. *Birmingham News,* Dec. 17, 1964, p. 41; *Newsweek* 64 (Dec. 28, 1964): pp. 16–19.

50. *Birmingham News,* Dec. 19, 1964, p. 6.

51. *Birmingham News,* Aug. 14, 1989, p. 4B; Letter, Robert McDavid Smith to the author, June 24, 1998.

52. *New York Times,* Dec. 15, 1964, pp. 1, 48. See also *Chicago Tribune,* Dec. 15, 1964, p. 20; *Los Angeles Times,* Dec. 16, 1964, pt. II, p. 4; *Christian Science Monitor,* Dec. 17, 1964, p. 20; Dec. 19, 1964, p. 20.

53. *New York Times,* Dec. 16, 1964, p. 42.

54. Ibid., Dec. 15, 1964, p. 48.

55. Ibid; LC, NAACP Papers, Part III, A67, Telegram, J. Francis Pohlhaus to Roy Wilkins, Dec. 14, 1964.

56. *New York Times,* Dec. 16, 1964, p. 50.

57. LBJL, John Macy File, Box 364, Burke Marshall.

58. White House Press Release, Dec. 18, 1964, ibid.

59. Archibald Cox, *The Warren Court: Constitutional Decision as an Instrument of Reform* (Cambridge: Harvard University Press, 1968), p. 40.

60. Ibid., p. 39.

61. *NLRB v. Jones and Laughlin Steel Corp.,* 301 U.S. 1 (1937).

62. The firm of Lange, Simpson, Robinson and Somerville ultimately spent $15,000 on the *McClung* case. The Birmingham Restaurant Association paid the firm $8,248.65 of this bill, while Ollie McClung Sr. paid a sum of $250. "While there remained a balance of $6,700.00 unpaid," Robert Smith said, "we never attached any further significance to that. We expected to be paid by the Birmingham Restaurant Association, and never expected to make any money out of the case—even at 1964 rates." Letter, Robert McDavid Smith to the author, June 24, 1998.

63. See, for example, "*Katzenbach v. McClung,*" in Kermit L. Hall, ed., *The Oxford Companion to the Supreme Court of the United States* (New York: Oxford University Press, 1992), p. 481.

64. Ibid.; 379 U.S. 294, 304–5 (1964).

65. Brian K. Landsberg, *Enforcing Civil Rights* (Lawrence: University Press of Kansas, 1997), pp. 97–98.

66. *Daniel v. Paul,* 395 U.S. 298 (1969).

67. Interestingly, Justice Black dissented in *Daniel v. Paul,* but Justice Harlan joined the majority opinion. See *Daniel v. Paul,* 395 U.S. 298, 309–15 (1969).

68. *National League of Cities v. Usery,* 426 U.S. 833 (1976).

69. *Garcia v. San Antonio Metropolitan Transit Authority,* 469 U.S. 528 (1985).

70. *New York v. United States,* 505 U.S. 144 (1992).

71. *Printz v. United States,* 521 U.S. 898 (1997).

72. The Court has also recently held that Congress lacks the power under the Commerce Clause to abrogate the Eleventh Amendment immunity of the states from suits against them in the federal courts. See *Seminole Tribe v. Florida,* 517 U.S. 44 (1996); *Alden v. Maine,* 144 L.Ed.2d 636 (1999).

73. *United States v. Lopez,* 131 L.Ed.2d 626 (1995).

74. Ibid., 643 (1995).

75. 379 U.S. 294, 303–4 (1964).

76. *Lochner v. New York,* 198 U.S. 45 (1905)

77. 131 L.E.2d 626, 668–69.

78. Ibid., 673–84.

79. See, for example, *United States v. Guest,* 383 U.S. 745 (1966).

80. *United States v. Morrison,* Bench Opinion of the Court, pp. 19–27.

81. Bench Opinion, Justice Souter dissenting, p. 2.

82. Ibid., p. 15.

83. See the concurring opinion of Justices Kennedy and O'Connor, 131 L.Ed.2d 626, 643–53; and the concurring opinion of Justice Thomas, 131 L.Ed.2d 626, 653–65.

INDEX